ANCIENT TALES &
FOLKLORE OF
JAPAN

ANCIENT TALES & FOLKLORE OF
JAPAN

RICHARD GORDON SMITH

SENATE

Ancient Tales and Folklore of Japan

First published in 1918 by A & C Black, London

This edition published in 1995 by Senate, an imprint of
Studio Editions Ltd, Princess House, 50 Eastcastle Street,
London W1N 7AP, England

Copyright © this edition Studio Editions Ltd 1995

Reprinted 1995

ISBN 1 85958 079 3

Printed and bound in Guernsey by
The Guernsey Press Co. Ltd

TO

THE RIGHT HONOURABLE

Sir ERNEST MASON SATOW, K.C.M.G.

IN REMEMBRANCE

OF HIS KINDNESS IN JAPAN

Preface

THE stories in this volume are transcribed from voluminous illustrated diaries which have been kept by me for some twenty years spent in travel and in sport in many lands— the last nine of them almost entirely in Japan, while collecting subjects of natural history for the British Museum; trawling and dredging in the Inland Sea, sometimes with success, sometimes without, but in the end contributing to the treasury some fifty things new to Science, and, according to Sir Edwin Ray Lankester, 'adding greatly to the knowledge of Japanese Ethnology.' As may be supposed, such a life has brought me into close contact with the people—the fisher, the farmer, the priest, the doctor, the children, and all others from whom there is a possibility of extracting information. Many and weird are the tales I have been told. In this volume the Publishers prefer to have a mixture—stories of Mountains, of Trees, of Flowers, of Places in History, and Legends. For the general results obtained in my diaries I have to thank our late Minister in Tokio, Sir Ernest Satow; the

Ancient Tales and Folklore of Japan

Ministers and Vice-Ministers of Foreign Affairs and of Agriculture, who gave me many letters of introduction; my dear friend Mr. Hattori, Governor of Hiogo Prefecture; the translators of the original notes and manuscripts (often roughly written in Japanese), among whom are Mr. Ando, Mr. Matsuzaki, and Mr. Watanabe; and Mr. Mo-No-Yuki, who drew and painted the illustrations from sketches of my own, which must often have grated on his artistic ideas, keeping him awake in reflection on the crudeness of the European sense of art.

To my faithful interpreter Yuki Egawa also are due my thanks for continual efforts to find what I wanted; and to many Japanese peasants and fishermen, whose good-nature, kindness, and hospitality have endeared them to me for ever. Well is it that they, so worthy a people, have so worthy a Sovereign.

R. GORDON SMITH.

June 1908.

viii

Contents

Ancient Tales and Folklore of Japan

Contents

List of Illustrations

xiii

Ancient Tales and Folklore of Japan

List of Illustrations

ANCIENT TALES AND FOLKLORE
OF JAPAN

I

THE GOLDEN HAIRPIN[1]

Up in the northern city of Sendai, whence come the best of Japanese soldiers, there lived a samurai named Hasunuma.

Hasunuma was rich and hospitable, and consequently much thought of and well liked. Some thirty-five years ago his wife presented him with a beautiful daughter, their first child, whom they called 'Ko,' which means 'Small' when applied to a child, much as we say 'Little Mary' or 'Little Jane.' Her full name was really 'Hasu-ko,' which means 'Little Lily'; but here we will call her 'Ko' for short.

Exactly on the same date, 'Saito,' one of Hasunuma's friends and also a samurai, had the good fortune to have a son. The fathers decided that, being such old friends, they would wed their children to each other when old enough to marry; they were very happy over the idea, and so were their wives. To make the engagement of the

[1] This story savours of 'Botan Dōrō,' or Peony Lantern story, told both by Mitford and by Lafcadio Hearn. In this instance, however, the spirit of the dead sister passes into the body of the living one, assumes her form, leaves her sick and ill for over a year, and then allows her to reappear as if she had never been ill at all. It is the first story of its kind I have heard.

babies more binding, Saito handed to Hasunuma a golden hairpin which had long been in his family, and said :

'Here, my old friend, take this pin. It shall be a token of betrothal from my son, whose name shall be Kōnojō, to your little daughter Ko, both of whom are now aged two weeks only. May they live long and happy lives together.'

Hasunuma took the pin, and handed it to his wife to keep ; then they drank saké to the health of each other, and to the bride and bridegroom of some twenty years thence.

A few months after this Saito, in some way, caused displeasure to his feudal lord, and, being dismissed from service, left Sendai with his family—whither no one knew.

Seventeen years later O Ko San was, with one exception, the most beautiful girl in all Sendai ; the exception was her sister, O Kei, just a year younger, and as beautiful as herself.

Many were the suitors for O Ko's hand ; but she would have none of them, being faithful to the engagement made for her by her father when she was a baby. True, she had never seen her betrothed, and (which seemed more curious) neither she nor her family had ever once heard of the Saito family since they had left Sendai, over sixteen years before ; but that was no reason why she, a Japanese girl, should break the word of her father, and therefore O Ko San remained faithful to her unknown lover, though she sorrowed greatly at his non-appearance ; in fact, she secretly suffered so much thereby that she sickened, and three months later died, to the grief of all who knew her and to her family's serious distress.

The Golden Hairpin

On the day of O Ko San's funeral her mother was seeing to the last attentions paid to corpses, and smoothing her hair with the golden pin given to Ko San or O Ko[1] by Saito in behalf of his son Kōnojō. When the body had been placed in its coffin, the mother thrust the pin into the girl's hair, saying :

'Dearest daughter, this is the pin given as a memento to you by your betrothed, Kōnojō. Let it be a pledge to bind your spirits in death, as it would have been in life ; and may you enjoy endless happiness, I pray.'

In thus praying, no doubt, O Ko's mother thought that Kōnojō also must be dead, and that their spirits would meet ; but it was not so, for two months after these events Kōnojō himself, now eighteen years of age, turned up at Sendai, calling first on his father's old friend Hasunuma.

'Oh, the bitterness and misfortune of it all!' said the latter. 'Only two months ago my daughter Ko died. Had you but come before then she would have been alive now. But you never even sent a message ; we never heard a word of your father or of your mother. Where did you all go when you left here ? Tell me the whole story.'

'Sir,' answered the grief-stricken Kōnojō, 'what you tell me of the death of your daughter, whom I had hoped to marry, sickens my heart, for I, like herself, had been faithful, and I hoped to marry her, and thought daily of her. When my father took my family away from Sendai, he took us to Yedo ; and afterwards we went north to

---

[1] 'O' means Honourable Miss ; 'San' means Miss. Either will do ; but *Ko* is the name.

3

Yezo Island, where my father lost his money and became poor. He died in poverty. My poor mother did not long survive him. I have been working hard to try and earn enough to marry your daughter Ko ; but I have not made more than enough to pay my journey down to Sendai. I felt it my duty to come and tell you of my family's misfortune and my own.'

The old samurai was much touched by this story. He saw that the most unfortunate of all had been Kōnojō.

'Kōnojō,' he said, 'often have I thought and wondered to myself, Were you honest or were you not ? Now I find that you have been truly faithful, and honest to your father's pledge. But you should have written— you should have written ! Because you did not do so, sometimes we thought, my wife and I, that you must be dead ; but we kept this thought to ourselves, and never told Ko San. Go to our Butsudan ;[1] open the doors of it, and burn a joss stick to Ko San's mortuary tablet. It will please her spirit. She longed and longed for your return, and died of that same longing—for love of you. Her spirit will rejoice to know that you have come back for her.'

Kōnojō did as he was bid.

Bowing reverently three times before the mortuary tablet of O Ko San, he muttered a few words of prayer in her behalf, and then lit the incense-stick and placed it before the tablet.

After this exhibition of sincerity Hasunuma told the young fellow that he should consider him as an adopted son, and that he must live with them. He could have

---

[1] Family shrine.

the small house in the garden. In any case, whatever his plans for the future might be, he must remain with them for the present.

This was a generous offer, worthy of a samurai. Kōnojō gratefully accepted it, and became one of the family. About a fortnight afterwards he settled himself in the little house at the end of the garden. Hasunuma, his wife, and their second daughter, O Kei, had gone, by command of the Daimio, to the Higan, a religious ceremony held in March; Hasunuma also always worshipped at his ancestral tombs at this time. Towards the dusk of evening they were returning in their palanquins. Kōnojō stood at the gate to see them pass, as was proper and respectful. The old samurai passed first, and was followed by his wife's palanquin, and then by that of O Kei. As this last passed the gate Kōnojō thought he heard something fall, causing a metallic sound. After the palanquin had passed he picked it up without any particular attention.

It was the golden hairpin; but of course, though Kōnojō's father had told him of the pin, Kōnojō had no idea that this was it, and therefore he thought nothing more than that it must be O Kei San's. He went back to his little house, closed it for the night, and was about to retire when he heard a knock at the door. 'Who is there?' he shouted. 'What do you want?' There came no answer, and Kōnojō lay down on his bed, thinking himself to have been mistaken. But there came another knock, louder than the first; and Kōnojō jumped out of bed, and lit the ando.[1] 'If not a fox or a badger,'

[1] Lamp.

thought he, 'it must be some evil spirit come to disturb me.'

On opening the door, with the ando in one hand, and a stick in the other, Kōnojō looked out into the dark, and there, to his astonishment, he beheld a vision of female beauty the like of which he had never seen before. 'Who are you, and what do you want?' quoth he.

'I am O Kei San, O Ko's younger sister,' answered the vision. 'Though you have not seen me, I have several times seen you, and I have fallen so madly in love with you that I can think of nothing else but you. When you picked up my golden pin to-night on our return, I had dropped it to serve as an excuse to come to you and knock. You must love me in return; for otherwise I must die!'

This heated and outrageous declaration scandalised poor Kōnojō. Moreover, he felt that it would be doing his kind host Hasunuma a great injustice to be receiving his younger daughter at this hour of the night and make love to her. He expressed himself forcibly in these terms.

'If you will not love me as I love you, then I shall take my revenge,' said O Kei, 'by telling my father that you got me to come here by making love to me, and that you then insulted me.'

Poor Kōnojō! He was in a nice mess. What he feared most of all was that the girl would do as she said, that the samurai would believe her, and that he would be a disgraced and villainous person. He gave way, therefore, to the girl's request. Night after night she visited him, until nearly a month had passed. During

6

The Golden Hairpin

this time Kōnojō had learned to love dearly the beautiful
O Kei. Talking to her one evening, he said :

'My dearest O Kei, I do not like this secret love of
ours. Is it not better that we go away? If I asked your
father to give you to me in marriage he would refuse,
because I was betrothed to your sister.'

'Yes,' answered O Kei : 'that is what I also have
been wishing. Let us leave this very night, and go to
Ishinomaki, the place where (you have told me) lives a
faithful servant of your late father's, called Kinzo.'

'Yes : Kinzo is his name, and Ishinomaki is the place.
Let us start as soon as possible.'

Having thrust a few clothes into a bag, they started
secretly and late that night, and duly arrived at their
destination. Kinzo was delighted to receive them, and
pleased to show how hospitable he could be to his late
master's son and the beautiful lady.

They lived very happily for a year. Then one day
O Kei said:

'I think we ought to return to my parents now.
If they were angry with us at first they will have got
over the worst of it. We have never written. They
must be getting anxious as to my fate as they grow
older. Yes : we ought to go.'

Kōnojō agreed. Long had he felt the injustice he
was doing Hasunuma.

Next day they found themselves back in Sendai, and
Kōnojō could not help feeling a little nervous as he
approached the samurai's house. They stopped at the
outer gate, and O Kei said to Kōnojō, 'I think it will
be better for you to go in and see my father and mother

7

first.   If they get very angry show them this golden pin.'

Kōnojō stepped boldly up to the door, and asked for an interview with the samurai.

Before the servant had time to return, Kōnojō heard the old man shout, 'Kōnojō San!   Why, of course! Bring the boy in at once,' and he himself came out to welcome him.

'My dear boy,' said the samurai, 'right glad am I to see you back again.   I am sorry you did not find your life with us good enough.   You might have said you were going.   But there—I suppose you take after your father in these matters, and prefer to disappear mysteriously.   You are welcome back, at all events.'

Kōnojō was astonished at this speech, and answered :

'But, sir, I have come to beg pardon for my sin.'

'What sin have you committed?' queried the samurai in great surprise, and drawing himself up, in a dignified manner.

Kōnojō then gave a full account of his love-affair with O Kei.   From beginning to end he told it all, and as he proceeded the samurai showed signs of impatience.

'Do not joke, sir!   My daughter O Kei San is not a subject for jokes and untruths.   She has been as one dead for over a year—so ill that we have with difficulty forced gruel into her mouth.   Moreover, she has spoken no word and shown no sign of life.'

'I am neither stating what is untrue nor joking,' said Kōnojō.   'If you but send outside, you will find O Kei in the palanquin, in which I left her.'

A servant was immediately sent to see, and returned,

stating that there was neither palanquin nor any one at the gate.

Kōnojō, seeing that the samurai was now beginning to look perplexed and angry, drew the golden pin from his clothes, saying :

'See ! if you doubt me and think I am lying, here is the pin which O Kei told me to give you ! '

' Bik-ku-ri-shi-ta- ! '[1] exclaimed O Kei's mother. ' How came this pin into your hands ? I myself put it into Ko San's coffin just before it was closed.'

The samurai and Kōnojō stared at each other, and the mother at both. Neither knew what to think, or what to say or do. Imagine the general surprise when the sick O Kei walked into the room, having risen from her bed as if she had never been ill for a moment. She was the picture of health and beauty.

' How is this ? ' asked the samurai, almost shouting. ' How is it, O Kei, that you have come from your sick-bed dressed and with your hair done and looking as if you had never known a moment of illness ? '

' I am not O Kei, but the spirit of O Ko,' was the answer. ' I was most unfortunate in dying before the return of Kōnojō San, for had I lived until then I should have become quite well and been married to him. As it was, my spirit was unhappy. It took the form of my dear sister O Kei, and for a year has lived happily in her body with Kōnojō. It is appeased now, and about to take its real rest.'

' There is one condition, however, Kōnojō, which I must make,' said the girl, turning to him. ' You must

---

[1] An exclamation, such as ' Great Scot ! '

marry my sister O Kei. If you do this my spirit will rest truly in peace, and then O Kei will become well and strong. Will you promise to marry O Kei?'

The old samurai, his wife, and Kōnojō were all amazed at this. The appearance of the girl was that of O Kei; but the voice and manners were those of O Ko. Then, there was the golden hairpin as further proof. The mother knew it well. She had placed it in Ko's hair just before the tub coffin was closed. Nobody could undeceive her on that point.

'But,' said the samurai at last, 'O Ko has been dead and buried for more than a year now. That you should appear to us puzzles us all. Why should you trouble us so?'

'I have explained already,' resumed the girl. 'My spirit could not rest until it had lived with Kōnojō, whom it knew to be faithful. It has done this now, and is prepared to rest. My only desire is to see Kōnojō marry my sister.'

Hasunuma, his wife, and Kōnojō held a consultation. They were quite prepared that O Kei should marry, and Kōnojō did not object.

All things being settled, the ghost-girl held out her hand to Kōnojō saying:

'This is the last time you will touch the hand of O Ko. Farewell, my dear parents! Farewell to you all! I am about to pass away.'

Then she fainted away, and seemed dead, and remained thus for half an hour; while the others, overcome with the strange and weird things which they had seen and heard, sat round her, hardly uttering a word.

The Golden Hairpin

At the end of half an hour the body came to life, and standing up, said :

'Dear parents, have no more fear for me. I am perfectly well again ; but I have no idea how I got down from my sick-room in this costume, or how it is that I feel so well.'

Several questions were put to her ; but it was quite evident that O Kei knew nothing of what had happened—nothing of the spirit of O Ko San, or of the golden hairpin !

A week later she and Kōnojō were married, and the golden hairpin was given to a shrine at Shiogama, to which, until quite recently, crowds used to go and worship.

II

THE SPIRIT OF THE WILLOW TREE

ABOUT one thousand years ago (but according to the dates of the story 744 years ago) the temple of 'San-jū-san-gen Dō' was founded. That was in 1132. 'San-jū-san-gen Dō' means hall of thirty-three spaces; and there are said to be over 33,333 figures of the Goddess Kwannon, the Goddess of Mercy, in the temple to-day. Before the temple was built, in a village near by stood a willow tree of great size. It marked the playing-ground of all the village children, who swung on its branches, and climbed on its limbs. It afforded shade to the aged in the heat of summer, and in the evenings, when work was done, many were the village lads and lasses who vowed eternal love under its branches. The tree seemed an influence for good to all. Even the weary traveller could sleep peacefully and almost dry under its branches. Alas, even in those times men were often ruthless with regard to trees. One day the villagers announced an intention to cut it down and use it to build a bridge across the river.

There lived in the village a young farmer named

The Spirit of the Willow Tree

Heitaro, a great favourite, who had lived near the old tree all his days, as his forefathers had done ; and he was greatly against cutting it down.

Such a tree should be respected, thought he. Had it not braved the storms of hundreds of years ? In the heat of summer what pleasure it afforded the children ! Did it not give to the weary shelter, and to the love-smitten a sense of romance ? All these thoughts Heitaro impressed upon the villagers. Sooner than approve your cutting it down,' he said, ' I will give you as many of my own trees as you require to build the bridge. You must leave this dear old willow alone for ever.'

The villagers readily agreed. They also had a secret veneration for the old tree.

Heitaro was delighted, and readily found wood with which to build the bridge.

Some days later Heitaro, returning from his work, found standing by the willow a beautiful girl.

Instinctively he bowed to her. She returned the bow. They spoke together of the tree, its age and beauty. They seemed, in fact, to be drawn towards each other by a common sympathy. Heitaro was sorry when she said that she must be going, and bade him good-day. That evening his mind was far from being fixed on the ordinary things of life. ' Who was the lady under the willow tree ? How I wish I could see her again !' thought he. There was no sleep for Heitaro that night. He had caught the fever of love.

Next day he was at his work early ; and he remained at it all day, working doubly hard, so as to try and forget the lady of the willow tree ; but on his way home in the

Ancient Tales and Folklore of Japan

evening, behold, there was the lady again! This time she came forward to greet him in the most friendly way.

'Welcome, good friend!' she said. 'Come and rest under the branches of the willow you love so well, for you must be tired.'

Heitaro readily accepted this invitation, and not only did he rest, but also he declared his love.

Day by day after this the mysterious girl (whom no others had seen) used to meet Heitaro, and at last she promised to marry him if he asked no questions as to her parents or friends. 'I have none,' she said. 'I can only promise to be a good and faithful wife, and tell you that I love you with all my heart and soul. Call me, then, "Higo," [1] and I will be your wife.'

Next day Heitaro took Higo to his house, and they were married. A son was born to them in a little less than a year, and became their absorbing joy. There was not a moment of their spare time in which either Heitaro or his wife was not playing with the child, whom they called Chiyodō. It is doubtful if a more happy home could have been found in all Japan than the house of Heitaro, with his good wife Higo and their beautiful child.

Alas, where in this world has complete happiness ever been known to last? Even did the gods permit this, the laws of man would not.

When Chiyodō had reached the age of five years—the most beautiful boy in the neighbourhood—the ex-Emperor Toba decided to build in Kyoto an immense temple to Kwannon. He would contribute 1001 images of the Goddess of Mercy. (Now, in 1907, as we said at

[1] Meaning goithe or willow.

14

The Spirit of the Willow Tree

the beginning, this temple is known as 'San-jū-san-gen Dō,' and contains 33,333 images.)

The ex-Emperor Toba's wish having become known, orders were given by the authorities to collect timber for the building of the vast temple ; and so it came to pass that the days of the big willow tree were numbered, for it would be wanted, with many others, to form the roof.

Heitaro tried to save the tree again by offering every other he had on his land for nothing ; but that was in vain. Even the villagers became anxious to see their willow tree built into the temple. It would bring them good luck, they thought, and in any case be a handsome gift of theirs towards the great temple.

The fatal time arrived. One night, when Heitaro and his wife and child had retired to rest and were sleeping, Heitaro was awakened by the sound of axes chopping. To his astonishment, he found his beloved wife sitting up in her bed, gazing earnestly at him, while tears rolled down her cheeks and she was sobbing bitterly.

'My dearest husband,' she said with choking voice, 'pray listen to what I tell you now, and do not doubt me. This is, unhappily, not a dream. When we married I begged you not to ask me my history, and you have never done so ; but I said I would tell you some day if there should be a real occasion to do so. Unhappily, that occasion has now arrived, my dear husband. I am no less a thing than the spirit of the willow tree you loved, and so generously saved six years ago. It was to repay you for this great kindness that I appeared to you in human form under the tree, hoping that I could

15

live with you and make you happy for your whole life. Alas, it cannot be! They are cutting down the willow. How I feel every stroke of their axes! I must return to die, for I am part of it. My heart breaks to think also of leaving my darling child Chiyodō and of his great sorrow when he knows that his mother is no longer in the world. Comfort him, dearest husband! He is old enough and strong enough to be with you now without a mother and yet not suffer. I wish you both long lives of prosperity. Farewell, my dearest! I must be off to the willow, for I hear them striking with their axes harder and harder, and it weakens me each blow they give.'

Heitaro awoke his child just as Higo disappeared, wondering to himself if it were not a dream. No: it was no dream. Chiyodō, awaking, stretched his arms in the direction his mother had gone, crying bitterly and imploring her to come back.

'My darling child,' said Heitaro, 'she has gone. She cannot come back. Come: let us dress, and go and see her funeral. Your mother was the spirit of the Great Willow.'

A little later, at the break of day, Heitaro took Chiyodō by the hand and led him to the tree. On reaching it they found it down, and already lopped of its branches. The feelings of Heitaro may be well imagined.

Strange! In spite of united efforts, the men were unable to move the stem a single inch towards the river, in which it was to be floated to Kyoto.

On seeing this, Heitaro addressed the men.

The Spirit of the Willow Tree

'My friends,' said he, 'the dead trunk of the tree which you are trying to move contains the spirit of my wife. Perhaps, if you will allow my little son Chiyodō to help you, it will be more easy for you; and he would like to help in showing his last respects to his mother.'

The woodcutters were fully agreeable, and, much to their astonishment, as Chiyodō came to the back end of the log and pushed it with his little hand, the timber glided easily towards the river, his father singing the while an 'Uta.'[1] There is a well-known song or ballad in the 'Uta' style said to have sprung from this event; it is sung to the present day by men drawing heavy weights or doing hard labour :—

> Muzan naru kana
> Motowa kumanono yanagino tsuyu de
> Sodate-agetaru kono midorigo wa
> Ȳoi, Ȳoi, Ȳoito na![2]

In Wakanoura the labourers sing a working or hauling song, which also is said to have sprung from this story of the 'Yanagi no Sé' :—

> Wakano urani wa meishoga gozaru
> Ichini Gongen
> Nini Tamatsushima

---

[1] Poetical song.

[2] Is it not sad to see the little fellow,
Who sprang from the dew of the Kumano Willow,
And is thus far budding well?
Heave ho, heave ho, pull hard, my lads.

17

Ancient Tales and Folklore of Japan

Sanni Sagari Matsu
Shini Shiogama yo
Ȳoi, Ȳoi, ȳoi to na.[1]

A third 'Uta' sprang from this story, and is often applied to small children helping.

The waggon could not be drawn when it came to the front of Heitaro's house, so his little five-year-old boy Chiyodō was obliged to help, and they sang :—

Muzan naru kana
Motowa Kumanono yanagino tsuyu de
Sodate-agetaru kono midorigo wa
Ȳoi, ȳoi, ȳoito na.[2]

---

[1] There are famous places in Wakanoura
First Gongen
Second Tamatsushima
Third, the pine tree with its hanging branches
Fourth comes Shiogama
Is it not good, good, good?

[2] Is it not sad to see the little fellow,
Who sprang from the dew of the Kumano Willow,
And is thus far budding well?
Heave ho, heave ho, pull hard, my lads.

III

GHOST OF THE VIOLET WELL [1]

In the wild province of Yamato, or very near to its borders, is a beautiful mountain known as Yoshino yama. It is not only known for its abundance of cherry blossom in the spring, but it is also celebrated in relation to more than one bloody battle. In fact, Yoshino might be called the staging-place of historical battles. Many say, when in Yoshino, 'We are walking on history, because Yoshino itself is history.' Near Yoshino mountain lay another, known as Tsubosaka ; and between them is the Valley of Shimizutani, in which is the Violet Well.

At the approach of spring in this tani [2] the grass assumes a perfect emerald green, while moss grows luxuriantly over rocks and boulders. Towards the end of April great patches of deep-purple wild violets show up in the lower parts of the valley, while up the sides pink and scarlet azaleas grow in a manner which beggars description.

Some thirty years ago a beautiful girl of the age of seventeen, named Shingé, was wending her way up

[1] Told to me by Shofukutei Fukuga. [2] Hollow.

19

Shimizutani, accompanied by four servants. All were out for a picnic, and all, of course, were in search of wild-flowers. O Shingé San was the daughter of a Daimio who lived in the neighbourhood. Every year she was in the habit of having this picnic, and coming to Shimizu-tani at the end of April to hunt for her favourite flower, the purple violet (sumire).

The five girls, carrying bamboo baskets, were eagerly collecting flowers, enjoying the occupation as only Japanese girls can. They raced in their rivalry to have the prettiest basketful. There not being so many purple violets as were wanted, O Shingé San said, 'Let us go to the northern end of the valley, where the Violet Well is.'

Naturally the girls assented, and off they all ran, each eager to be there first, laughing as they went.

O Shingé outran the rest, and arrived before any of them; and, espying a huge bunch of her favourite flowers, of the deepest purple and very sweet in smell, she flung herself down, anxious to pick them before the others came. As she stretched out her delicate hand to grasp them—oh, horror!—a great mountain snake raised his head from beneath his shady retreat. So frightened was O Shingé San, she fainted away on the spot.

In the meanwhile the other girls had given up the race, thinking it would please their mistress to arrive first. They picked what they most fancied, chased butterflies, and arrived fully fifteen minutes after O Shingé San had fainted.

On seeing her thus laid out on the grass, a great fear

filled them that she was dead, and their alarm increased when they saw a large green snake coiled near her head.

They screamed, as do most girls amid such circumstances; but one of them, Matsu, who did not lose her head so much as the others, threw her basket of flowers at the snake, which, not liking the bombardment, uncoiled himself and slid away, hoping to find a quieter place. Then all four girls bent over their mistress. They rubbed her hands and threw water on her face, but without effect. O Shingé's beautiful complexion became paler and paler, while her red lips assumed the purplish hue that is a sign of approaching death. The girls were heartbroken. Tears coursed down their faces. They did not know what to do, for they could not carry her. What a terrible state of affairs!

Just at that moment they heard a man's voice close behind them:

'Do not be so sad! I can restore the young lady to consciousness if you will allow me.'

They turned, and saw a remarkably handsome youth standing on the grass not ten feet away. He appeared as an angel from Heaven.

Without saying more, the young man approached the prostrate figure of O Shingé, and, taking her hand in his, felt her pulse. None of the servants liked to interfere in this breach of etiquette. He had not asked permission; but his manner was so gentle and sympathetic that they could say nothing.

The stranger examined O Shingé carefully, keeping silence. Having finished, he took out of his pocket a little case of medicine, and, putting some white powder from this into a paper, said :

'I am a doctor from a neighbouring village, and I have just been to see a patient at the end of the valley. By good fortune I returned this way, and am able to help you and save your mistress's life. Give her this medicine, while I hunt for and kill the snake.'

O Matsu San forced the medicine, along with a little water, into her mistress's mouth, and in a few minutes she began to recover.

Shortly after this the doctor returned, carrying the dead snake on a stick.

'Is this the snake you saw lying by your young mistress?' he asked.

'Yes, yes,' they cried : 'that is the horrible thing.'

'Then,' said the doctor, 'it is lucky I came, for it is very poisonous, and I fear your mistress would soon have died had I not arrived and been able to give her the medicine. Ah! I see that it is already doing the beautiful young lady good.'

On hearing the young man's voice O Shingé San sat up.

'Pray, sir, may I ask to whom I am indebted for bringing me thus back to life?' she asked.

The doctor did not answer, but in a proud and manly way contented himself by smiling, and bowing low and respectfully after the Japanese fashion ; and departed as quietly and unassumingly as he had arrived, disappearing in the sleepy mist which always appears in the afternoons of spring time in the Shimizu Valley.

The four girls helped their mistress home ; but indeed she wanted little assistance, for the medicine had done her much good, and she felt quite recovered. O Shingé's father and mother were very grateful for their daughter's recovery; but the name of the handsome young doctor remained a secret to all except the servant girl Matsu.

For four days O Shingé remained quite well; but on the fifth day, for some cause or another, she took to her bed, saying she was sick. She did not sleep, and did not wish to talk, but only to think, and think, and think. Neither father nor mother could make out what her illness was. There was no fever.

Doctors were sent for, one after another; but none of them could say what was the matter. All they saw was that she daily became weaker. Asano Zembei, Shingé's father, was heartbroken, and so was his wife. They had tried everything and failed to do the slightest good to poor O Shingé.

One day O Matsu San craved an interview with Asano Zembei—who, by the by, was the head of all his family, a Daimio and great grandee. Zembei was not accustomed to listen to servants' opinions; but, knowing that O Matsu was faithful to his daughter and loved her very nearly as much as he did himself, he consented to hear her, and O Matsu was ushered into his presence.

'Oh, master,' said the servant, 'if you will let me find a doctor for my young mistress, I can promise to find one who will cure her.'

'Where on earth will you find such a doctor? Have we not had all the best doctors in the province and some even from the capital? Where do you propose to look for one?'

O Matsu answered :

'Ah, master, my mistress is not suffering from an illness which can be cured by medicines—not even if they be given by the quart. Nor are doctors of much use. There is, however, one that I know of who could cure her. My mistress's illness is of the heart. The doctor I know of can cure her. It is for love of him that her heart suffers ; it has suffered so from the day when he saved her life from the snake-bite.'

Then O Matsu told particulars of the adventure at the picnic which had not been told before,—for O Shingé had asked her servants to say as little as possible, fearing they would not be allowed to go to the Valley of the Violet Well again.

'What is the name of this doctor?' asked Asano Zembei, 'and who is he?'

'Sir,' answered O Matsu, 'he is Doctor Yoshisawa, a very handsome young man, of most courtly manners ; but he is of low birth, being only of the eta.[1] Please think, master, of my young mistress's burning heart, full of love for the man who saved her life—and no wonder, for he is very handsome and has the manners of a proud samurai. The only cure for your daughter, sir, is to be allowed to marry her lover.'

O Shingé's mother felt very sad when she heard this. She knew well (perhaps by experience) of the illnesses caused by love. She wept, and said to Zembei :

'I am quite with you in sorrow, my lord, at the terrible trouble that has come to us ; but I cannot see my daughter die thus. Let us tell her we will make

---

[1] The eta are the lowest people or caste in Japan—skinners and killers of animals.

inquiries about the man she loves, and see if we can make him our son-in-law. In any case, it is the custom to make full inquiries, which will extend over some days; and in this time our daughter may recover somewhat and get strong enough to hear the news that we cannot accept her lover as our son-in-law.'

Zembei agreed to this, and O Matsu promised to say nothing to her mistress of the interview.

O Shingé San was told by her mother that her father, though he had not consented to the engagement, had promised to make inquiries about Yoshisawa.

O Shingé took food and regained much strength on this news; and when she was strong enough, some ten days later, she was called into her father's presence, accompanied by her mother.

'My sweet daughter,' said Zembei, 'I have made careful inquiries about Dr. Yoshisawa, your lover. Deeply as it grieves me to say so, it is impossible that I, your father, the head of our whole family, can consent to your marriage with one of so low a family as Yoshisawa, who, in spite of his own goodness, has sprung from the eta. I must hear no more of it. Such a contract would be impossible for the Asano family.'

No one ventured to say a word to this. In Japan the head of a family's decision is final.

Poor O Shingé bowed to her father, and went to her own room, where she wept bitterly; O Matsu, the faithful servant, doing her best to console her.

Next morning, to the astonishment of the household, O Shingé San could nowhere be found. Search was made everywhere; even Dr. Yoshisawa joined in the search.

Ancient Tales and Folklore of Japan

On the third day after the disappearance one of the searchers looked down the Violet Well, and saw poor O Shingé's floating body.

Two days later she was buried, and on that day Yoshisawa threw himself into the well.

The people say that even now, on wet, stormy nights, they see the ghost of O Shingé San floating over the well, while some declare that they hear the sound of a young man weeping in the Valley of Shimizutani.

IV

GHOST STORY OF THE FLUTE'S TOMB [1]

LONG ago, at a small and out-of-the-way village called Kumedamura, about eight miles to the south-east of Sakai city, in Idsumo Province, there was made a tomb, the Fuezuka or Flute's Tomb, and to this day many people go thither to offer up prayer and to worship, bringing with them flowers and incense-sticks, which are deposited as offerings to the spirit of the man who was buried there. All the year round people flock to it. There is no season at which they pray more particularly than at another.

The Fuezuka tomb is situated on a large pond called Kumeda, some five miles in circumference, and all the places around this pond are known as of Kumeda Pond, from which the village of Kumeda took its name.

Whose tomb can it be that attracts such sympathy? The tomb itself is a simple stone pillar, with nothing artistic to recommend it. Neither is the surrounding scenery interesting; it is flat and ugly until the mountains of Kiushu are reached. I must tell, as well as I can, the story of whose tomb it is.

[1] Told to me by Fukuga.

27

Ancient Tales and Folklore of Japan

Between seventy and eighty years ago there lived near the pond in the village of Kumedamura a blind amma[1] called Yoichi. Yoichi was extremely popular in the neighbourhood, being very honest and kind, besides being quite a professor in the art of massage—a treatment necessary to almost every Japanese. It would be difficult indeed to find a village that had not its amma.

Yoichi was blind, and, like all men of his calling, carried an iron wand or stick, also a flute or 'fuezuka'—the stick to feel his way about with, and the flute to let people know he was ready for employment. So good an amma was Yoichi, he was nearly always employed, and, consequently, fairly well off, having a little house of his own and one servant, who cooked his food.

A little way from Yoichi's house was a small teahouse, placed upon the banks of the pond. One evening (April 5 ; cherry-blossom season), just at dusk, Yoichi was on his way home, having been at work all day. His road led him by the pond. There he heard a girl crying piteously. He stopped and listened for a few moments, and gathered from what he heard that the girl was about to drown herself. Just as she entered the lake Yoichi caught her by the dress and dragged her out.

'Who are you, and why in such trouble as to wish to die ?' he asked.

'I am Asayo, the teahouse girl,' she answered. 'You know me quite well. You must know, also, that it is not possible for me to support myself out of the small pittance which is paid by my master. I have eaten nothing for two days now, and am tired of my life.'

[1] Shampooer.

Ghost Story of the Flute's Tomb

'Come, come!' said the blind man. 'Dry your tears. I will take you to my house, and do what I can to help you. You are only twenty-five years of age, and I am told still a fair-looking girl. Perhaps you will marry! In any case, I will take care of you, and you must not think of killing yourself. Come with me now; and I will see that you are well fed, and that dry clothes are given you.'

So Yoichi led Asayo to his home.

A few months found them wedded to each other. Were they happy? Well, they should have been, for Yoichi treated his wife with the greatest kindness; but she was unlike her husband. She was selfish, bad-tempered, and unfaithful. In the eyes of Japanese infidelity is the worst of sins. How much more, then, is it against the country's spirit when advantage is taken of a husband who is blind?

Some three months after they had been married, and in the heat of August, there came to the village a company of actors. Among them was Sawamura Tamataro, of some repute in Asakusa.

Asayo, who was very fond of a play, spent much of her time and her husband's money in going to the theatre. In less than two days she had fallen violently in love with Tamataro. She sent him money, hardly earned by her blind husband. She wrote to him love-letters, begged him to allow her to come and visit him, and generally disgraced her sex.

Things went from bad to worse. The secret meetings of Asayo and the actor scandalised the neighbourhood. As in most such cases, the husband knew nothing about

29

them. Frequently, when he went home, the actor was in his house, but kept quiet, and Asayo let him out secretly, even going with him sometimes.

Every one felt sorry for Yoichi; but none liked to tell him of his wife's infidelity.

One day Yoichi went to shampoo a customer, who told him of Asayo's conduct. Yoichi was incredulous.

'But yes: it is true,' said the son of his customer. 'Even now the actor Tamataro is with your wife. So soon as you left your house he slipped in. This he does every day, and many of us see it. We all feel sorry for you in your blindness, and should be glad to help you to punish her.'

Yoichi was deeply grieved, for he knew that his friends were in earnest; but, though blind, he would accept no assistance to convict his wife. He trudged home as fast as his blindness would permit, making as little noise as possible with his staff.

On reaching home Yoichi found the front door fastened from the inside. He went to the back, and found the same thing there. There was no way of getting in without breaking a door and making a noise. Yoichi was much excited now; for he knew that his guilty wife and her lover were inside, and he would have liked to kill them both. Great strength came to him, and he raised himself bit by bit until he reached the top of the roof. He intended to enter the house by letting himself down through the 'tem-mado.'[1] Unfortunately, the straw rope he used in doing this was rotten, and gave way, precipitating him below, where he

[1] Hole in the roof of a Japanese house, in place of a chimney.

fell on the kinuta.[1] He fractured his skull, and died instantly.

Asayo and the actor, hearing the noise, went to see what had happened, and were rather pleased to find poor Yoichi dead. They did not report the death until next day, when they said that Yoichi had fallen downstairs and thus killed himself.

They buried him with indecent haste, and hardly with proper respect.

Yoichi having no children, his property, according to the Japanese law, went to his bad wife, and only a few months passed before Asayo and the actor were married. Apparently they were happy, though none in the village of Kumeda had any sympathy for them, all being disgusted at their behaviour to the poor blind shampooer Yoichi.

Months passed by without event of any interest in the village. No one bothered about Asayo and her husband ; and they bothered about no one else, being sufficiently interested in themselves. The scandal-mongers had become tired, and, like all nine-day wonders, the history of the blind amma, Asayo, and Tamataro had passed into silence.

However, it does not do to be assured while the spirit of the injured dead goes unavenged.

Up in one of the western provinces, at a small village called Minato, lived one of Yoichi's friends, who was closely connected with him. This was Okuda Ichibei. He and Yoichi had been to school together. They had promised when Ichibei went up to the north-west always

[1] A hard block of wood used in stretching cotton cloth.

31

to remember each other, and to help each other in time of need, and when Yoichi had become blind Ichibei came down to Kumeda and helped to start Yoichi in his business of amma, which he did by giving him a house to live in—a house which had been bequeathed to Ichibei. Again fate decreed that it should be in Ichibei's power to help his friend. At that time news travelled very slowly, and Ichibei had not immediately heard of Yoichi's death or even of his marriage. Judge, then, of his surprise, one night on awaking, to find, standing near his pillow, the figure of a man whom by and by he recognised as Yoichi!

'Why, Yoichi! I am glad to see you,' he said; 'but how late at night you have arrived! Why did you not let me know you were coming? I should have been up to receive you, and there would have been a hot meal ready. But never mind. I will call a servant, and everything shall be ready as soon as possible. In the meantime be seated, and tell me about yourself, and how you travelled so far. To have come through the mountains and other wild country from Kumeda is hard enough at best; but for one who is blind it is wonderful.'

'I am no longer a living man,' answered the ghost of Yoichi (for such it was). 'I am indeed your friend Yoichi's spirit, and I shall wander about until I can be avenged for a great ill which has been done me. I have come to beg of you to help me, that my spirit may go to rest. If you listen I will tell my story, and you can then do as you think best.'

Ichibei was very much astonished (not to say a little

1. IGANOSUKE DIVES FOR THE PIPE AND FINDS THE IDOL

2. THE SPIRIT OF O KO APPEARS TO KONOJO AS O KEI SAN

3. HEITARO MEETS HIGO UNDER THE WILLOW TREE

4. SHIMIZUTANI. THE SERVANTS FIND THEIR MISTRESS LYING INSENSIBLE

5. THE GHOST OF YOICHI APPEARS TO THE THREE AS THEY TALK

6. JOGEN SIGHTS THE HAUNTED TEMPLE

7. ROSETSU WATCHES THE CARP

8. THE FIRE-BALL OR 'SHITO DAMA' OF AKECHI

nervous) to know that he was in the presence of a ghost; but he was a brave man, and Yoichi had been his friend. He was deeply grieved to hear of Yoichi's death, and realised that the restlessness of his spirit showed him to have been injured. Ichibei decided not only to listen to the story but also to revenge Yoichi, and said so.

The ghost then told all that had happened since he had been set up in the house at Kumedamura. He told of his success as a masseur; of how he had saved the life of Asayo, how he had taken her to his house and subsequently married her; of the arrival of the accursed acting company which contained the man who had ruined his life; of his own death and hasty burial; and of the marriage of Asayo and the actor. 'I must be avenged. Will you help me to rest in peace?' he said in conclusion.

Ichibei promised. Then the spirit of Yoichi disappeared, and Ichibei slept again.

Next morning Ichibei thought he must have been dreaming; but he remembered the vision and the narrative so clearly that he perceived them to have been actual. Suddenly turning with the intention to get up, he caught sight of the shine of a metal flute close to his pillow. It was the flute of a blind amma. It was marked with Yoichi's name.

Ichibei resolved to start for Kamedamura and ascertain locally all about Yoichi.

In those times, when there was no railway and a rickshaw only here and there, travel was slow. Ichibei took ten days to reach Kamedamura. He immediately went to the house of his friend Yoichi, and was there told the whole history again, but naturally in another way. Asayo said :

'Yes : he saved my life. We were married, and I helped my blind husband in everything. One day, alas, he mistook the staircase for a door, falling down and killing himself. Now I am married to his great friend, an actor called Tamataro, whom you see here.'

Ichibei knew that the ghost of Yoichi was not likely to tell him lies, and to ask for vengeance unjustly. Therefore he continued talking to Asayo and her husband, listening to their lies, and wondering what would be the fitting procedure.

Ten o'clock passed thus, and eleven. At twelve o'clock, when Asayo for the sixth or seventh time was assuring Ichibei that everything possible had been done for her blind husband, a wind storm suddenly arose, and in the midst of it was heard the sound of the amma's flute, just as Yoichi played it ; it was so unmistakably his that Asayo screamed with fear.

At first distant, nearer and nearer approached the sound, until at last it seemed to be in the room itself. At that moment a cold puff of air came down the tem-mado, and the ghost of Yoichi was seen standing beneath it, a cold, white, glimmering and sad-faced wraith.

Tamataro and his wife tried to get up and run out of the house ; but they found that their legs would not support them, so full were they of fear.

Tamataro seized a lamp and flung it at the ghost ; but the ghost was not to be moved. The lamp passed through him, and broke, setting fire to the house, which burned instantly, the wind fanning the flames.

Ghost Story of the Flute's Tomb

Ichibei made his escape; but neither Asayo nor her husband could move, and the flames consumed them in the presence of Yoichi's ghost. Their cries were loud and piercing.

Ichibei had all the ashes swept up and placed in a tomb. He had buried in another grave the flute of the blind amma, and erected on the ground where the house had been a monument sacred to the memory of Yoichi. It is known as Fuezuka no Kwaidan.[1]

[1] The flute ghost tomb.

V

A HAUNTED TEMPLE IN INABA PROVINCE[1]

ABOUT the year 1680 there stood an old temple on a wild pine-clad mountain near the village of Kisaichi, in the Province of Inaba. The temple was far up in a rocky ravine. So high and thick were the trees, they kept out nearly all daylight, even when the sun was at its highest. As long as the old men of the village could remember the temple had been haunted by a shito dama and the skeleton ghost (they thought) of some former priestly occupant. Many priests had tried to live in the

[1] In many stories in MS. volumes I have told of shito dama or astral spirits. So much evidence have I got from personal acquaintances as to their existence, and even frequent occurrence, that I almost believe in them myself. Some say that there are two shapes—the roundish oblong tadpole shape, and the more square-fronted eyed shape. Priests declare the shapes and sexes to be all alike, indistinguishable from each other and square-fronted, as in No. 2. My hunter, Oto of Itami, who, with his son, saw the old barber's wife's shito dama after she had died, declared that the shape was like an egg with a tail. At Tsuboune, near Naba, two or three dozen people who had seen the shito dama of a deaf man and that of a fisher-girl there declared both to be square-fronted. Again: At Toshi Shima the old men declare that there was a carpenter whose shito dama appeared five or six times some fifteen years ago, and that it was red, instead of having the ordinary phosphorescent smoky-white appearance. Shito dama, I take it, is the astral form that a spirit can assume if it wishes to wander the earth after death. This is the story of a dissatisfied spirit which haunted a temple and also showed itself as a ghost.

36

temple and make it their home; but all had died. No one could spend a night there and live.

At last, in the winter of 1701, there arrived at the village of Kisaichi a priest who was on a pilgrimage. His name was Jogen, and he was a native of the Province of Kai.

Jogen had come to see the haunted temple. He was fond of studying such things. Though he believed in the shito dama form of spiritual return to earth, he did not believe in ghosts. As a matter of fact, he was anxious to see a shito dama, and, moreover, wished to have a temple of his own. In this wild mountain temple, with a history which fear and death prevented people from visiting or priests inhabiting, he thought that he had (to put it in vulgar English) 'a real good thing.' Thus he had found his way to the village on the evening of a cold December night, and had gone to the inn to eat his rice and to hear all he could about the temple.

Jogen was no coward; on the contrary, he was a brave man, and made all inquiries in the calmest manner.

'Sir,' said the landlord, 'your holiness must not think of going to this temple, for it means death. Many good priests have tried to stay the night there, and every one has been found next morning dead, or has died shortly after daybreak without coming to his senses. It is no use, sir, trying to defy such an evil spirit as comes to this temple. I beg you, sir, to give up the idea. Badly as we want a temple here, we wish for no more deaths, and often think of burning down this old haunted one and building a new.'

Jogen, however, was firm in his resolve to find and see the ghost.

'Kind sir,' he answered, 'your wishes are for my preservation; but it is my ambition to see a shito dama, and, if prayers can quiet it, to reopen the temple, to read its legends from the old books that must lie hidden therein, and to be the head priest of it generally.'

The innkeeper, seeing that the priest was not to be dissuaded, gave up the attempt, and promised that his son should accompany him as guide in the morning, and carry sufficient provisions for a day.

Next morning was one of brilliant sunshine, and Jogen was out of bed early, making preparations. Kosa, the innkeeper's twenty-year-old son, was tying up the priest's bedding and enough boiled rice to last him nearly two full days. It was decided that Kosa, after leaving the priest at the temple, should return to the village, for he as well as every other villager refused to spend a night at the weird place; but he and his father agreed to go and see Jogen on the morrow, or (as some one grimly put it) 'to carry him down and give him an honourable funeral and decent burial.'

Jogen entered fully into this joke, and shortly after left the village, with Kosa carrying his things and guiding the way.

The gorge in which the temple was situated was very steep and wild. Great moss-clad rocks lay strewn everywhere. When Jogen and his companion had got half-way up they sat down to rest and eat. Soon they heard voices of persons ascending, and ere long the innkeeper and some eight or nine of the village elders presented themselves.

A Haunted Temple in Inaba Province

'We have followed you,' said the innkeeper, 'to try once more to dissuade you from running to a sure death. True, we want the temple opened and the ghosts appeased; but we do not wish it at the cost of another life. Please consider!'

'I cannot change my mind,' answered the priest. 'Besides, this is the one chance of my life. Your village elders have promised me that if I am able to appease the spirit and reopen the temple I shall be the head priest of the temple, which must hereafter become celebrated.'

Again Jogen refused to listen to advice, and laughed at the villagers' fears. Shouldering the packages that had been carried by Kosa, he said:

'Go back with the rest. I can find my own way now easily enough. I shall be glad if you return to-morrow with carpenters, for no doubt the temple is in sad want of repairs, both inside and out. Now, my friends, until to-morrow, farewell. Have no fear for me: I have none for myself.'

The villagers made deep bows. They were greatly impressed by the bravery of Jogen, and hoped that he might be spared to become their priest. Jogen in his turn bowed, and then began to continue his ascent. The others watched him as long as he remained in view, and then retraced their steps to the village; Kosa thanking the good fortune that had not necessitated his having to go to the temple with the priest and return in the evening alone. With two or three people he felt brave enough; but to be here in the gloom of this wild forest and near the haunted temple alone—no: that was not in his line.

As Jogen climbed he came suddenly in sight of the

39

temple, which seemed to be almost over his head, so precipitous were the sides of the mountain and the path. Filled with curiosity, the priest pressed on in spite of his heavy load, and some fifteen minutes later arrived panting on the temple platform, or terrace, which, like the temple itself, had been built on driven piles and scaffolding.

At first glance Jogen recognised that the temple was large ; but lack of attention had caused it to fall into great dilapidation. Rank grasses grew high about its sides ; fungi and creepers abounded upon the damp, sodden posts and supports ; so rotten, in fact, did these appear, the priest mentioned in his written notes that evening that he feared the spirits less than the state of the posts which supported the building.

Cautiously Jogen entered the temple, and saw that there was a remarkably large and fine gilded figure of Buddha, besides figures of many saints. There were also fine bronzes and vases, drums from which the parchment had rotted off, incense-burners, or koros, and other valuable or holy things.

Behind the temple were the priests' living quarters ; evidently, before the ghost's time, the temple must have had some five or six priests ever present to attend to it and to the people who came to pray.

The gloom was oppressive, and as the evening was already approaching Jogen bethought himself of light. Unpacking his bundle, he filled a lamp with oil, and found temple-sticks for the candles which he had brought with him. Having placed one of these on either side of the figure of Buddha, he prayed earnestly for two hours, by which time it was quite dark. Then he took his simple meal of rice, and settled himself to watch and listen. In order that he might see inside and outside the temple at the same time, he had chosen the gallery. Concealed behind an old column, he waited, in his heart disbelieving in ghosts, but anxious, as his notes said, to see a shito dama.

For some two hours he heard nothing. The wind—such little as there was—sighed round the temple and through the stems of the tall trees. An owl hooted from time to time. Bats flew in and out. A fungusy smell pervaded the air.

Suddenly, near midnight, Jogen heard a rustling in the bushes below him, as if somebody were pushing through. He thought it was a deer, or perhaps one of the large red-faced apes so fond of the neighbourhood of high and deserted temples ; perhaps, even, it might be a fox or a badger.

The priest was soon undeceived. At the place whence the sound of the rustling leaves had come, he saw the clear and distinct shape of the well-known shito dama. It moved first one way and then another, in a hovering and jerky manner, and from it a voice as of distant buzzing proceeded ; but—horror of horrors !—what was that standing among the bushes ?

The priest's blood ran cold. There stood the luminous skeleton of a man in loose priest's clothes, with glaring eyes and a parchment skin ! At first it remained still ; but as the shito dama rose higher and higher the ghost moved after it — sometimes visible, sometimes not.

Higher and higher came the shito dama, until finally

the ghost stood at the base of the great figure of Buddha, and was facing Jogen.

Cold beads of sweat stood out on the priest's forehead; the marrow seemed to have frozen in his bones; he shook so that he could hardly stand. Biting his tongue to prevent screaming, he dashed for the small room in which he had left his bedding, and, having bolted himself in, proceeded to look through a crack between the boards. Yes! there was the figure of the ghost, still seated near the Buddha; but the shito dama had disappeared.

None of Jogen's senses left him; but fear was paralysing his body, and he felt himself no longer capable of moving—no matter what should happen. He continued, in a lying position, to look through the hole.

The ghost sat on, turning only its head, sometimes to the right, sometimes to the left, and sometimes looking upwards.

For full an hour this went on. Then the buzzing sound began again, and the shito dama reappeared, circling and circling round the ghost's body, until the ghost vanished, apparently having turned into the shito dama; and after circling round the holy figures three or four times it suddenly shot out of sight.

Next morning Kosa and five men came up to the temple. They found the priest alive but paralysed. He could neither move nor speak. He was carried to the village, dying before he got there.

Much use was made of the priest's notes. No one else ever volunteered to live at the temple, which, two years later, was struck by lightning and burned to the ground. In digging among the remains, searching for bronzes and metal Buddhas, villagers came upon a skeleton buried, only a foot deep, near the bushes whence Jogen had first heard the sounds of rustling.

Undoubtedly the ghost and shito dama were those of a priest who had suffered a violent death and could not rest.

The bones were properly buried and masses said, and nothing has since been seen of the ghost.

All that remains of the temple are the moss-grown pedestals which formed the foundations.

VI

A CARP GIVES A LESSON IN PERSEVERANCE[1]

BETWEEN the years 1750 and 1760 there lived in Kyoto a great painter named Okyo-Maruyama Okyo. His paintings were such as to fetch high prices even in those days. Okyo had not only many admirers in consequence, but had also many pupils who strove to copy his style; among them was one named Rosetsu, who eventually became the best of all.

When first Rosetsu went to Okyo's to study he was, without exception, the dullest and most stupid pupil that Okyo had ever had to deal with. His learning was so slow that pupils who had entered as students under Okyo a year and more after Rosetsu overtook him. He was one of those plodding but unfortunate youths who work hard, harder perhaps than most, and seem to go backwards as if the very gods were against them.

[1] One day my old painter Busetsu was talking with me about Japan's greatest painters, and of one of them he told a strange story. It was interesting in one thing especially, and that was that the name of *Rosetsu* I could not find mentioned in Louis Gonse's book, though, of course, Maruyama Okyo was. Five names were given as those of the best pupils of Okyo; but Rosetsu was not mentioned. I wrote to my friend the Local Governor, who is an authority on Japanese paintings. His answer was, 'You are quite right: Rosetsu was one of Okyo's best pupils, perhaps the best.'

44

A Carp gives a Lesson in Perseverance

I have the deepest sympathy with Rosetsu. I myself became a bigger fool day by day as I worked; the harder I worked or tried to remember the more manifestly a fool I became.

Rosetsu, however, was in the end successful, having been greatly encouraged by his observations of the perseverance of a carp.

Many of the pupils who had entered Okyo's school after Rosetsu had left, having become quite good painters. Poor Rosetsu was the only one who had made no progress whatever for three years. So disconsolate was he, and so little encouragement did his master offer, that at last, crestfallen and sad, he gave up the hopes he had had of becoming a great painter, and quietly left the school one evening, intending either to go home or to kill himself on the way. All that night he walked, and half-way into the next, when, tired out from want of sleep and of food, he flung himself down on the snow under the pine trees.

Some hours before dawn Rosetsu awoke, hearing a strange noise not thirty paces from him. He could not make it out, but sat up, listening, and glancing towards the place whence the sound—of splashing water—came.

As the day broke he saw that the noise was caused by a large carp, which was persistently jumping out of the water, evidently trying to reach a piece of sembei (a kind of biscuit made of rice and salt) lying on the ice of a pond near which Rosetsu found himself. For full three hours the fish must have been jumping thus unsuccessfully, cutting and bruising himself against the edges of the ice until the blood flowed and many scales had been lost.

45

Rosetsu watched its persistency with admiration. The fish tried every imaginable device. Sometimes it would make a determined attack on the ice where the biscuit lay from underneath, by charging directly upwards; at other times it would jump high in the air, and hope that by falling on the ice bit by bit would be broken away, until it should be able to reach the sembei; and indeed the carp did thus break the ice, until at last he reached the prize, bleeding and hurt, but still rewarded for brave perseverance.

Rosetsu, much impressed, watched the fish swim off with the food, and reflected.

'Yes,' he said to himself: 'this has been a moral lesson to me. I will be like this carp. I will not go home until I have gained my object. As long as there is breath in my body I will work to carry out my intention. I will labour harder than ever, and, no matter if I do not progress, I will continue in my efforts until I attain my end or die.'

After this resolve Rosetsu visited the neighbouring temple, and prayed for success; also he thanked the local deity that he had been enabled to see, through the carp's perseverance, the line that a man should take in life.

Rosetsu then returned to Kyoto, and to his master, Okyo, told the story of the carp and of his determination.

Okyo was much pleased, and did his best for his backward pupil. This time Rosetsu progressed. He became a well-known painter, the best man Okyo ever taught, as good, in fact, as his master; and he ended by being one of Japan's greatest painters.

Rosetsu took for crest the leaping carp.

VII

LEGENDS TOLD BY A FISHERMAN ON LAKE BIWA, AT ZEZE

WHILE up fishing on Lake Biwa, and later shooting in the vicinity (shooting is not allowed on the lake itself, the water being considered a holy place), I often made Zeze my head-quarters. At the edge of the lake, just there, stands the cottage of an old old fisherman and his sons. They have made a little harbour for their boats ; but they cultivate no ground, their cottage standing in wild grass near a solitary willow. The reason of this is that they are rich, or comparatively so, being the owners of an immense fish-trap, which runs out into the lake nearly a mile, and is a disgrace to all civilised ideas of conservation. They bought the rights from the Daimio, who owned Zeze Castle a hundred years or more ago (this is my own guess at the date, for I never asked or noted it). The trap catches enough to keep the whole of four families comfortable.

Two or three interesting little legends (*truths* the old

senior fisherman called them) I got, either from himself
or from his son while visiting his trap, or sitting under
his willow, fishing myself—for stories.

'Surely the Danna San could not be interested in the
simple old stories of bygone days? Even my sons do
not care for them nowadays!'

'I care for anything of interest,' I said. 'And you
will greatly please me by telling me any fishermen's
legends of hereabouts, or even of the north-western end
of the lake if you know any.'

'Well, there is our Fire Ball,' said the old fisherman.
'That is a curious and unpleasant thing. I have seen it
many times myself. I will begin with that.'

LEGEND

'Many years ago there was a Daimio who had con-
structed at the foot of the southern spur of Mount Hiyei
a castle, the ruins of which may still be seen just to the
north of the military barracks of the Ninth Regiment in
Otsu. The name of the Daimio was Akechi Mitsuhide,
and it is his shito dama that we see now in wet weather on
the lake. It is called the spirit of Akechi.

'The reason of it is this. When Akechi Mitsuhide
defended himself against the Toyotomi, he was closely
invested; but his castle held out bravely, and could not
be taken in spite of Toyotomi's greater forces. As time
went on, the besiegers became exasperated, and prevailed
upon a bad fisherman from Magisa village to tell where
was the source of water which supplied Akechi's castle.
The water having been cut off, the garrison had to

48

capitulate, but not before Akechi and most of his men had committed suicide.

'From that time, in rain or in rough weather, there has come from the castle a fire-ball, six inches in diameter or more. It comes to wreak vengeance on fishermen, and causes many wrecks, leading boats out of their course. Sometimes it comes almost into the boat. Once a fisherman struck it with a bamboo pole, breaking it up into many fiery bits; and on that occasion many boats were lost.

'In full it is called "The Spider Fire of the Spirit of the Dead Akechi." That is all, sir, that I can tell of it —except that often have I seen it myself, and feared it.'

'That is very interesting,' said I, 'and quite what I like. Can you tell me any more?'

'Perhaps, if Danna San found interest in that simple story, he would like to know the reason of why we always have such a terrible storm over the lake on February 25 : so I will tell of that also.'

LEGEND

'Long ago there lived in the village of Komatsu, on the south-eastern side of the lake, a beautiful girl called O Tani. She was the daughter of a wealthy farmer, and of a studious nature as far as it was possible for a girl to be so in those days; that is to say, she was for ever wishing to learn and to know things which were not always within the province of women to know. With the intention of inquiring and learning, she frequently crossed the lake in a boat alone, to visit a certain talented and clever young monk, who was the chief priest at one of the smaller temples situated at the foot of Mount Hiyei San, just over there where you are looking now.

'So deeply impressed was O Tani San with the priest's knowledge, she lost her heart and fell in love with him. Her visits became more frequent. Often she crossed the lake alone, in spite of her parents' protests, when the waves were too high for the safety even of a hardy fisherman like myself.

'At last O Tani could resist no longer. She felt that she must tell the good priest of her love for him, and see if she could not persuade him to renounce the Church and run away with her.

'The monk was greatly sorrowed, and did not quite know what to say, or how to put the girl off. At last he thought that he would give her an impossible task. Knowing that the weather on Lake Biwa towards the end of February is nearly impossible as far as the navigation of small boats is concerned, he said, probably not for a moment meaning it seriously :

' "O Tani San, if you successfully crossed the lake on the evening of February 25 in a washing-tub, it might be possible that I should cast off my robes and forget my calling to carry out your wishes."

'O Tani did not think of the impossible, nor did she quite understand the depth of the priest's meaning; young and foolish as she was with her blind love, she sculled herself home, thinking that the next time she crossed the lake it would be in the washing-tub and to carry off the young priest as her husband. She was supremely happy.

Legends told by a Fisherman

'At last the 25th of February arrived. O Tani had taken care that the best and largest washing-tub had been left near the borders of the lake. After dark she embarked in her frail craft, and without the least fear started.

'When she was about half-way across a fearful storm broke over Hiyei Mountain. The waves arose, and the wind blew with blinding force. Moreover, the light that was usually burning on the Hiyei San side of the lake, which the priest had promised should be especially bright this night, had been blown out. It was not long before poor O Tani's tub was capsized, and in spite of her efforts to keep afloat she sank beneath the waves to rise no more.

'It is said by some that the priest himself put out the light, so as to cut off the last possible chance of O Tani's reaching the shore, being over-zealous in his thoughts of good and evil.

'Since the night that O Tani was drowned, every 25th of February has been wild and stormy, and fishermen fear to be out on that day. People say that the cause is the dissatisfied spirit of poor O Tani, who, though she did not fear death, died disconsolate at being deceived by the monk she loved.

'The washing-tub that O Tani used drifted ashore at Kinohama village, in Eastern Omi. It was picked up by Gensuke, a match-maker, who split it up and made matches of it. When this became known to the villagers of Kinohama, including Gensuke himself, they resolved that every 25th of February should be a holiday, and that a prayer should be said at their shrine for the spirit of

O Tani. They call the day "Joya" (Dealer in Matches Festival), and on it no men work.'

'That is a capital story,' said I to the old fisherman; 'but I should greatly have liked to put the monk in another tub on the following 25th of February, and anchored him out, so that he should be sure of being drowned in the same way.'

'Does the Danna San know why all the little papers are tied in the black rocks at Ishiyama-dera?'

'No: I do not,' I answered; 'and, moreover, when I went there no one would or could tell me.'

'Well, it is not an uninteresting story, and I will tell it to you, for it is short.'

LEGEND

'As the Danna San has been to Ishiyama-dera, he will know about the temple and monastery, which has a history eleven hundred years long;[1] but few people know the real reason why the bits of paper with prayers on them are tied to the black rocks.

'The origin or the reason of tying these paper prayers —*musubi no kami*, as they are called—is pretty, if suicide for the romance of love can make it so.

'Many years ago in Baba Street of Otsu, then known as Shibaya Street, there was a teahouse called Kagiya, which kept very beautiful geisha. Among them was one, named O Taga hana, whose loveliness surpassed all imagination. Though scarcely seventeen, her heart was

---

[1] The temple was founded A.D. 749 by the monk Ryoben Sojo at the command of the Emperor Shomei. It is the thirteenth of the Thirty-Three Holy Places.

no longer her own. It had gone as completely to her lover Denbei as had his to her. It is difficult to imagine how this desperate affair came about at first, for Denbei was only the clerk of a rice-merchant in Otsu, and had but little money to spend on geisha, especially in such an expensive teahouse as Kagiya.

'Jealousy and unhappiness crept into the heart of Denbei, not on account of any unfaithfulness on the part of O Taga hana San, but because he felt jealous of others being well enough off to go to the Kagiya teahouse and hear her sing and see her dance while they ate costly dinners.

'So much did these sorrows tell upon Denbei's heart at last, he used to falsify his master's account-books, frequently taking money, which he spent, of course, at the Kagiya teahouse in seeing the beloved O Taga hana.

'This state of affairs could not last long, and when Denbei told O Taga hana how he had procured the money to come and see her she was shocked beyond measure.

'"My dearest," she said, "the wrong which you have done out of love for me is sure to be discovered, and even were it not it would be wrong. Our love is so great that there remains but one chance for our future happiness—shinju (suicide together). Nothing else will enable us to become united, for if I ran away with you they would soon recapture me, most probably before a day and night had passed."

'"Will you leave with me to-night?" said Denbei.

'"I will meet you at two o'clock in the morning, when all are asleep, down at the flat-growing pine tree near the east end of the town. From there we will go to Ishiyama-dera, and after praying at that holy temple to our good Kwannon we will do shinju in the Hotaru Dani (Firefly Valley), and our souls will depart together."

'Denbei bowed to his sweetheart, and spoke words of gratitude for her faithfulness in recognising his love for her as the cause of his sin, and he promised that at the appointed hour he would meet her by the pine tree near the lake and take her off to Ishiyama, there to carry out their final act and die together.

'To save time, Danna San, in telling this story it is only necessary to say that Denbei and O Taga hana met, and that, after passing over the flat and uninteresting plain known as Awatsu, they reached and passed the Seta Bridge, and that shortly after, about daybreak, they found themselves at Ishiyama. There, in one of the tea-houses, they remained some hours in bliss, and then went to the temple to pray to Kwannon. Then they went to the Hotaru Dani, and, after embracing each other for the last time on this earth, they each wrote a prayer on a piece of paper, twisted it into a piece of string, and fastened it in a double knot with their thumbs and little fingers through a small hole bored in the soft black rocks. Their being able to do this successfully was taken as an omen that all would be well with them after death, and was an answer to their prayer.

'Their spirits passed away together, just as the leaves of fragrant flowers blown off by autumn winds pass together under Seta Bridge.

'That, Danna San, is the origin and reason of tying

Legends told by a Fisherman

these pieces of paper to the black rocks and other places at Ishiyama-dera. The custom is still followed by many country folks, who go to worship and pray for the spirits of Denbei and O Taga hana in the Firefly Valley itself.'

VIII

A MIRACULOUS SWORD

ABOUT the year 110 B.C. there lived a brave prince known in Japanese history as Yamato-dake no Mikoto.[1] He was a great warrior, as was his son, who is said to have been a husband to the Empress Jingo—I presume a second one, for it could not have been the Emperor who was assassinated before the Empress's conquest of Korea. However, that does not very much matter to my story, which is merely the legend attached to the miraculous sword known as the Kusanagi no Tsurugi (the grass-cutting sword), which is held as one of the three sacred treasures, and is handed down from father to son in the Imperial Family. The sword is kept at the Atsuta Shrine, in Owari Province.

At the date given by my interpreter, 110 B.C. (I should

[1] Yamato-dake no Mikoto, one of the eighty children of the Emperor Keiko, was a great hero of the prehistoric age. While yet a stripling he was sent by his father to destroy the rebels of Western Japan. In order to accomplish this end he borrowed the gown of his aunt, who was high priestess of Ise, and, thus disguised, made the rebel chieftains fall in love with him while carousing in the cave where they dwelt. Then, suddenly drawing a sword from his bosom, he smote them to death. He next subdued the province of Izumo, and finally conquered Eastern Japan, which was at that time a barbarous waste. After many adventures, both warlike and amorous, he died on the homeward march to Yamato, where the Emperor, his father, held Court.

56

add 'or thereabouts,' allowing large margins), Yamato-dake no Mikoto had been successful at all events in suppressing the revolutionists known as the Kumaso in Kyushu. Being a man of energy, and possessing a strong force of trained men, he resolved that he would suppress the revolutionists up on the north-eastern coasts.

Before starting, Yamato-dake no Mikoto thought he should go to Ise to worship in the temples, to pray for divine aid, and to call on an aunt who lived near. Yamato-dake spent five or six days with his aunt, Princess Yamato Hime, to whom he announced his intention of subduing the rebels. She presented him with her greatest treasure —the miraculous sword—and also with a tinder-and-flint-box.

Before parting with her nephew Yamato Hime no Mikoto said : 'This sword is the most precious thing which I could give you, and will guard you safely through all dangers. Value it accordingly, for it will be one of the sacred treasures.'

(Legend says that in the age of the gods Susanoo-no Mikoto once found an old man and a woman weeping bitterly because a mammoth eight-headed snake had devoured seven of their daughters, and there remained only one more, whom, they felt sure, the eighth serpent's head would take. Susanoo-no Mikoto asked if they would give him the daughter if he killed the snake ; to which they gladly assented. Susanoo filled eight buckets with sake-wine, and put them where the serpent was likely to come, and, hiding himself in the vicinity, awaited events. The monster came, and the eight heads drank the eight buckets full of sake, and became, naturally, dead-drunk. Susanoo then dashed in and cut the beast to bits. In the tail he found a sword—the celebrated and miraculous sword 'Kusanagi no Tsurugi,' the grass-cutting sword of our story.)

After bidding farewell to Yamato Hime no Mikoto, the Prince took his departure, setting out for the province of Suruga, on the eastern coast, to find what he could hear, it being in a turbulent state ; and it was there that he ran into his first danger, and that his enemies laid a trap for him, through their knowledge that he was fond of hunting.

There were some immense rush plains in Suruga Province where now stands the village of Yaitsu Mura ('Yaita' means 'burning fields'). It was resolved by the rebels that one of them should go and invite Yamato-dake to come out and hunt, while they were to scatter and hide themselves in the long grass, until the guide should lead him into their midst, when they would jump up and kill him. Accordingly, they sent to Yamato-dake a plausible and clever man, who told him that there were many deer on the grass plains. Would he come and hunt them? The man volunteered to act as guide.

The invitation was tempting ; and, as he had found the country less rebellious than he had expected, the Prince accepted.

When the morning arrived the Prince, in addition to carrying his hunting-bow, carried the sword given him by his aunt, the Princess Yamato. The day was windy, and it was thought by the rebels that as the rushes were so dry it would be more sure, and less dangerous to themselves, to fire the grass, for it was certain that the guide would make the Prince hunt up-wind, and if they fired the grass properly the flames would rush with lightning speed towards him and be absolutely safe for themselves.

Yamato-dake did just as they had expected. He came quietly on, suspecting nothing. Suddenly the rushes took fire in front and at the sides of him. The Prince realised that he had been betrayed. The treacherous guide had disappeared. The Prince stood in danger of suffocation and death. The smoke, dense and choking, rushed along with rapidity and great roaring.

Yamato-dake tried to run for the only gap, but was too late. Then he began cutting the grass with his sword, to prevent the fire from reaching him. He found that whichever direction he cut in with his sword, the wind changed to that direction. If to the north he cut, the wind changed to the south and prevented the fire from advancing farther; if to the south, the wind changed to the north; and so on. Taking advantage of this, Yamato-dake retaliated upon his enemies. He got fire from his aunt's tinder-box, and where there was no fire in the rushes he lit them, cutting through the grass at the same time in the direction in which he wished the fire to go. Rushing thus from point to point, he was successful in the endeavour to turn the tables on his enemies, and destroyed them all.

It is important to note that there is in existence a sword, said to be this sword, in the Atsuta Shrine, Owari Province; a great festival in honour of it is held on June 21 every year.

From that place Yamato-dake no Mikoto went on

to Sagami Province. Finding things quiet there, he took a ship to cross to Kazusa Province, accompanied by a lady he deeply loved, who was given the title of Hime (Princess) because of Yamato-dake's rank. Her name was Tachibana. They had not got more than ten miles from shore when a terrible storm arose. The ship threatened to go down.

'This,' said Tachibana Hime, 'is the doing of one of the sea-goddesses who thirst for men's lives. I will give her mine, my lord; perhaps that may appease her until you have safely crossed the wicked sea.'

Without further warning, Tachibana Hime cast herself into the sea; the waves closed over her head, to the consternation and grief of all, and to the breaking of Yamato-dake's heart.

As Tachibana Hime had expected, the sea-goddess was appeased. The wind went down, the water calmed, and the ship reached Kazusa Province in safety. Yamato-dake went as far as Yezo, putting down small rebellions on the way.

Several years afterwards, accompanied by many of his old officers, he found himself back on the side of a hill in Sagami Province overlooking the place where poor Tachibana Hime had given up her life for him by throwing herself into the sea. The Prince gazed sadly at the sea, and thrice exclaimed, with tears flowing down his cheeks,—brave though he was—'Azuma waya!' (Alas, my dearest wife!); and Eastern Japan, about the middle, has since then been called 'Azuma.'

IX

'THE PROCESSION OF GHOSTS'[1]

SOME four or five hundred years ago there was an old temple not far from Fushimi, near Kyoto. It was called the Shozenji temple, and had been deserted for many years, priests fearing to live there, on account of the ghosts which were said to haunt it. Still, no one had ever seen the ghosts. No doubt the story came into the people's minds from the fact that the whole of the priests had been killed by a large band of robbers many years beyond the memory of men—for the sake of loot, of course.

So great a horror did this strike into the minds of all, that the temple was allowed to rot and run to ruin.

[1] Somewhere between the years 1400 and 1550 there lived a family of celebrated painters covering three generations, and consequently difficult to be accurate about. There were Tosa Mitsunobu, Kano Mitsunobu, and Hasegawa Mitsunobu; sometimes Tosa Mitsunobu signed his pictures as Fujiwara Mitsunobu. When to this I add that there were other celebrated painters—Kano Masanobu, Kano Motonobu, besides their families, imitators, and name forgers—you will realise the difficulties into which one may fall in fixing on names and dates; but, as usual, I have been placed safely on high ground by a kind friend, H.E. Mr. Hattori, the Governor, whose knowledge of Art is great. Undoubtedly it was Tosa Mitsunobu who painted the picture known as the Hiyakki Yakō, or as The One Hundred Ghosts' Procession, which is celebrated, and has served as a map of instruction in the drawing of hobgoblins and ghosts, 'spooks,' 'eries,' or whatever you may choose to call them. As far as I can judge, the picture was painted about the end of the first half of the fifteenth century.

61

One year a priest, a pilgrim and a stranger, passed by the temple, and, not knowing its history, went in and sought refuge from the weather, instead of continuing his journey to Fushimi. Having cold rice in his wallet, he felt that he could not do better than pass the night there; for, though the weather might be cold, he would at all events save drenching the only clothes which he had, and be well off in the morning.

The good man took up his quarters in one of the smaller rooms, which was in less bad repair than the rest of the place; and, after eating his meal, said his prayers and lay down to sleep, while the rain fell in torrents on the roof and the wind howled through the creaky buildings. Try as he might, the priest could not sleep, for the cold draughts chilled him to the marrow. Somewhere about midnight the old man heard weird and unnatural noises. They seemed to proceed from the main building.

Prompted by curiosity, he arose; and when he got to the main building he found Hiyakki Yakō (meaning a procession of one hundred ghosts)—a term, I believe, which had been generally applied to a company of ghosts. The ghosts fought, wrestled, danced, and made merry. Though greatly alarmed at first, our priest became interested. After a few moments, however, more awful spirit-like ghosts came on the scene. The priest ran back to the small room, into which he barred himself; and he spent the rest of the night saying masses for the souls of the dead.

At daybreak, though the weather continued wet, the priest departed. He told the villagers what he had seen, and they spread the news so widely that within three or four days the temple was known as the worst-haunted temple in the neighbourhood.

It was at this time that the celebrated painter Tosa Mitsunobu heard of it. Having ever been anxious to paint a picture of Hiyakki Yakō, he thought that a sight of the ghosts in Shozenji temple might give him the necessary material : so off to Fushimi and Shozenji he started.

Mitsunobu went straight to the temple at dusk, and sat up all night in no very happy state of mind ; but he saw no ghosts, and heard no noise.

Next morning he opened all the windows and doors and flooded the main temple with light. No sooner had he done this than he found the walls of the place covered, as it were, with the figures or drawings of ghosts of indescribable complexity. There were far more than two hundred, and all different.

Could he but remember them ! That was what Tosa Mitsunobu thought. Drawing his notebook and brush from his pocket, he proceeded to take them down minutely. This occupied the best part of the day.

During his examination of the outlines of the various ghosts and goblins which he had drawn, Mitsunobu saw that the fantastic shapes had come from cracks in the damp deserted walls ; these cracks were filled with fungi and mildew, which in their turn produced the toning, colouring, and eventually the figures from which he compiled his celebrated picture Hiyakki Yakō.[1] Grateful

[1] It is well known that certain fungi and mildews produce phosphorescent light amid certain circumstances. No doubt the priest saw the cracks in the wall amid these

was he to the imaginative priest whose stories had led him to the place. Without him never would the picture have been drawn ; never could the horrible aspects of so many ghosts and goblins have entered the mind of one man, no matter how imaginative.

My painter's illustration gives a few, copied from a first-hand copy of Mitsunobu's.

circumstances, and the noise he heard was made by rats. I once read a story about a haunted country-house in England, the ghost in which was eventually found to be a luminous fungus.

9. O TANI SAN'S TUB GETS SWAMPED

10. THE BLACK ROCKS AT ISHIYAMA-DERA WHERE PRAYERS ARE TIED

11. YAMATO-DAKE NO MIKOTO DESTROYS HIS ENEMIES AND SAVES HIMSELF FROM BEING BURNED BY THE AID OF THE MIRACULOUS SWORD

12. THE PROCESSION OF GHOSTS

13. MATSUO DECLARES THE HEAD TO BE THAT OF KANSHUSAI

14. OKAWA PLUNGES THE HOSOKAWA DEED INTO HIS STOMACH

15. ISHIDOMARO MEETS HIS FATHER, BUT FAILS TO IDENTIFY HIM FOR SURE

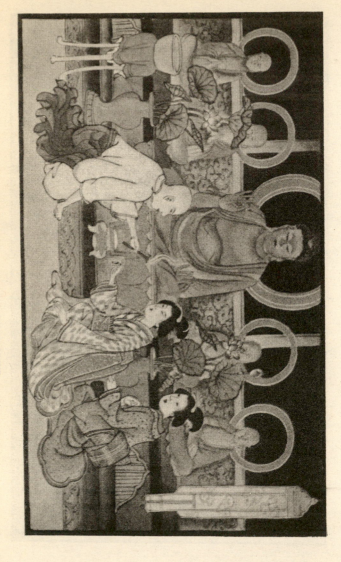

16. O SAME SEES THE HANDSOME YOUNG PRIEST

X

A FAITHFUL SERVANT[1]

IN the reign of the Emperor Engi, which began in the year 901 A.D., there lived a man whose name has ever since been celebrated on account of his beautiful writings, poetic and other. He was the Emperor's great favourite, and consequently he was the strong man of the day; his name was Sugawara Michizane. Needless to say, it was not very long before, with all these things in his favour, he was the head of the Government, living in luxury.

Things went well enough for a time; but the inevitable came at last. Not all the people agreed with Michizane's ideas or his politics. Secret enemies lurked at every corner. Among them was one particularly bad man named Tokihira, whose poisonous intrigues at Court were constant.

Tokihira held a Government position under Michizane, and hated him in his heart, thinking that if he could but arrange to get Michizane into the bad graces of the

---

[1] This little tragedy, showing the deep loyalty which was general 1000 years ago, was told to me by Mr. Matsuzaki of the Kencho (Government Office).

Emperor he himself might become leader of the Government.

Michizane was a man with whom little fault could be found, and so it came to pass that Tokihira was unable to find any cause for starting evil reports about him; but as time went on he became more determined to do evil in the end.

At last an opportunity arrived. Tokihira, who had many secret agents trying to discover something to be reported to the Emperor against Michizane, heard a statement that Prince Toki (Toki no Miya) had fallen secretly in love with the beautiful daughter of Michizane, and that they held secret meetings.

Tokihira was overjoyed at the news, and went straightway to the Emperor, who received him, hearing that he had a marvellous tale of intrigue to tell.

'Your Majesty,' said Tokihira, 'much as I grieve to tell it, a serious plot is about. Sugawara Michizane has so arranged it that your Majesty's younger brother, Prince Toki, has fallen in love with his daughter. Deeply as I regret to say it, they hold secret meetings. Moreover, Michizane, your Majesty's Premier, is scheming that your Majesty may be assassinated, or at least dethroned in favour of Prince Toki, who is to marry Michizane's daughter.'

Naturally the Emperor Engi was infuriated. He was a good and sound monarch, and had ruled the people, with the aid of Michizane, fairly, firmly, and well. He had looked upon Michizane as a personal friend; and to think of Michizane conspiring his assassination, or at all events so scheming as to place Prince Toki on the throne, and to marry his own daughter to the Prince, was more than he could stand.

He sent for Michizane.

Michizane protested his innocence. True it was, he said, that the Prince had fallen in love with his daughter; but that was not much to be wondered at. His daughter was beautiful; the Prince and she were much of the same age, and had seen much of each other from their childhood. Now that they had grown older, they found that their friendship had turned to love. That was all. It was not easy for a Prince of the blood royal to meet the lady of his heart quite so openly as another might; and, no doubt, they had met, for his daughter had told him so. As to the plot asserted by Tokihira, that was absolutely fanciful, and it was an astonishment to hear of so dastardly an accusation.

Tokihira perceived the temper of the Emperor. By loud words and unscrupulous lies he upset all the unfortunate Michizane's protests; and the Emperor ordered Michizane to be sent for the rest of his life to Tsukushi, in the island of Kyushu.

Accompanied only by his faithful servant Matsuo, Michizane went into exile. The punishment of Michizane, unjust as it was, broke up the employment of many others. All those who had been closely associated with him were dismissed. Among them was Takebayashi Genzo, who had been one of Michizane's chief attendants. Genzo had been one of Michizane's literary pupils; consequently it is not astonishing that on losing employment, Genzo fled to a small town, and out of duty took with him Michizane's wife and young son Kanshusai, aged ten. All changed their names, and Genzo, to support them as well as his own family, established a small school.

Thus it was that for some time Kanshusai escaped the wicked designs against his life that had been planned by Tokihira.

Matsuo, the faithful servant who had followed his master Michizane into banishment, heard of a vile plot to assassinate his master's son, and after many weary days of thought as to how he could prevent it he perceived that the only way would be to sacrifice his own son instead.

First he told his banished master of his intention, and having obtained leave he journeyed back to Kyoto, and sought out Tokihira himself, to whom he offered his services both as a servant and as a hunter of Michizane's son Kanshusai. Tokihira readily engaged him, thinking that now he would be sure to find the boy whom he wished to have beheaded. Tokihira had taken the place of Michizane in the Emperor's favour, and had great power ; his will was almost law.

So well did Matsuo play his part in Tokihira's household and among his servants, it was not long before they were all agreed that Matsuo was most faithful to his new master, and the greatest confidence was placed in him.

Shortly after this, it came to the knowledge of Tokihira that Kanshusai was hidden, under a different name, in the school which belonged to Genzo. Genzo was ordered to send the boy's head to Tokihira within forty-eight hours.

Matsuo, ever faithful, hearing of this, went to Genzo's

school in disguise and disclosed to the schoolmaster, who readily assented, his scheme for saving Kanshusai. Then Matsuo sent his son Kotaro to Genzo's school, from which he never returned alive, poor boy; and though (in all honour be it said) Genzo did not like the killing of this boy, he steeled his nerves, for the sake of his former master and to save Kanshusai's life.

With one blow of his sword he took off the innocent head.

At the appointed time Tokihira's officials called at the school to fetch it, and they carried it back to Tokihira, saying : 'Now, Lord Tokihira, there is no longer fear for the future from Michizane's son, for here is his head in this box. See ! And here is the schoolmaster Take-bayashi Genzo, who followed your lordship's orders and cut it off.'

Tokihira was pleased, but not perfectly assured that the head was the right one : so, knowing that Matsuo had previously been employed by Michizane, and that he must know if it were Kanshusai's head or not, he called him, ordering him to take the head out of the box and identify it.

Poor Matsuo ! Imagine his feelings at having to draw his only son Kotaro's head from the box, and hold it up by the hair, and assure the Lord Tokihira that it was indeed the head of Kanshusai, Michizane's son ! He did so, however, with great nerve and splendid fortitude, thus saving the life of Kanshusai, and fulfilling his duty to his banished master Michizane.

Matsuo's fidelity is still adored by those who know the story.

Ancient Tales and Folklore of Japan

Not long after a terrible thunderstorm came over Kyoto. A thunderbolt crashed through Tokihira's palace and killed him. To this day people say that Michizane's spirit came down in the shape of that thunderbolt to be avenged.

XI

PRINCE HOSOKAWA'S MOST VALUABLE
TITLE-DEEDS[1]

SEVERAL hundred years ago there dwelt in lands of the Hosokawas a widow and her daughter, a beautiful girl of seventeen, named Kazuye. O Kazuye San's father had been foully murdered some six months before, and both Kazuye and her mother had made up their minds to devote their fortune and their lives to bringing the criminals to justice. In these efforts they received no help, but spent the whole of their money, until at last they were almost forced to beg in the street for food. Day after day, however, they continued to pray in the temple for help, and never once lost heart or weakened in their purpose. O Kazuye told her mother that were she fortunate enough to gain the affections of a man, even he should be sacrificed in the effort after vengeance.

One day it came to pass that the poverty-stricken appearance of Kazuye and her mother, returning as usual from praying in the temple, aroused the mirth of a party

[1] Told to me by Mr. Matsuzaki, and said to be perfectly true, the document in question being in possession of the present Prince Hosokawa.

of roughs, who proceeded to insult them. A handsome young samurai, Okawa Jomoyemon, happened to come along. Drawing his sword, he very soon put the roughs to flight. Having done this, and bowing low, he asked whom he had the honour of serving.

O Kazuye answered for her mother, and quickly recognised that this handsome youth was just such as she had longed to meet, so that he might fall in love and wish to help her in seeking out the murderer of her father. Therefore, not unnaturally, she encouraged him; and he fell in love with her. In the meanwhile an old friend of Kazuye's father, feeling great sorrow for her, had found a place for her in Prince Hosokawa's household; and there she won such favour in the eyes of the Prince (or, as the title then was, Daimio) that the other maids began to be jealous.

It happened that one evening Okawa, now desperately in love with O Kazuye, in spite of being the retainer of another Daimio, felt that he must see her at all costs. He arranged a secret meeting, and eventually found his way to Kazuye's apartment. Still full of desire for vengeance, she seized upon the occasion to pour forth her story and implore assistance.

Okawa, being a true knight-errant, vowed that he would speak no more of love until he himself had hunted down and killed the murderers of Kazuye's father. Just as he had finished making this vow, one of the jealous maids (who had been listening) made her presence known, and rushed off to tell her mistress.

What was to be done? Okawa, the retainer of another Daimio, caught in the castle secretly conversing with one of the Hosokawa maids of honour! Surely both he and she would suffer death! O Kazuye was not long in thinking. She hid her lover in an old armour-case. That, however, was no use. She was instantly summoned into the presence of the Daimio, and the armour-chest was carried in as well.

The Daimio, furiously angry, ordered that O Kazuye should be killed. Okawa spoke up. He said that she was in no way responsible for this secret meeting, that the fault was entirely his; and begged that he might be allowed to die in place of her. Moreover, he told the whole story of Kazuye's life, and mentioned that her ambition in life was to avenge the death of her father.

The Daimio was greatly touched. Recognising the chivalry on both sides, he took Okawa into his own service, promising at the same time to aid them both in fulfilling their purpose.

Tears of gratitude came into Okawa's eyes, and he vowed there and then to sacrifice his life for Hosokawa on the very first opportunity.

After about a year had passed a great fire broke out in the castle. It was so sudden that nothing could be done. The wind, fanning the flames, barely gave time for the people to escape, much less to carry off the family valuables.

When all were clear of the burning mass the Daimio suddenly remembered that his title-deeds would be lost, and that such a disaster would be dangerous for his family. Realising this, he jumped from his horse, and was about to dash back to try and recover them; but his retainers held him, fearing that he would die.

Okawa, hearing this, thought with delight that now an opportunity had come to him to save his new master and pay him for the kindness to himself and Kazuye. He rushed into the burning mass, and, having broken open the iron safe, seized the valuable documents. Then he found escape impossible. He was cut off by fire on all sides, and plainly saw that both he and the papers must be burned. At this moment a thought came to him. Though he must be burned, possibly his body might save the documents. Drawing his short sword, he deliberately disembowelled himself, and thrust the roll of papers into his stomach. Then he flung himself on the flaming floor and died. The fire went on. Poor Okawa was charred beyond recognition.

When the fire was over his body was recovered, and inside the roasted corpse was found the blood-stained roll of papers on which the Hosokawa family depended. From that time on, the document has been called 'Hosokawa no chi daruma' — the blood-stained document of the Hosokawas.

XII

THE STORY OF KATO SAYEMON[1]

In the days when Ashikaga was Shogun there served under him a knight of good family, Kato Sayemon, of whom he was especially fond. Things went well with Sayemon. He lived in what might almost be called a palace. Money he possessed in plenty. He had a charming wife who had borne him a son, and, according to old custom, he had many others who lived as wives within his mansion. There was no war in the land.

[1] Told to me by Mr. Matsuzaki. I cannot say that I think much of the story. Sayemon is made a hero; but he must appear to most as a rather cowardly and low creature. I remarked upon this to Mr. Matsuzaki, saying: 'I do not see that the story is finished. You make Sayemon out a model person, whereas to me he appears the worst one in the story. Surely the wife and the son should have come out as the good people; but you laud and praise Sayemon for leaving his family, and refusing to recognise them when they had no sin against themselves.' 'I do not admit the difficulty,' said Mr. Matsuzaki. 'It is the same as the Lord Buddha. He also left his wife, and devoted his life to religious affairs just as Sayemon did.' Well, I could not agree with this. Buddha was Buddha, a benefactor and helper to the whole of Asia. Sayemon was a poor miserable weakling who simply sought personal peace. As far as the story goes I defy anybody to find him a hero, or a person who in any way emulated Buddha—unless he did so from an entirely Japanese point of view. The story, however, is quite a celebrated one, referred to in many Japanese books: so Mr. Matsuzaki tells me.

Sayemon found no trouble in his household. Peace and contentment reigned. He enjoyed life accordingly, by feasting and so forth. ' Oh that such a life could last ! ' thought he ; but fate decreed otherwise.

One evening, when Sayemon was strolling about in his lovely garden, watching the fireflies and listening to singing insects and piping toads, of which he was extremely fond, he happened to pass his wife's room and to look up.

There he saw his dear wife and his favourite concubine playing chess ('go,' in Japanese). What struck him most was that they appeared perfectly happy and contented in each other's society. While Sayemon looked, however, their hair seemed to rear up from behind in the shapes of snakes which fought desperately. This filled him with fear.

Sayemon, in amazement, stealthily approached in order to see better ; but he found the vision just the same. His wife and the other lady, when moving their men, smiled at each other, showing every sign of great courtesy ; nevertheless, there remained the indistinct outlines of their hair assuming the forms of fighting snakes. Hitherto Sayemon had thought of them as almost sisters to each other, and so outwardly had they in fact appeared ; but, now that he had seen the mysterious sign of the snakes, he knew that they hated each other more than could be understood by a man.

He became uneasy in his mind. Until then his life had been rendered doubly happy because he thought his home was peaceful ; but now, he reflected, hatred and malice must be rampant in the house. Sayemon felt as if he were a rudderless boat, being drawn towards a cataract, from which no means of escape seemed possible.

He spent a sleepless night in meditation, during which he decided that to run away would be the safest course in the end. Peace was all that he craved for. To obtain it, he would devote himself to religious work for the rest of his life.

Next morning Kato Sayemon was nowhere to be found. There was consternation in the household. Men were dispatched here, there, and everywhere; but Sayemon could not be found. On the fifth or sixth day after the disappearance his wife reduced the establishment, but continued herself, with her little son Ishidomaro, to live in the house. Even the Shogun Ashikaga was greatly disconcerted at Sayemon's disappearance. No news of him came, and time passed on until a year had gone, and then another, when Sayemon's wife resolved to take Ishidomaru, aged five, and go in search.

For five weary years they wandered about, this mother and son, making inquiries everywhere; but not the slightest clue could they get, until at last one day they were staying at a village in Kishu, where they met an old man who told them that a year before he had seen Kato Sayemon at the temple of Koya San. 'Sure,' he said, 'I knew him, for I was once a palanquin-bearer for the Shogun, and often and often saw Sayemon San. I cannot say if he is at the temple; but he was a priest there a year ago.'

For Ishidomaro and his mother there was but little sleep that night. They were in a fever of excitement. Ishidomaro was now eleven years of age, and was most anxious to have his father at home ; both mother and son, happy after their long years of searching, eagerly looked forward to the morrow.

Unfortunately, according to ancient regulations, Koya San temple and mountain were only for men. No woman was allowed to ascend to worship the image of Buddha on this mountain. Thus Ishidomaro's mother had to remain in the village while he went in quest of his father.

At daybreak he started, full of hope, and telling his mother not to fear. 'I will bring back father this very evening,' said he ; 'and how happy we shall all be ! Farewell for the time being, and fear not for me !' So saying, Ishidomaro went off. 'True,' he said, 'I do not know my father by sight ; but he has a black mole over his left eye, and so have I ; besides, I feel that it is my father I am going to meet.' With that and such other thoughts in his mind the boy plodded upwards through the tall and gloomy forests, stopping here and there at some wayside shrine to pray for success.

Higher and higher Ishidomaro climbed—Koya San is near 1100 feet in height—until he reached the outer gates of the temple, of which the true name is 'Kongobuji,' for 'Koya San' means only 'Koya Mountain.'

Arrived at the first priest's house, Ishidomaro espied an old man mumbling prayers.

'Please, sir,' said he, doffing his hat and bowing low, 'could you tell me if there is a priest here called Kato Sayemon? Greatly should I be obliged if you could direct me to him. He has only been a priest for five years. For all that time my dear mother and myself have been in search of him. He is my father, and we both love him much, and wish him to come back to us!'

'Ah, my lad, I feel sorry for you,' answered Sayemon (for it was indeed he). 'I know of no man called Kato Sayemon in these temples.' Delivering himself of this speech, Sayemon showed considerable emotion. He fully recognised that the boy he was addressing was his son, and he was under sore distress to deny him thus, and not to recognise and take him to his heart; but Sayemon had made up his mind that the rest of his life should be sacrificed for the sake of Buddha, and that all worldly things should be cast aside. Ishidomaro and his wife needed no money or food, but were well provided for; thus he need not trouble on those grounds. Sayemon determined to remain as he was, a poor monk, hidden in the monastery on Koya San. With a desperate effort he continued:

'I don't remember ever hearing of a Kato Sayemon's having been here, though, of course, I have heard of the Kato Sayemon who was the great friend of the Shogun Ashikaga.'

Ishidomaro was not at all satisfied with this answer. He felt somehow or other that he was in the presence of his father. Moreover, the priest had a black mole over his left eye, and he, Ishidomaro, had one exactly the same.

'Sir,' said he, again addressing the priest, 'my mother has always particularly drawn my attention to the mole over my left eye, saying, "My son, your father has such a mark over his left eye, the exact counterpart; now, remember this, for when you go forth to seek him this will be a sure sign to you." You, sir, have the exact mark that I have. I know and feel that you are my father !'

With that, tears came into the eyes of Ishidomaro, and, outstretching his arms, he cried, 'Father, father, let me embrace you !'

Sayemon trembled all over with emotion ; but haughtily held up his head and, recovering himself, said :

'My lad, there are many men and many boys who have moles over their left eyebrows, and even over their right. I am not your father. You must go elsewhere to seek him.'

At this moment the chief priest came and called Sayemon to the evening services, which were held in the main temple. Thus it was that Sayemon preferred to devote his life to Buddha, and (as Mr. Matsuzaki tells me) to emulate Buddha, rather than return to the ways of the world or to his family, or even to recognise his one and only son !

My sympathies are with Ishidomaro, of whom, as of his poor mother, we are told nothing further. To end in Mr. Matsuzaki's words :

'What became of Ishidomaro and his mother is not known ; but it is told to this day that Kato Sayemon passed the rest of his life in peace and purity, entirely sacrificing his body and soul to Buddha, and did these things without any person to mourn over him, but in perfect contentment.'

In the third book of Sir Edwin Arnold's *Light of Asia* are the following verses, which were addressed to Buddha, when he was a Prince, by the winds :—

The Story of Kato Sayemon

We are the voices of the wandering wind ;
Wander thou too, O Prince, thy rest to find ;
Leave love for love of lovers, for woe's sake
Quit state for sorrow, and deliverance make.
So sigh we, passing o'er the silver strings,
To thee who know'st not yet of earthly things ;
So say we ; mocking, as we pass away,
Those lovely shadows wherewith thou dost play.

No one, I feel sure, will fail to agree with me that
Sayemon appears as a weak, selfish, and unheroic personage
—not as a hero, much less as a Buddha.

XIII

GREAT FIRE CAUSED BY A LADY'S DRESS

SOME 120 years ago, in the year of Temmei, a most terrible fire broke out in the western corner of Yedo,—the worst fire, probably, that is known to the world's history, for it is said to have destroyed no fewer than 188,000 persons.

At that time there lived in Yedo, now Tokio, a very rich pawnbroker, Enshu Hikoyemon, the proud possessor of a beautiful daughter aged sixteen, whose name was O Same, which in this instance is probably derived from the word 'sameru' (to fade away), for in truth O Same San did fade away.

Enshu Hikoyemon loved his daughter dearly, and, he being a widower with no other child, his thoughts and affections were concentrated on her alone. He had long been rich enough to cast aside the mean thoughts and characteristics which had enabled him to reach his present position. From being a hard-hearted relentless money-grubber, Enshu Hikoyemon had become soft-hearted and generous—as far, at all events, as his daughter was concerned.

One day the beautiful O Same went to pray at her

ancestors' graves. She was accompanied by her maid, and, after saying her prayers, passed the Temple of Hommyoji, which is in the same grounds at Hongo Maru Yama, and there, as she repeated her prayers before the image of Buddha, she saw a young priest, with whom she fell instantly in love. Thitherto she had had no love-affair; nor, indeed, did she fully realise what had happened, beyond the fact that the youth's face pleased her to gaze upon. It was a solemn and noble face. As O Same lit a joss-stick and handed it to the priest, to be placed before Buddha, their hands met, and she felt pass through her body a thrill the like of which she had never experienced. Poor O Same was what is known as madly in love at first sight,—in love so much that as she arose and left the temple all she could see was the face of the young priest; wherever she looked she saw nothing else. She spoke not a word to her maid on the way home, but went straight to her room.

Next morning she announced to the maid that she was indisposed. 'Go,' she said, 'and tell my dear father that I shall remain in bed. I do not feel well this day.'

Next day was much the same, and so were the next and the next.

Hikoyemon, disconsolate, tried every means to enliven his daughter. He sought to get her away to the seaside. He offered to take her to the Holy Temple of Ise or to Kompira. She would not go. Doctors were called, and could find nothing wrong with O Same San. 'She has something on her mind, and when you can get it off she will be well,' was all that they could say.

At last O Same confessed to her father that she had

lost her heart to a young priest in the Hommyoji Temple. 'Nay,' she said : 'be not angry with me, father, for I do not know him, and have seen him only once. In that once I loved him, for he has a noble face, which haunts me night and day ; and so it is that my heart is heavy, and my body sickens for the want of him. Oh, father, if you love me and wish to save my life, go and find him and tell him that I love him, and that without him I must die !'

Poor Hikoyemon ! Here was a nice business—his daughter in love—dying of love for an unknown priest! What was he to do ? First he humoured his daughter, and at last, after several days, persuaded her to accompany him to the temple. Unfortunately, they did not see the priest in question ; nor did they on a second visit ; and after this O Same became more disconsolate than ever, absolutely refusing to leave her room. Night and day her sobs were heard all over the house, and her father was utterly wretched, especially as he had now found out secretly that the priest with whom his daughter had fallen in love was one of the most strict of Buddha's followers, and not likely to err from the disciplinarian rules of religion.

In spite of this, Hikoyemon determined to make an effort in behalf of his daughter. He ventured to the temple alone, saw the priest, told him of his daughter's love, and asked if a union would be possible.

The priest spurned the idea, saying, 'Is it not evident to you by my robes that I have devoted my love to Buddha? It is an insult that you should make such a proposition to me !'

Hikoyemon returned to his home deeply mortified at

the rebuff; but felt it his duty to be candid with his daughter.

O Same wept herself into hysterics. She grew worse day by day. Hoping to distract her mind, her father had got made for her a magnificent dress which cost nearly yen 4000. He thought that O Same would be vain enough to wish to put it on, and to go out and show it.

This was no use. O Same was not like other women. She cared not for fine raiment or for creating sensations. She put the costume on in her room, to please her father; but then she took it off again, and went back to her bed, where, two days later, she died of a broken heart.

Hikoyemon felt the loss of his pretty daughter very much. At the funeral there must have been half a mile of flower-bearers.

The superb dress was presented to the temple. Such dresses are carefully kept; they remind the priests to say prayers for their late owners as, every two or three months, they are being dusted and cleaned.

The Vicar or Head Priest of this temple, however, was not a good man. He stole this particular dress of O Same's, knowing the value, and sold it secretly to a second-hand dealer in such things.

Some twelve months later the dress was again donated to the same temple by another father whose daughter had died of a love-affair, he having bought the dress at the second-hand clothes-shop. (This girl died and was buried on the same day of the same month as O Same.)

The priest of the temple was not sorry to see the valuable garment return as a gift to his church, and, being mercenary, he sold it again. It seemed, indeed, a sort of gold-mine to himself and his church. Imagine, therefore, the feeling among the priests when, in the following year, in the same month and on exactly the same day as that on which O Same and the other girl had died, another girl of exactly the same age was buried in their cemetery, having died also of a love-affair, and having also worn the splendid dress that O Same was given, which was duly presented to the temple, at the conclusion of her burial service, for the third time.

To say that the chief priest was astonished would be to say little. He and the rest of them were sorely perplexed and troubled.

There were the honest priests, who had had nothing to do with the selling of the garment, and the dishonest head priest or vicar. The honest men were puzzled. The vicar was frightened into thinking honesty the best policy amid the circumstances. Accordingly, he assembled all the priests of the temple, made a hasty confession, and asked for advice.

The priests came to one conclusion, and that was that the spirit of O Same San was in the dress, and that it must be burned, and burned with some ceremony, so as to appease her spirit. Accordingly a time was fixed. When the day arrived many people came to the temple. A great ceremony was held, and finally the valuable garment was placed upon a stone cut in the shape of a lotus flower and lighted.

The weather was calm at the time; but as the garment took fire a sudden gust of wind came, instantly fanning the whole into flame. The gust increased into

Great Fire caused by a Lady's Dress

a storm, which carried one of the sleeves of the dress up to the ceiling of the temple, where it caught between two rafters and burned viciously. In less than two or three minutes the whole temple was on fire. The fire went on for seven days and seven nights, at the expiration of which time nearly the whole of the south and western portions of Yedo were gone ; and gone also were 188,000 people.

The charred remains (as far as possible) were collected and buried, and a temple (which now exists), called 'Eko In,' was built at the spot, to invoke the blessing of Buddha on their souls.

NOTE BY MATSUZAKI.—At the present day the Eko In Temple is well known. Games and wrestling are held there twice a year. Visitors to the temple see the wrestling-place; but no one asks why the temple was built there.

XIV

HISTORY OF AWOTO FUJITSUNA[1]

Hojo Tokiyori—who, my *Murray* says, was born in 1246 A.D., and died seventeen years later, in 1263—was Regent for a time, young as he was.

One day he went to worship at the shrine of Tsurugaoka in Kamakura. That same evening he dreamed that one of the gods appeared to him and said :

'Hojo Tokiyori, you are very young for a ruler, and there are some who will try to deceive you, for honest men are scarce. There is one man who is of exceptional honesty, however, and if you wish to govern the people successfully it would be advisable to employ him. His name is Awoto Fujitsuna.'

Hojo Tokiyori told him of his dream. 'Nay,' said he ; 'it was more than a dream : it was a vision that called upon me to appoint you to the post, which I have done.'

'Ah, indeed !' quoth Awoto Fujitsuna. 'Then, sir, if you appoint high officials as the result of dreams and visions, it is a risky matter, for by those dreams we may some day be ordered to be beheaded !'

[1] Told to me by my friend Mr. Matsuzaki.

History of Awoto Fujitsuna

Hojo Tokiyori laughed at this, and said he hoped not. Awoto Fujitsuna turned out a most excellent and trustworthy official, popular, just, and honest. No one had a word against him, and Hojo Tokiyori was delighted.

One day Fujitsuna was carrying over a bridge a bag of money belonging to the Government. He fell, and the bag burst. Fujitsuna collected the money—with the exception of a half-cent piece, which had rolled in some way over the edge of the bridge and fallen into the river.

Fujitsuna could have let it go, putting another in its place; but that course would not have been up to the high standard of his morals in such matters. He had lost a half-cent which belonged to the Government. It was, he knew, in the river. Consequently, he refused to move on until it was recovered. That was clearly his duty. Awoto Fujitsuna ran to the houses at either end of the bridge, telling the villagers merely that he had dropped some Government money into the river—would they come and help him to find it? Of course they would, ready to help as the Japanese country-men have been from time immemorial. All followed Fujitsuna into the river—men, women, and children—and a diligent search was kept up by several hundreds for many hours, without result, when at last, just as the sun was setting, an old farmer picked up the half-cent, which he presented to Fujitsuna.

Fujitsuna was delighted, and told the people that things were all right now : he had recovered the money —thanks to the quick sight of the farmer.

'But,' they cried, 'that is only a half-cent. Where is the rest?'

'My friends,' said Fujitsuna, 'the half-cent is all that was lost; but that half-cent was not mine; it was part of the Government treasure, and was entrusted to me, and it was my duty to recover it. Here are thirty yen for you who have helped me to find it, to spend in sake. That is my money; and remember what I tell you — that, no matter how small a thing is entrusted to you by the Government, you must not lose it, but give up your life and fortune sooner.'

The villagers were much impressed with this great honesty and way of reasoning.

Hojo Tokiyori, on hearing the little story, sent for and promoted Awoto Fujitsuna to a higher position than he had held before; but, in spite of his advances and riches, the minister continued to work hard, to eat simple food, and to put on plain raiment, living in a cottage instead of occupying a palace, and devoting his life to his country.

XV

A LIFE SAVED BY A SPIDER AND
TWO DOVES

OF Yoritomo *Murray* says that 'he lived from 1147 to
1199. He was the founder of the Shogunate—the first
Japanese Mayor of the Palace, if one may so phrase it.
A scion of the great house of Minamoto, as shrewd and
ambitious as he was unscrupulous and inhuman, he was
left an orphan at an early age, and barely escaped death
as a lad at the hands of Kiyomori, the then all-powerful
minister who belonged to the rival house of Taira.'

In this excellently-concentrated epitome of Yoritomo's
fifty-two years of life, it will readily be seen that he
must have had innumerable adventures. Fighting went
on throughout his career ; yet oddly enough, in spite of
all this, he died comfortably in bed.

In the earlier half of Yoritomo's time he was once
severely defeated at a battle against Oba Kage-chika in
the Ishibashi mountains, in the province of Izu. So bad
had been his defeat that Yoritomo, with six of his most
faithful followers, to use vulgar language, made a bolt of
it. They ran, not over-boldly, but to save their skins,

and in their haste to escape Oba Kage-chika's men they took, like hunted hares, to a large forest, hoping there to escape by lying concealed. After they had pushed their way into the thickest and heaviest part of the forest, they came to an enormous hi no ki tree, partly rotten, and containing a hollow which was large enough to hide them all. Yoritomo and his six followers eagerly sought refuge within the tree, for in their state of tiredness they could not long hope to escape the large and active forces of Oba Kage-chika, which were following up their victory by hunting out and cutting off all those who had fled. When he reached the edge of the forest, Oba Kage-chika sent his cousin Oba Kagetoki to search for Yoritomo, saying: 'Go, my cousin, and bring in our enemy Yoritomo. It is the opportunity of your life, for sure it is that he must be in this forest. I myself will endeavour, as our men come up, to place them so as to surround the forest.' Oba Kagetoki was not pleased with his mission, for at one time he had known and been friendly with Yoritomo. However, he bowed low to his cousin and went off. Half an hour after starting Oba Kagetoki came to the enormous tree, and found his old friend Yoritomo and his six faithful attendants. His heart softened, and, instead of carrying out his duty, he returned to Oba Kage-chika, saying that he had been unable to find the enemy, and that in his opinion Yoritomo had escaped from the wood.

Oba Kage-chika was very angry, and openly said that he did not believe his cousin—that to escape from the wood was impossible in such a short time.

'Come!' said he. 'Follow me, some fifteen or twenty

of you ; and you, my cousin, lead the way and show us where you went, and play fair, or you shall suffer for it ! '

Thus bid, Kagetoki led the way, carefully avoiding the big tree, for he was determined to save the life of Yoritomo if he could. By some misfortune, however, he chose an abominably bad path, and Kage-chika, having on a particularly heavy suit of armour, cried out, 'Enough of your leading ! Let us stick to the road by which we started. It is more likely to be the one which our fugitives took. In any case, this is no road at all where you lead us, and with heavy armour on it is impossible.'

Thus it was that in due time they reached the huge tree. Kagetoki was much afraid that his cousin would go into the hollow and find Yoritomo, and set to think how he could save him.

Kage-chika was about to enter the hollow tree when a bright idea occurred to Kagetoki.

'Hold ! ' said he. 'It is no use wasting time by going in there. Can't you see that there is a spider's web right across the entrance ? It would have been quite impossible for any one to get inside without breaking it.

Kage-chika was half-inclined to agree that his cousin was right ; but, being still a little suspicious about him, he put in his bow to feel what was inside. Just as his bow was about to be thrust against Yoritomo's heavy armour (which would naturally have revealed his presence), two beautiful white doves flew out of the top of the hole.

'You are right, cousin,' said Kage-chika, laughing, when he saw the doves : 'I am wasting time here, for no

93

one can be in this tree with wild doves in it, besides the entrance being closed by a cobweb.'

Thus it was that Yoritomo's life was saved by a spider and two doves. When he became Shogun in later years, and fixed upon Kamakura as his place of residence and as the seat of government, two shrines were built in the temple of Tsuru-ga-oka, which itself is dedicated to Hachiman, the God of War. One is dedicated to the Emperor Nintoku, son of Ojin, the God of War, and the other to Yoritomo, called Shirahata Jinja. The shrines were erected to show Yoritomo's gratitude to the God of War, for doves are known in Japan as the messengers of war, not of peace.

NOTE.—I think that the shrine called by *Murray* 'Shirahata,' which means *White Flag*, is really ' *Shiro hato*,' *the white doves.* The following is from *Murray* :—

The Temple of Hachiman, the God of War, dating from the end of the twelfth century, stands in a commanding position on a hill called Tsuru-ga-oka, and is approached by a stately avenue of pine trees leading up the whole way from the seashore. Though both avenue and temple have suffered from the ravages of time, enough still remains to remind one of the ancient glories of the place. Three stone *torii* lead up to the temple, which stands at the head of a broad flight of stone steps. Notice the magnificent icho tree, nearly 20 feet in circumference, and said to be over a thousand years old, and the flowering trees scattered about the grounds.

Before ascending the flight of steps, the minor shrines to the rear deserve notice. The nearer one, painted red and called Wakamiya, is dedicated to the Emperor Nintoku, son of the God of War. The farther one, renovated in 1890, is called Shirahata Jinja, and dedicated to Yoritomo. The style and structure are

A Life saved by a Spider and Two Doves

somewhat unusual, black and gold being the only colours employed, and iron being the material of the four main pillars. The interior holds a small wooden image of Yoritomo.

A side path leads up hence to the main temple, which is enclosed in a square colonnade painted red. The temple, which was re-erected in 1828, after having been destroyed by fire seven years previously, is in the Ryobu Shinto style, with red pillars, beams, and rafters, and is decorated with small painted carvings, chiefly of birds and animals. In the colonnade are several religious palanquins (mikoshi) used on the occasion of the semi-annual festivals (April 15 and December 15), a wooden image of Sumiyoshi by Unkei, and a few relics of Yoritomo. Most of the relics once preserved in the temple have been removed to the residence of the Chief Priest (Hakozaki Oyatsu-kwan), and are only exhibited at festival times.

Immediately behind the temple of Hachiman is a small hill called Shirabata-yama, whence Yoritomo is said to have often admired the prospect. The base of the hill is enclosed and laid out as a garden.

XVI

MURAKAMI YOSHITERU'S FAITHFULNESS

MURAKAMI YOSHITERU—we shall call him Yoshiteru for short — was one of the faithful retainers of Prince Morinaga, third son of the Emperor Godaigo, who reigned from 1319 to 1339. When I say 'reigned,' I mean that Godaigo was Emperor; but there was a Regent at the time, Hojo Takatoki, who ruled with harshness and great selfishness.

With the exception of young Prince Morinaga, the Imperial family appeared to take things easily. They preferred quietude and comfort to turbulence and quarrelling. Prince Morinaga was different. Fiery-tempered and proud, he thought that Hojo Takatoki was usurping the Emperor's rights. The man, he said, was nothing more by birth than one of the Emperor's subjects, and had no business to be made Regent.

Naturally these opinions led to trouble, and it was not very long before Prince Morinaga was obliged to leave the capital suddenly, with his followers, of whom there were some hundreds, not enough to fight Hojo Takatoki at the time.

96

17. AWOTO FUJITSUNA ORDERS EVERY ONE TO SEARCH FOR THE HALF-CENT

18. OBA KAGE-CHIKA FEELS IN THE TREE WITH HIS BOW

19. MURAKAMI YOSHITERU DOES 'HARAKIRI' AND THROWS HIS ENTRAILS AT THE ENEMY

20. O TOKOYO SEES THE GIRL ABOUT TO BE THROWN OVER CLIFF

21. O TOKOYO SEES YOFUNÉ-NUSHI COMING TOWARDS HER

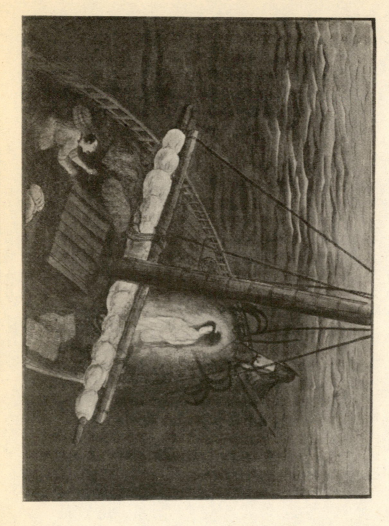

22. TARADA SEES THE MYSTERIOUS FIGURE OF A GIRL

23. YOGODAYU SAVES THE BEE'S LIFE IN KIZUGAWA VALLEY

Murakami Yoshiteru's Faithfulness

Prince Morinaga had made up his mind that it would be better to live independently in Yamato than to be under the sway of Hojo Takatoki, as were his father and his elder brothers. Having collected the most faithful of his followers—of whom the most notable was the hero of our story, Murakami Yoshiteru,—the Prince left the capital in disguise, and started for Yoshino in Yamato. There, in the wild mountains, he intended to build a castle, in which to dwell for the rest of his days independent of the Regent, whom he held in much loathing.

Prince Morinaga carried with him an Imperial flag, which, he expected, would gain for him sympathy and help even in the wild Yamato Province. Though from Kioto the then capital to the borders of Yamato is, in a direct line, only about thirty miles, the whole country is mountainous and wild ; roads are non-existent, mountain paths taking their place. Consequently, it was noon on the fifth day before the Prince found himself at a little border village called Imogase. Here he found his way blocked as it were by a guard-house, the soldiery of which had been chosen from among Imogase villagers, headed by one Shoji, a rough and disagreeable man.

When Prince Morinaga and his party of about eighty followers dressed as *yamabushi* (fighting monks) arrived, flying the standard, they were called to a halt by the village guard, and told that they could go no farther into Yamato without leaving one of themselves as hostage. The Prince was too haughty to speak to the villagers and explain, and, unfortunately, Murakami Yoshiteru, his most trusted leader, could not be found, for he had remained some miles behind to gather straw and make a new pair of waraji (straw shoes). Shoji, leader of the Imogase villagers, was firm in his demand that one of the party should be left behind until their return. For some twenty minutes matters stood thus. Neither side wanted to fight. At last Shoji said :

'Well, you may say that you are a prince! I am a simple villager, and I don't know. You may carry the Imperial flag ; but when you are dressed like *yamabushi* it does not look exactly as if you were a prince. As I don't want trouble, and you want to pass without trouble, —my orders being that out of all parties of over ten armed people I am to hold one as a hostage,—the only suggestion that I can make is that I keep as hostage this Imperial flag.'

The prince, glad enough to save leaving one of his faithful followers, gave the standard to Shoji as hostage, and then he and his party were allowed to pass into Yamato. They proceeded on their way. Not half-an-hour after they had passed, Murakami Yoshiteru arrived at the guard-house, having made himself a pair of straw shoes, to take the place of his old ones ; and his surprise at seeing his master's flag in such low hands was equalled by his anger.

'What is the meaning of this ?' he asked.

Shoji explained what had happened.

On hearing the story Murakami lost control of his temper. He flew into a violent passion. He reviled Shoji and his men as a set of low blackguards who scarcely had a right to look at the Imperial standard of Japan, much less to dare to touch it ; and with that he began a general assault on the village guard, killing three or four and putting the rest to flight. Murakami then seized the standard, and ran on with it until, towards evening, he came up with the Prince and his party, who were overjoyed at what he had done and at the recovery of the flag.

Two days later the party reached Yoshino, and in the vicinity of this place they built a fortress, where for some months they dwelt in peace. It was not long, however, before the Regent heard of the prince's whereabouts, and he soon sent a small army after him. For two days the fort was desperately attacked ; on the third the outer gates were taken ; two-thirds of the prince's men were dead. Murakami had been wounded three times, and his life could not last long. Faithful to the end, he rushed to his prince, saying, ' Master, I am wounded unto death. In less than half-an-hour our enemies will have conquered us, for we have but few men left. Your Highness is unwounded, and can in disguise escape when the end comes. Give me quick your armour, and let me pretend that I am your Highness. I will show our enemies how a prince can die.'

Changing clothes hastily, and donning the prince's armour, Murakami, bleeding badly from his wounds, and already more dead than alive with weakness from the loss of blood, regained the wall, and struggling up the last steps he reached a point where he could see and be seen by the whole of the enemy.

' I am Prince Morinaga ! ' shouted he. ' Fate is against me, though I am in the right. Sooner or later Heaven's punishment will come down on you. Until then my curses upon you, and take a lesson as to how a prince can die, emulating it, if you dare, when your time comes!'

With this Murakami Yoshiteru drew his short sword across his abdomen, and, seizing his quivering entrails, he flung them into the midst of his enemies, his dead body falling directly afterwards.

His head was taken to the Regent in Kioto as the head of Prince Morinaga, who escaped to plot in the future.

XVII

A STORY OF OKI ISLANDS

THE Oki Islands, some forty-five miles from the mainland of Hoki Province, were for centuries the scene of strife, of sorrow, and of banishment ; but to-day they are fairly prosperous and highly peaceful. Fish, octopus, and cuttlefish form the main exports. They are a weird, wild, and rocky group, difficult of access, and few indeed are the Europeans who have visited them. I know of only two—the late Lafcadio Hearn and Mr. Anderson (who was there to collect animals for the Duke of Bedford). I myself sent Oto, my Japanese hunter, who was glad to return.

In the Middle Ages—that is, from about the year 1000 A.D.—there was much fighting over the islands by various chieftains, and many persons were sent thither in banishment.

In the year 1239 Hojo Yoshitoshi defeated the Emperor Go Toba and banished him to Dogen Island.

Another Hojo chieftain banished another Emperor, Go Daigo, to Nishi-no-shima. Oribe Shima, the hero of our story, was probably banished by this same Hojo chieftain, whose name is given to me as Takatoki (Hojo), and the date of the story must be about 1320 A.D.

At the time when Hojo Takatoki reigned over the country with absolute power, there was a samurai whose name was Oribe Shima. By some misfortune Oribe (as we shall call him) had offended Hojo Takatoki, and had consequently found himself banished to one of the islands of the Oki group which was then known as Kami-shima (Holy Island). So the relater of the story tells me; but I doubt his geographical statement, and think the island must have been Nishi-no-shima (Island of the West, or West Island [1]).

Oribe had a beautiful daughter, aged eighteen, of whom he was as fond as she was of him, and consequently the banishment and separation rendered both of them doubly miserable. Her name was Tokoyo, O Tokoyo San.

Tokoyo, left at her old home in Shima Province, Ise, wept from morn till eve, and sometimes from eve till morn. At last, unable to stand the separation any longer, she resolved to risk all and try to reach her father or die in the attempt; for she was brave, as are most girls of Shima Province, where the women have much to do with the sea. As a child she had loved to dive with the women whose daily duty is to collect awabi and pearl-oyster shells, running with them the risk of life in spite of her higher birth and frailer body. She knew no fear.

Having decided to join her father, O Tokoyo sold what property she could dispose of, and set out on her

---

[1] Since writing this, I have found that there is a very small island, called Kamishima, between the two main islands of the Oki Archipelago, south-west of the eastern island.

long journey to the far-off province of Hoki, which, after many weeks she reached, striking the sea at a place called Akasaki, whence on clear days the Islands of Oki can be dimly seen. Immediately she set to and tried to persuade the fishermen to take her to the Islands; but nearly all her money had gone, and, moreover, no one was allowed to land at the Oki Islands in those days—much less to visit those who had been banished thence. The fishermen laughed at Tokoyo, and told her that she had better go home. The brave girl was not to be put off. She bought what stock of provisions she could afford, at night went down to the beach, and, selecting the lightest boat she could find, pushed it with difficulty into the water, and sculled as hard as her tiny arms would allow her. Fortune sent a strong breeze, and the current also was in her favour. Next evening, more dead than alive, she found her efforts crowned with success. Her boat touched the shore of a rocky bay.

O Tokoyo sought a sheltered spot, and lay down to sleep for the night. In the morning she awoke much refreshed, ate the remainder of her provisions, and started to make inquiries as to her father's whereabouts. The first person she met was a fisherman. 'No,' he said: 'I have never heard of your father, and if you take my advice you will not ask for him if he has been banished, for it may lead you to trouble and him to death!'

Poor O Tokoyo wandered from one place to another, subsisting on charity, but never hearing a word of her father.

One evening she came to a little cape of rocks, whereon stood a shrine. After bowing before Buddha and imploring his help to find her dear father, O Tokoyo lay down, intending to pass the night there, for it was a peaceful and holy spot, well sheltered from the winds, which, even in summer, as it was now (the 13th of June), blow with some violence all around the Oki Islands.

Tokoyo had slept about an hour when she heard, in spite of the dashing of waves against the rocks, a curious sound, the clapping of hands and the bitter sobbing of a girl. As she looked up in the bright moonlight she saw a beautiful person of fifteen years, sobbing bitterly. Beside her stood a man who seemed to be the shrine-keeper or priest. He was clapping his hands and mumbling 'Namu Amida Butsu's.' Both were dressed in white. When the prayer was over, the priest led the girl to the edge of the rocks, and was about to push her over into the sea, when O Tokoyo came to the rescue, rushing at and seizing the girl's arm just in time to save her. The old priest looked surprised at the intervention, but was in no way angered or put about, and explained as follows :—

'It appears from your intervention that you are a stranger to this small island. Otherwise you would know that the unpleasant business upon which you find me is not at all to my liking or to the liking of any of us. Unfortunately, we are cursed with an evil god in this island, whom we call Yofuné-Nushi. He lives at the bottom of the sea, and demands, once a year, a girl just under fifteen years of age. This sacrificial offering has to be made on June 13, Day of the Dog, between eight and nine o'clock in the evening. If our villagers neglect this, Yofuné-Nushi becomes angered, and causes great storms, which drown many of our fishermen. By sacrificing one young girl annually much is saved. For the last seven years it has been my sad duty to superintend the ceremony, and it is that which you have now interrupted.'

O Tokoyo listened to the end of the priest's explanation, and then said :

'Holy monk, if these things be as you say, it seems that there is sorrow everywhere. Let this young girl go, and say that she may stop her weeping, for I am more sorrowful than she, and will willingly take her place and offer myself to Yofuné-Nushi. I am the sorrowing daughter of Oribe Shima, a samurai of high rank, who has been exiled to this island. It is in search of my dear father that I have come here ; but he is so closely guarded that I cannot get to him, or even find out exactly where he has been hidden. My heart is broken, and I have nothing more for which to wish to live, and am therefore glad to save this girl. Please take this letter, which is addressed to my father. That you should try and deliver it to him is all I ask.'

Saying which, Tokoyo took the white robe off the younger girl and put it on herself. She then knelt before the figure of Buddha, and prayed for strength and courage to slay the evil god, Yofuné-Nushi. Then she drew a small and beautiful dagger, which had belonged to one of her ancestors, and, placing it between her pearly teeth, she dived into the roaring sea and disappeared, the priest and the other girl looking after her with wonder and admiration, and the girl with thankfulness.

As we said at the beginning of the story, Tokoyo had been brought up much among the divers of her own country in Shima ; she was a perfect swimmer, and knew, moreover, something of fencing and jujitsu, as did many girls of her position in those days.

Tokoyo swam downwards through the clear water, which was illuminated by bright moonlight. Down, down she swam, passing silvery fish, until she reached the bottom, and there she found herself opposite a submarine cave resplendent with the phosphorescent lights issuing from awabi shells and the pearls that glittered through their openings. As Tokoyo looked she seemed to see a man seated in the cave. Fearing nothing, willing to fight and die, she approached, holding her dagger ready to strike. Tokoyo took him for Yofuné-Nushi, the evil god of whom the priest had spoken. The god made no sign of life, however, and Tokoyo saw that it was no god, but only a wooden statue of Hojo Takatoki, the man who had exiled her father. At first she was angry and inclined to wreak her vengeance on the statue ; but, after all, what would be the use of that ? Better do good than evil. She would rescue the thing. Perhaps it had been made by some person who, like her father, had suffered at the hands of Hojo Takatoki. Was rescue possible ? Indeed it was more : it was probable. So perceiving, Tokoyo undid one of her girdles and wound it about the statue, which she took out of the cave. True, it was waterlogged and heavy ; but things are lighter in the water than they are out, and Tokoyo feared no trouble in bringing it to the surface—she was about to tie it on her back. However, the unexpected happened.

She beheld, coming slowly out of the depths of the cavern, a horrible thing, a luminous phosphorescent creature of the shape of a snake, but with legs and small scales on its back and sides. The thing was twenty-seven or eight shaku (about twenty-six feet) in length. The eyes were fiery.

Tokoyo gripped her dagger with renewed determination, feeling sure that this was the evil god, the Yofuné-Nushi that required annually a girl to be cast to him. No doubt the Yofuné-Nushi took her for the girl that was his due. Well, she would show him who she was, and kill him if she could, and so save the necessity of further annual contributions of a virgin from this poor island's few.

Slowly the monster came on, and Tokoyo braced herself for the combat. When the creature was within six feet of her, she moved sideways and struck out his right eye. This so disconcerted the evil god that he turned and tried to re-enter the cavern; but Tokoyo was too clever for him. Blinded by the loss of his right eye, as also by the blood which flooded into his left, the monster was slow in his movements, and thus the brave and agile Tokoyo was able to do with him much as she liked. She got to the left side of him, where she was able to stab him in the heart, and, knowing that he could not long survive the blow, she headed him off so as to prevent his gaining too far an entrance into the cave, where in the darkness she might find herself at a disadvantage. Yofuné-Nushi, however, was unable to see his way back to the depths of his cavern, and after two or three heavy gasps died, not far from the entrance.

Tokoyo was pleased at her success. She felt that she had slain the god that cost the life of a girl a-year to the people of the island to which she had come in search of her father. She perceived that she must take it and the wooden statue to the surface, which, after several attempts, she managed to do,—having been in the sea for nearly half-an-hour.

In the meantime the priest and the little girl had continued to gaze into the water where Tokoyo had disappeared, marvelling at her bravery, the priest praying for her soul, and the girl thanking the gods. Imagine their surprise when suddenly they noticed a struggling body rise to the surface in a somewhat awkward manner! They could not make it out at all, until at last the little girl cried, 'Why, holy father, it is the girl who took my place and dived into the sea! I recognise my white clothes. But she seems to have a man and a huge fish with her.'

The priest had by this time realised that it was Tokoyo who had come to the surface, and he rendered all the help he could. He dashed down the rocks, and pulled her half-insensible form ashore. He cast his girdle round the monster, and put the carved image of Hojo Takatoki on a rock beyond reach of the waves.

Soon assistance came, and all were carefully removed to a safe place in the village. Tokoyo was the heroine of the hour. The priest reported the whole thing to Tameyoshi, the lord who ruled the island at the time, and he in his turn reported the matter to the Lord Hojo Takatoki, who ruled the whole Province of Hoki, which included the Islands of Oki.

Takatoki was suffering from some peculiar disease quite unknown to the medical experts of the day. The recovery of the wooden statue representing himself made it clear that he was labouring under the curse of some one to whom he had behaved unjustly—some one who had carved his figure, cursed it, and sunk it in the sea. Now that it had been brought to the surface, he felt that the curse was over, that he would get better; and he did. On hearing that the heroine of the story was the daughter of his old enemy Oribe Shima, who was confined in prison, he ordered his immediate release, and great were the rejoicings thereat.

The curse on the image of Hojo Takatoki had brought with it the evil god, Yofuné-Nushi, who demanded a virgin a-year as contribution. Yofuné-Nushi had now been slain, and the islanders feared no further trouble from storms. Oribe Shima and his brave daughter O Tokoyo returned to their own country in Shima Province, where the people hailed them with delight; and their popularity soon re-established their impoverished estates, on which men were willing to work for nothing.

In the island of Kamijima (Holy Island) in the Oki Archipelago peace reigned. No more virgins were offered on June 13 to the evil god, Yofuné-Nushi, whose body was buried on the Cape at the shrine where our story begins. Another small shrine was built to commemorate the event. It was called the Tomb of the Sea Serpent.

The wooden statue of Hojo Takatoki, after much travelling, found a resting-place at Honsōji, in Kamakura.

XVIII

CAPE OF THE WOMAN'S SWORD [1]

Down in the Province of Higo are a group of large islands, framing with the mainland veritable little inland seas, deep bays, and narrow channels. The whole of this is called Amakusa. There are a village called Amakusa mura, a sea known as Amakusa umi, an island known as Amakusa shima, and the Cape known as Joken Zaki, which is the most prominent feature of them all, projecting into the Amakusa sea.

History relates that in the year 1577 the Daimio of the province issued an order that every one under him was to become a Christian or be banished.

During the next century this decree was reversed; only, it was ordered that the Christians should be executed. Tens of thousands of Christianised heads were collected and sent for burial to Nagasaki, Shimabara and Amakusa.

This—repeated from *Murray*—has not much to do

---

[1] The title to this old and hitherto untold legend is not much less curious than the story itself, which was told to me by a man called Fukuga, who journeys much up and down the southern coast in search of pearls and coral.

with my story. After all, it is possible that at the time the Amakusa people became Christian the sword in question, being in some temple, was with the gods cast into the sea, and recovered later by a coral or pearl diver in the Bunroku period, which lasted from 1592 to 1596. A history would naturally spring from a sword so recovered. But to the story.

The Cape of Joken Zaki (the Woman's Sword Cape) was not always so called. In former years, before the Bunroku period, it had been called Fudozaki (Fudo is the God of Fierceness, always represented as surrounded by fire and holding a sword) or Fudo's Cape. The reason of the change of names was this.

The inhabitants of Amakusa lived almost entirely on what they got out of the sea, so that when it came to pass that for two years of the Bunroku period no fish came into their seas or bay and they were sorely distressed, many actually starved, and their country was in a state of desolation. Their largest and longest nets were shot and hauled in vain. Not a single fish so large as a sardine could they catch. At last things got so bad that they could not even see fish schooling outside their bay. Peculiar rumbling sounds were occasionally heard coming from under the sea off Cape Fudo; but of these they thought little, being Japanese and used to earthquakes.

All the people knew was that the fish had completely gone—where they could not tell, or why, until one day an old and much-respected fisherman said :

' I fear, my friends, that the noise we so often hear off Cape Fudo has nothing to do with earthquakes, but that the God of the Sea has been displeased.'

One evening a few days after this a sailing junk, the *Tsukushi-maru*, owned by one Tarada, who commanded her, anchored for the night to the lee of Fudozaki.

After having stowed their sails and made everything snug, the crew pulled their beds up from below (for the weather was hot) and rolled them out on deck. Towards the middle of the night the captain was awakened by a peculiar rumbling sound seeming to come from the bottom of the sea. Apparently it came from the direction in which their anchor lay ; the rope which held it trembled visibly. Tarada said the sound reminded him of the roaring of the falling tide in the Naruto Channel between Awa and Awaji Island. Suddenly he saw towards the bows of the junk a beautiful maid clothed in the finest of white silks (he thought). She seemed, however, hardly real, being surrounded by a glittering haze.

Tarada was not a coward ; nevertheless, he aroused his men, for he did not quite like this. As soon as he had shaken the men to their senses, he moved towards the figure, which, when but ten or twelve feet away, addressed him in the most melodious of voices, thus :

'Ah ! could I but be back in the world ! That is my only wish.'

Tarada, astonished and affrighted, fell on his knees, and was about to pray, when a sound of roaring waters was heard again, and the white-clad maiden disappeared into the sea.

Next morning Tarada went on shore to ask the people of Amakusa if they had ever heard of such a thing before, and to tell them of his experiences.

'No,' said the village elder. 'Two years ago we never

heard the noises which we hear now off Fudo Cape almost daily, and we had much fish here before then ; but we have even now never seen the figure of the girl whom (you say) you saw last night. Surely this must be the ghost of some poor girl that has been drowned, and the noise we hear must be made by the God of the Sea, who is in anger that her bones and body are not taken out of this bay, where the fish so much liked to come before her body fouled the bottom.'

A consultation was held by the fishermen. They concluded that the village elder was right—that some one must have been drowned in the bay, and that the body was polluting the bottom. It was her ghost that had appeared on Tarada's ship, and the noise was naturally caused by the angry God of the Sea, offended that his fish were prevented from entering the bay by its uncleanness.

What was to be done was quite clear. Some one must dive to the bottom in spite of the depth of water, and bring the body or bones to the surface. It was a dangerous job, and not a pleasant one either,—the bringing up of a corpse that had lain at the bottom for well over a year.

As no one volunteered for the dive, the villagers suggested a man who was a great swimmer—a man who had all his life been dumb and consequently was a person of no value, as no one would marry him and no one cared for him. His name was Sankichi or (as they called him) Oshi-no-Sankichi, Dumb Sankichi. He was twenty-six years of age ; he had always been honest ; he was very religious, attending at the temples and shrines constantly; but he kept to himself, as his infirmity did not appeal to the community. As soon as this poor fellow heard that in the opinion of most of them there was a dead body at the bottom of the bay which had to be brought to the surface, he came forward and made signs that he would do the work or die in the attempt. What was his poor life worth in comparison with the hundreds of fishermen who lived about the bay, their lives depending upon the presence of fish? The fishermen consulted among themselves, and agreed that they would let Oshi-no-Sankichi make the attempt on the morrow; and until that time he was the popular hero.

Next day, when the tide was low, all the villagers assembled on the beach to give Dumb Sankichi a parting cheer. He was rowed out to Tarada's junk, and, after bidding farewell to his few relations, dived into the sea off her bows.

Sankichi swam until he reached the bottom, passing through hot and cold currents the whole way. Hastily he looked, and swam about; but no corpse or bones did he come across. At last he came to a projecting rock, and on the top of that he espied something like a sword wrapped in old brocade. On grasping it he felt that it really was a sword. On his untying the string and drawing the blade, it proved to be one of dazzling brightness, with not a speck of rust.

'It is said,' thought Sankichi, 'that Japan is the country of the sword, in which its spirit dwells. It must be the Goddess of the Sword that makes the roaring sound which frightens away the fishes—when she comes to the surface.'

Cape of the Woman's Sword

Feeling that he had secured a rare treasure, Sankichi lost no time in returning to the surface. He was promptly hauled on board the *Tsukushi-maru* amid the cheers of the villagers and his relations. So long had he been under water, and so benumbed was his body, he promptly fainted. Fires were lit, and his body was rubbed until he came to, and gave by signs an account of his dive. The head official of the neighbourhood, Naruse Tsushimanokami, examined the sword ; but, in spite of its beauty and excellence, no name could be found on the blade, and the official expressed it as his opinion that the sword was a holy treasure. He recommended the erection of a shrine dedicated to Fudo, wherein the sword should be kept in order to guard the' village against further trouble. Money was collected. The shrine was built. Oshi-no-Sankichi was made the caretaker, and lived a long and happy life.

The fish returned to the bay, for the spirit of the sword was no longer dissatisfied by being at the bottom of the sea.

XIX

HOW YOGODAYU WON A BATTLE

DURING the reign of the Emperor Shirakawa, which was between the years 1073 and 1086 A.D., there lived a general whose name was Yogodayu. He had built a fort for himself and his small army in the wilds of Yamato, not far from the Mountain of Kasagi, where, about the year 1380, the unfortunate Emperor Go-Daigo camped among the same rocky fastnesses and eventually perished. Even to-day, as one winds in and out of the narrow gorge where the railway passes Kasagi, in the Kizugawa valley, one is struck by the extreme wildness of the scenery. Here it was that Yogodayu built his fort. Some months later he was attacked by his wife's brother, whom he detested, and got badly beaten, so much so as to have only some twenty warriors left alive. With these he escaped to Kasagi Mountain, and hid himself for two days in a cave, in fear and trembling that he should be discovered. On the third day Yogodayu, finding that he was not pursued, ventured forth to admire the scenery. While thus occupied he saw a bee in a large spider's-web struggling in vain to free itself. Struggle as it might, it

116

only made things worse. Yogodayu, feeling sympathy for the bee, relieved it from its captivity and let it fly, saying :

'Ah, little bee! fly back to liberty and to your hive. I wish I could do the same. It is a pleasure to relieve those in captivity, even though one is at the mercy of one's enemy, as I am.'

That night Yogodayu dreamed that a man dressed in black and yellow saluted him, and said : 'Sir, I have come to tell you that it is my desire to help you and fulfil the resolve which I came to this morning.'

'And who, pray, may you be?' answered Yogodayu in his dream.

'I am the bee whom you released from the spider's web, and deeply grateful ; so much so that I have thought out a plan by which you can defeat your enemy and regain your lost fortune.'

'How is it possible for me to defeat my enemy with only a remnant of my force—some twenty warriors?' quoth Yogodayu.

'It is very simple,' was the answer. 'Follow exactly the instructions I give you, and you shall see.'

'But I have no walls behind which the few friends I have can make a show of fighting. It is impossible for me to attack my enemy.'

The bee smiled and said : 'You shall not want walls. You shall be attacked, and, with the help of some ten millions of the bees of Yamato, you shall put your enemies to rout. Listen ! When you have fixed upon the day and the place where you will fight your brother-in-law, build a wooden house, place in it as many hundred empty jars and receptacles as your men can find, so that we bees may come and hide in them. You must live in the house with your twenty and odd men, and manage to let your enemy know where you are, and that you are collecting a force to attack him. It will then not be long before he attacks you. When he does, we bees will come out in our millions and help you. You are sure of victory. Fear nothing ; but do as I say.'

As Yogodayu was about to speak the bee disappeared, and he awoke from his dream. Deeply impressed, he related it to his men. It was arranged that these should split themselves up into couples and return to their native province, collect what men they could, and be back at the cave some thirty days later. Yogodayu went off alone. Thirty days later they all met again at the cave on Kasagi yama. Altogether they were now eighty men. Quietly they set to, and, following the bee's advice, built a wooden house at the entrance of the valley, and put therein some two thousand jars. No sooner had this been done than the bees arrived in countless thousands, until there must have been well-nigh two millions. One of Yogodayu's men was sent to propagate reports that he was strongly fortifying himself.

Two days later his brother-in-law came to attack him.

Yogodayu began fighting carelessly, so as to draw the enemy, who, seeing this, came on in full force and in a most unguarded way. As soon as the whole of the enemy's force lay revealed, the bees swarmed out of their hiding-places, and flew among them in such blinding swarms—stinging as they went here, there, and everywhere —that there was no standing against them. The enemy,

without a single exception, turned and ran. They were
pursued by the bees, and by Yogodayu's eighty men, who
simply cut them down as they liked, for each of the enemy
had fully 3000 bees attending him. Many lost their
minds and went mad.

Thus, after completely defeating his old enemy,
Yogodayu became repossessed of his fortress; and, to commemorate the event, he built a small temple at the back
of Kasagi yama. All the dead bees that could be found
were collected and buried there, and once a-year during
the rest of his life Yogodayu used to go and worship
there.

XX

THE ISOLATED OR DESOLATED ISLAND

MANY years ago the Lord of Kishu, head of one of the three families of the Tokugawas, ordered his people to hold a hunting-party on Tomagashima (Toma Island). In those days such hunting-parties were often ordered, more for the purpose of improving drill and organisation than for sport. It brought men together, and taught others to handle them both on land and at sea. It made men recognise their commanders and superiors, and it disclosed what men were worthy of being made such. Hunting-parties of this kind were considered as military manœuvres.

On this particular hunt or manœuvre, the Lord of Kishu was to make a kind of descent by water on the island of Toma, and kill all the game that his landing-party could beat up.

Boats and junks were armed as if for war, and so were the men—except that they wore no armour.

The day for the entertainment was fine. Some sixty boats put to sea, and landed successfully about eight hundred men on Toma Island ; and busy indeed were they chasing boar and deer the whole morning.

The Isolated or Desolated Island

Towards afternoon, however, a storm of great violence came on and completely stopped the sport. The men were ordered to return to the shore and regain their boats before these should be smashed on the beach.

On embarking they put out to sea with the intention of gaining the mainland. On shore trees were being uprooted, columns of sand flew high in the air, and the gale was indeed terrific; if on shore it was as bad as this, it must be much worse at sea. The Lord of Kishu's boats and junks were tossed about as if they were floating leaves.

One of the party was a notedly brave man, Makino Heinei, who had been nicknamed 'Ino shishi' (Wild Boar) on account of his reckless bravery. Seeing that neither junks nor boats were making headway against the storm, he pushed the small boat off the junk, jumped into it alone, took the oars, laughed at every one, and cried : 'See here ! You all seem to be too frightened to make headway. Look at what I do and follow me. I am not afraid of the waves, and none of you should be if you are to serve our Lord of Kishu faithfully.'

With that Makino Heinei shot out into the wild sea, and by extraordinary exertion managed to get some three hundred yards ahead of the rest of the fleet. Then the gale increased to such violence that he was incapable of doing anything. For fear of being blown out of the boat, he was obliged to hold tight to the mast and otherwise abandon his fate to good fortune. At times even the heart of the Wild Boar quailed. Often his boat was lifted clean out of the water by the wind ; waves towered over him ; he closed his eyes and awaited his fate.

121

Finally, one squall more powerful than the rest blew his boat out of the water, and it was seen from the other boats (which lay at anchor) to disappear into the horizon. Heinei clung to the boat tightly. When the mast blew away he held on to the ribs. He prayed hard and earnestly. Some eight hours after the storm began, Heinei found the boat in comparatively smooth water. She was flooded, and she was a wreck; but still she floated, and that was all he cared for at the moment. Moreover, Heinei felt encouraged, because between two dark clouds he could see an opening and some stars, though at present it was absolutely dark and the driving rain had not ceased. Suddenly, when Heinei was wondering how far he had been blown from shore or from his friends, crack!—he felt his boat plump into a rock. The shock was so violent (for the boat was still being driven fast by the gale) that our hero lost his balance and was thrown fully ten feet away. Falling on soft stuff, Heinei thought he was in the sea; but his hands suddenly realised that it was soft wet sand. Delighted at this discovery, he looked at the clouds and the sky, and came to the conclusion that in another hour it would be daylight. In the meantime he thanked the gods for his deliverance, and prayed for his friends and for his lord and master.

As morning broke Heinei arose stiff, weary, and hungry. Before the sun appeared he realised that he was on an island. No other land was in sight, and it puzzled him sorely to guess where he could be, for from all the Kishu islands the mainland could be easily seen.

'Oh, here is a new tree! I have never seen that in

Kishu,' said he. 'And this flower—that also is new—while here is a butterfly more brilliant than any I know.'

So saying and thinking, Heinei began looking about for food, and, being a Japanese, easily satisfied his appetite with the shellfish which were abundantly strewn everywhere after the storm.

The island on which Heinei had been cast was fair in size—some two miles across and ten in circumference. There was one small hill in the middle, which Heinei resolved to ascend, to see if he could discover Kishu from the top of it. Accordingly he started. The undergrowth of bush was so great that Heinei made a detour to another bay. The trees were quite different from any he had ever seen before, and there were many kinds of palms. At last he found to his delight a well-worn path leading up the mountain. He took it ; but when he came to a damp place in the way he was in no whit reassured, for there he saw footmarks which could have been made by no one who was not a giant—they were fully eighteen inches in length. A warrior belonging to Kishu must fear nothing, thought Heinei, and, arming himself with a stout stick, he proceeded. Near the top he found the opening to a somewhat large cave, and, nothing daunted, began to enter, prepared to meet anything. What was his surprise when an enormous man, fully eight feet in height, appeared before him, not more than ten feet from the entrance ! He was a hideous, wild-looking creature, nearly black, with long unkempt hair, flashing angry eyes, and a mouth that stretched from ear to ear, showing two glittering rows of teeth ; and he wore no clothes except the skin of a wild-cat tied round his loins.

As soon as he saw Heinei he came to a standstill, and said, in Japanese, 'Who are you? how have you got here? and what have you come for?'

Makino Heinei answered these questions as fully as he thought necessary by telling his name and adding, 'I am a retainer of the Lord of Kishu, and was blown away by the storm after we had been hunting and holding manœuvres on Toma Island.'

'And where are these places you speak of? Remember that this island is unknown to the world and has been for thousands of years. I am its sole occupant, and wish to remain so. No matter how I came. I am here. My name is Tomaru, and my father was Yamaguchi Shoun, who died, with his master Toyotomi Hidetsugu, on Koyasan Mountain in 1563. Both died by their own hands; and I got here, no matter how, and here I intend to remain undisturbed. I heard of your Lord of Kishu and of the Tokugawa family before I left Japan, and for that reason I will help you by giving you my old boat, in which I arrived. Come to the beach. I will send you off in the right direction, and if you continue sailing north-west you shall in time reach Kishu. But it is a long way off—a very long way.'

With that they walked down to the beach.

'See,' said Tomaru: 'the boat is well-nigh rotten, for it is many years since she was put here; but with luck you may reach Kishu. Stay—you must have some provision. I can give only dry fish and fruits; but to these you are welcome. And I must give you a present for your master, the Lord of Kishu. It is a kind of seaweed. You shall have some for yourself also. It is

The Isolated or Desolated Island

my great discovery on this island. No matter how bad
a sword-cut you may get, it will stop the blood flowing
and cure at once. Now, jump into the boat and row
away. I like to be alone. You may speak of your
adventure; but you are not to mention my name.
Farewell!'

Heinei could only do as he was bid. Consequently,
he made off. Rowing night and day and aided by
favourable currents, he found himself off the coast of
Kishu on the third day after leaving the island. The
people were much astonished to see him alive, and the
Lord of Kishu rejoiced, especially at the sword-cut-healing
seaweed, which he had planted in the sea at a part of the
coast which he renamed and called Nagusa-gori (District
of the famous Seaweed).

Later Makino Heinei sailed again by permission of
his Lord to get more seaweed. The island was found;
but the giant had disappeared.

Note.—Mujinto Island, in the Pacific, is the group called
Bonin Islands by Europeans.

XXI

CHIKUBU ISLAND, LAKE BIWA

MANY years ago, when I was a boy, there was a song about a Chinaman.   It began :

> In China once there lived a man,
> And his name was Ding-dong-dang.
> His legs were long, and his feet were small,
> And this Chinese man couldn't walk at all.

Chorus :

> Chi-chi-Maree, Chi-chi-Marah,
> Ding-dong, ding-dong, ding-dong dah,
> Kossi-kossi-ki, kossi-kossi-ka,
> Chikubu, Chikubu, Chikubu Chang.

Little in those days did I think that I should come across an island—or any other place, for the matter of that—which bore the name of part of this wild and idiotic chorus, 'Chikubu, Chikubu, Chikubu Chang.' It sounds truly wild. Well, so it is. I have found an island on Lake Biwa which is pronounced and spelt exactly as in the chorus of this song of my youth. 'Chikubu' is there, and I am puzzled to know where the composer found it. In my Japanese I can't find it.

Chikubu Island, Lake Biwa

However, let us to the story. It is not a very good one ; but, as it relates to the only island of importance in the lake, it is worth chronicling.

Chikubu-shima is situated about two-thirds up towards the north-western end of Lake Biwa, in Omi Province. The lake is some thirty-five miles long and twelve broad. The island is holy, I believe, and it is said to have been caused by an earthquake nearly 600 years B.C. Fuji Mountain made its appearance at the same time. Thus we have (so far as we like to believe it) the geographical pedigree of Lake Biwa and its principal island.

The nearest land to Chikubu is Tsuzurao Cape, which is about two miles away. There, some three hundred years ago, dwelt two sisters, O Tsuru and Kame. They were fifteen and eleven respectively, and dwelt with their old and only uncle, their father and mother and all their other relations being dead. Tsuru (the crane) and Kame (the turtle) were devoted to each other ; in fact, the poor girls clung to each other as the remnants of a family should cling. They loved each other. They were inseparable.

At that time there was much fear among the inhabitants of Tsuzurao Point of a large carp—a carp of such size that it was called ' The Master of Lake Biwa.' It was said that this fish ate dogs, cats, and sometimes people, if they were unwise enough to swim into water sufficiently deep for him to manoeuvre in. His principal hover was in the waters surrounding Chikubu Island, at the northern end of the lake.

When O Tsuru reached the age of fifteen, and her sister O Kame was eleven, O Tsuru became sick with consumption; from bad she grew worse, and her poor little sister O Kame became quite disconsolate; she cried because of her sister's illness, and went by herself to pray at all the temples in the neighbourhood. Day after day she thought of nothing but her sister's illness; but all she did, poor child, was in vain. O Tsuru became worse.

In her great distress O Kame thought that she should venture to the wild and sacred island of Chikubu, there to pray to the Goddess of Mercy, Kwannon. To do so with any chance of her prayers being heard, it was necessary that she should go alone. She would row off secretly that night.

After darkness had come and her uncle's household had gone to sleep, O Kame crept forth and went down to the edge of the lake, where her uncle's boat and many others lay. Getting into one, the lightest she could find, she sculled towards Chikubu Island. The sky was clear and the water glistened.

In less than an hour this whole-hearted child of Nippon was kneeling before the ever-pleasing and soothing figure of Kwannon, the goddess ever ready to listen to the prayers of the unhappy; and there she prayed to the full extent of her feelings, weeping between-times in sorrow for the sickness of her sister.

When poor O Kame had finished praying she got into her boat and began to row back to Tsuzurao. She had got within half-a-mile of that place when a terrible storm arose, and in the third squall her boat was capsized. O Kame was no swimmer, and as she sank into the depths of the lake the giant carp saw her, and instantly carried her off and devoured her.

25. O TSURU SEES THE GIANT CARP DEAD

26. THE MONKEYS LISTEN TO THE PRIEST'S SERMON

27. THE PRIEST WRITES THE FIRST FIVE VOLUMES

28. O KINU SAN INSPECTS THE PLACE WHERE TAKADAI JIRO COMMITTED SUICIDE

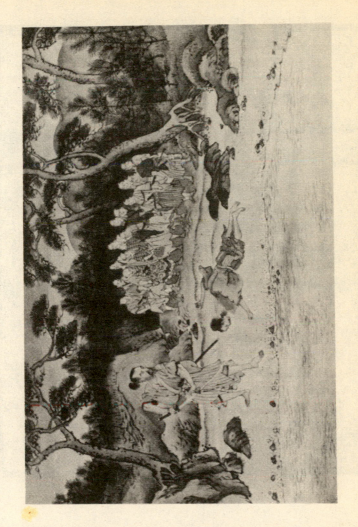

29. FURUZUKA IGA CUTS OFF THE HEAD OF THE EX-EMPEROR SHUTOKU, WHO IS HIS OWN SON

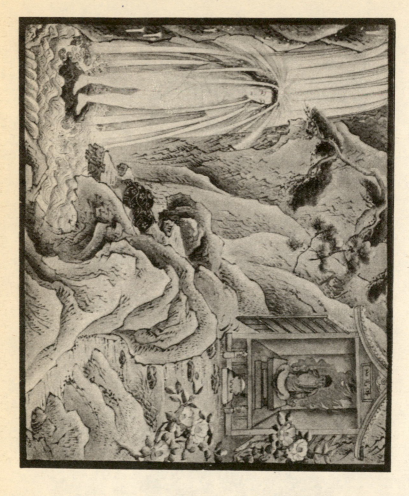

30. O AI SAN CONTINUES HER PRAYERS UNDER THE FALL

31. O CHO SAN COMMITS SUICIDE

32. KUME SLAYS THE EAGLE, TORIJIMA

Chikubu Island, Lake Biwa

Next morning there was consternation at Tsuzurao. When it was found that both O Kame San and one of the fishermen's boats were missing it was naturally surmised that she had gone out on the lake, and probably to Chikubu Island to pray to Kwannon.

Boats went off in search ; but nothing could be found, save the marks of her footsteps from the shore to the shrine dedicated to Kwannon. On hearing this sad news, O Tsuru, who lay nigh unto death, became worse ; but in spite of her sad condition she could not bear the idea of lingering on in the world without her sister O Kame. Consequently she resolved to destroy her life as near as she could think to the place where O Kame had died, so that her spirit might journey with hers until perhaps they should become born again together. At all events, it was clearly her duty to follow her sister.

When the dusk of evening arrived O Tsuru crept out from her room and gained the beach, where she, like her little sister, took the lightest boat which she could find, and rowed herself out, in spite of her weakness, to a spot where she thought that the carp might have killed her sister. There, standing in the bows of the boat, she cried aloud :

'Oh, mighty carp, that hast devoured my sister, devour me also, that our spirits may follow the same path and become reunited. It is for this I cast myself into the lake !'

So saying, O Tsuru shut her eyes and jumped into the water. Down, down, down she went, until she reached the bottom. No sooner had she alighted there, feeling (curiously enough) no effects of being under water, than she heard her name called.

'Strange indeed,' thought she, 'that I should hear my name at the bottom of Lake Biwa!'

She opened her eyes, and beheld standing beside her an old priest. O Tsuru asked him who he was, and why he had called her.

'I was a priest,' he explained. 'Perhaps I am one now. At all events, I often come to the bottom of the lake. I know all about your little sister Kame, of her faithfulness and affection for you, and of yours for her; I know also of the storm which capsized her boat when she had been praying to Kwannon on Chikubu Island, and of her being taken and eaten by that horrible carp. Believe me, none of these are reasons why you should take your own life. Go back on earth, rather, and pray to Buddha for your sister's blessing and for her soul. I will see that you are avenged on the carp, and I will see that you get well and strong. Take my hand, so, and I will take you back on shore.'

Having said this and carried Tsuru to land, the priest disappeared. For some time she lay unconscious; but when she came fully to her senses O Tsuru found herself on Chikubu Island, and, feeling considerably stronger than she had felt for some time, she went to the shrine dedicated to Kwannon, and passed the remainder of the night in prayer.

In the morning, having gone to the beach, she saw boats in the distance coming from Tsuzurao Point; but (what was more extraordinary) there lay, not ten feet from the shore where she stood, an enormous carp, fully nine feet in length, dead!

Chikubu Island, Lake Biwa

Among the search-boats that arrived was one containing her uncle and a priest.

Tsuru told her story. The carp was buried at a small promontory on the island, which is called Miyazaki. It was named Koizuka Miya-zaki (the Carp's Grave at Temple Cape).

O Tsuru lived to a ripe old age, and was never ill again. History tells of her at the age of seventy informing Ota Nobunaga, who came to destroy temples in the neighbourhood, that if he touched the shrines on Chikubu Island she herself would see to his destruction.

XXII

REINCARNATION

In the far-north and mountainous portion of Echigo Province is a temple which during the reign of the Emperor Ichijo had a curious story attached to it; and, though the Emperor Ichijo reigned so long ago as between the years 987 and 1011 A.D., the teller of the story assured me that he believed the temple to be in existence still.

The temple's name is Kinoto, and it is situated in the hills in wild woods, which in those days must have been almost virgin forest.

The monk who reigned supreme over the Kinoto Temple was a youngish man, but very devout; he read sacred sermons from the holy Buddhist Bible, aloud, twice a-day.

One day the good youth perceived that two monkeys had come down from the mountain and sat listening to his reading with serious faces and no tricks. He was amused, and, taking no notice, continued to read. As soon as he had finished, the monkeys went off into the hills.

Reincarnation

The monk was surprised to see the monkeys appear at both his sermons next day; and when on the third day they came again he could not help asking why they came so regularly.

'We have come, holy father, because we like to hear the words and sermons of Buddha as read by yourself, and greatly do we desire to retain all the wisdom and virtues which we have heard you recite. Is it possible for you to copy out the great and holy Buddhist book?'

'It would be a very laborious affair,' answered the priest, highly astonished; 'but, so rare an interest is it that you animals take in the sermons of our Great Lord Buddha, I will make an effort to satisfy your wish, hoping that thereby you may be benefited.'

The monkeys bowed and left the priest, pleased with themselves and the promise they had obtained, while the priest set to at his gigantic labours of copying the Buddhist Bible. Some six or seven days later about five hundred monkeys came to the temple, each bearing parchment paper, which they laid before the priest, their foreman saying how deeply grateful they would be when they had got the copy of the Bible, so that they might know the laws and mend their ways; and, bowing again before the priest, they retired, all except the first two monkeys. These two set diligently to work to find food for the priest while he wrote. Day after day they went into the mountains, returning with wild fruits and potatoes, honey and mushrooms; and the priest wrote steadily on, being thus attended, until he had copied five volumes of the sacred book.

When he had reached the end of the fifth volume

133

the monkeys, for some unaccountable reason, failed to come, and the good priest was quite nervous on their account. The second day of their absence he went in search of them, fearing that they must have been overcome by some misfortune. Everywhere the priest found traces of their forages in his behalf,—branches broken off the wild fruit trees, scratchings and holes where they had been looking for wild potatoes. Evidently the monkeys had worked hard, and the poor priest felt deeply anxious on their account.

At last, when near the top of the mountain, his heart gave a bound and was filled with sorrow when he came to a hole which the monkeys had made in looking for wild potatoes—so deep that they had been unable to get out. No doubt both of them had died of broken hearts, fearing that the priest would think they had deserted him.

There remained nothing to do but to bury the monkeys and pray for their blessing ; which he did. Shortly after this the priest was called away from the temple to another : so, as he saw no necessity to continue copying the Buddhist Bible, he put the five volumes he had copied into one of the pillars of the temple, which had a sort of shelf cupboard cut in it.

Forty years later there arrived at the temple one Kinomi-ta-ka Ason, who had become Governor or Lord of Echigo Province. He came with half of his retainers and domestics, and asked the priests if they knew anything of the unfinished copy of the Buddhist Bible. Was it in the temple still ?

'No,' they said, 'we were none of us here at the

time your Lordship mentions. But there is one old man, a servant, who is eighty-five years of age, and he may be able to tell you something. We will send for him.'

Shortly afterwards a man with flowing white beard was ushered in.

'Is it the old document that a priest began copying out for the monkeys you want? Well, if so, that has never been touched since, and is a matter of so little importance that I had nearly forgotten about it. The document is in a little secret shelf which is hollowed out in one of the main pillars of the temple. I will fetch it.'

Some ten minutes later the documents were in the hands of Kinomi-ta-ka Ason, who was in ecstasy of delight at the sight of them. He told the priests and the old man that he was the Lord of Echigo Province, and that he had journeyed all the way to their temple to see if unfinished volumes of the Bible remained there. 'For,' he said, 'I was the senior of the two monkeys who were so anxious to obtain copies of the whole of our Lord Buddha's sermons ; and, now that I have been born a man, I wish to complete them.'

Kinomi-ta-ka Ason was allowed to take the five volumes away with him, and for five years he kept copying out the sacred book. He copied three thousand volumes in all, and it is said that they are now kept in the Temple of Kinoto, in Echigo, as its most sacred treasure.

XXIII

THE DIVING-WOMAN OF OISO BAY

Oiso, in the Province of Sagami, has become such a celebrated place as the chosen residence of the Marquis Ito and of several other high Japanese personages, that a story of a somewhat romantic nature, dating back to the Ninan period, may be interesting.

During one of the earlier years of the period, which lasted from 1116 to 1169 A.D., a certain knight, whose name was Takadai Jiro, became ill in the town of Kamakura, where he had been on duty, and was advised to spend the hot month of August at Oiso, and there to give himself perfect rest, peace, and quietness.

Having obtained permission to do this, Takadai Jiro lost no time in getting to the place and settling himself down, as comfortably as was possible, in a small inn which faced the sea. Being a landsman who (with the exception of his service at Kamakura) had hardly ever seen the sea, Takadai was pleased to dwell in gazing at it both by day and by night, for, like most Japanese of high birth, he was poetical and romantic.

After his arrival at Oiso, Takadai felt weary and dusty. As soon as he had secured his room he threw off his

136

clothes and went down to bathe. Takadai, whose age was about twenty-five years, was a good swimmer, and plunged into the sea without fear, going out for nearly half-a-mile. There, however, misfortune overtook him. He was seized with a violent cramp and began to sink. A fishing-boat sculled by a man and containing a diving-girl happened to see him and went to the rescue; but by this time he had lost consciousness, and had sunk for the third time.

The girl jumped overboard and swam to the spot where he had disappeared, and, having dived deep, brought him to the surface, holding him there until the boat came up, when by the united efforts of herself and her father Takadai was hauled on board, but not before he had realised that the soft arm that clung round his neck was that of a woman.

When he was thoroughly conscious again, before they had reached the shore, Takadai saw that his preserver was a beautiful ama (diving-girl) aged not more than seventeen. Such beauty he had never seen before—not even in the higher circles in which he was accustomed to move. Takadai was in love with his brave saviour before the boat had grounded on the pebbly beach. Determined in some way to repay the kindness he had received, Takadai helped to haul their boat up the steep beach and then to carry their fish and nets to their little thatched cottage, where he thanked the girl for her noble and gallant act in saving him, and congratulated her father on the possession of such a daughter. Having done this, he returned to his inn, which was not more than a few hundred yards away.

From that time on the soul of Takadai knew no peace. Love of the maddest kind was on him. There was no sleep for him at night, for he saw nothing but the face of the beautiful diving-girl, whose name (he had ascertained) was Kinu. Try as he might, he could not for a moment put her out of his mind. In the daytime it was worse, for O Kinu was not to be seen, being out at sea with her father, diving for the haliotis shell and others ; and it was generally the dusk of evening before she returned, and then, in the dim light, he could not see her.

Once, indeed, Takadai tried to speak to O Kinu ; but she would have nothing to say to him, and continued busying herself in assisting her father to carry the nets and fish up to their cottage. This made Takadai far worse, and he went home wild, mad, and more in love than ever.

At last his love grew so great that he could endure it no longer. He felt that at all events it would be a relief to declare it. So he took his most confidential servant into the secret, and despatched him with a letter to the fisherman's cottage. O Kinu San did not even write an answer, but told the old servant to thank his master in her behalf for his letter and his proposal of marriage. ' Tell him also,' said she, ' that no good could come of a union between one of so high a birth as he and one so lowly as I. Such a badly matched pair could never make a happy home.' In answer to the servant's ex-postulation, she merely added, ' I have told you what to tell your master : take him the message.'

Takadai Jiro, on hearing what O Kinu had said, was not angry. He was simply astonished. It was beyond his belief that a fisher-girl could refuse such an offer in marriage as himself — a samurai of the upper class. Indeed, instead of being angry, Takadai was so startled as to be rather pleased than otherwise ; for he thought that perhaps he had taken the fair O Kinu San a little too suddenly, and that this first refusal was only a bit of coyness on her part that was not to be wondered at. 'I will wait a day or two,' thought Takadai. 'Now that Kinu knows of my love, she may think of me, and so become anxious to see me. I will keep out of the way. Perhaps then she will be as anxious to see me as I am to see her.'

Takadai kept to his own room for the next three days, believing in his heart that O Kinu must be pining for him. On the evening of the fourth day he wrote another letter to O Kinu, more full of love than the first, despatched his old servant, and waited patiently for the answer.

When O Kinu was handed the letter she laughed and said :

'Truly, old man, you appear to me very funny, bringing me letters. This is the second in four days, and never until four days ago have I had a letter addressed to me in my life. What is this one about, I wonder ?'

Saying this, she tore it open and read, and then, turning to the servant, continued : 'It is difficult for me to understand. If you gave my message to your master correctly he could not fail to know that I could not marry him. His position in life is far too high. Is your master quite right in his head ?'

'Yes : except for the love of you, my young master is

quite right in his head; but since he has seen you he talks and thinks of nothing but you, until even I have got quite tired of it, and earnestly pray to Kwannon daily that the weather may get cool, so that we may return to our duties at Kamakura. For three full days have I had to sit in the inn listening to my young master's poems about your beauty and his love. And I had hoped that every day would find us fishing from a boat for the sweet aburamme fish, which are now fat and good, as every other sensible person is doing. Yes: my master's head was right enough; but you have unsettled it, it seems. Oh, do marry him, so that we shall all be happy and go out fishing every day and waste no more of this unusual holiday.'

'You are a selfish old man,' answered O Kinu. 'Would you that I married to satisfy your master's love and your desire for fishing? I have told you to tell your master that I will not marry him, because we could not, in our different ranks of life, become happy. Go and repeat that answer.'

The servant implored once more; but O Kinu remained firm, and finally he was obliged to deliver the unpleasant message to his master.

Poor Takadai! This time he was distressed, for the girl had even refused to meet him. What was he to do? He wrote one more imploring letter, and also spoke to O Kinu's father; but the father said, 'Sir, my daughter is all I have to love in the world: I cannot influence her in such a thing as her love. Moreover, all our diving-girls are strong in mind as well as in body, for constant danger strengthens their nerves: they are not like the weak farmers' girls, who can be influenced and even ordered to marry men they hate. Their minds are, oftener than not, stronger than those of us men. I always did what Kinu's mother told me I was to do, and could not influence Kinu in such a thing as her marriage. I might give you my advice, and should do so ; but, sir, in this case I must agree with my daughter, that, great as the honour done to her, she would be unwise to marry one above her own station in life.'

Takadai's heart was broken. There was nothing more that he could say and nothing more that he could do. Bowing low, he left the fisherman and retired forthwith to his room in the inn, which he never left, much to the consternation of his servant.

Day by day he grew thinner, and as the day approached for his return from leave, Takadai was far more of an invalid than he had been on his arrival at Oiso. What was he to do? The sentiment of the old proverb that ' there are as good fish in the sea as ever came out of it ' did not in any way appeal to him. He felt that life was no longer worth having. He resolved to end it in the sea, where his spirit might perhaps linger and catch sight occasionally of the beautiful diving-girl who had bewitched his heart.

Takadai that evening wrote a last note to Kinu, and as soon as the villagers of Oiso were asleep he arose and went to the cottage, slipping the note under the door. Then he went to the beach, and, after tying a large stone to a rope and to his neck, he got into a boat and rowed himself about a hundred yards from shore, where he took the stone in his arms and jumped overboard.

Next morning O Kinu was shocked to read in the note that Jiro Takadai was to kill himself for love of her. She rushed down to the beach, but could see only an empty fishing-boat some three or four hundred yards from shore, to which she swam. There she found Takadai's tobacco box and his juro (medicine box). O Kinu thought that Takadai must have thrown himself into the sea somewhere hereabouts : so she began to dive, and was not long before she found the body, which she brought to the surface, after some trouble on account of the weight of the stone which the arms rigidly grasped. O Kinu took the body back to shore, where she found Takadai's old servant wringing his hands in grief.

The body was taken back to Kamakura, where it was buried. O Kinu was sufficiently touched to vow that she would never marry any one. True, she had not loved Takadai ; but he had loved, and had died for her. If she married, his spirit would not rest in peace.

No sooner had O Kinu mentally undertaken this generous course than a strange thing came to pass.

Sea-gulls, which were especially uncommon in Oiso Bay, began to swarm into it ; they settled over the exact spot where Takadai had drowned himself. In stormy weather they hovered over it on the wing ; but they never went away from the place. Fishermen thought it extraordinary ; but Kinu knew well enough that the spirit of Takadai must have passed into the gulls, and for it she prayed regularly at the temple, and out of her small savings built a little tomb sacred to the memory of Takadai Jiro.

By the time Kinu was twenty years of age her beauty

The Diving-Woman of Oiso Bay

was celebrated, and many were the offers she had in
marriage; but she refused them all, and kept her vow of
celibacy. During her entire life the sea-gulls were always
on the spot where Takadai had been drowned. She died
by drowning in a severe typhoon some nine years later
than Takadai; and from that day the sea-gulls disappeared, showing that his spirit was now no longer in
fear of O Kinu marrying.

XXIV

THEFT AND RECOVERY OF A GOLDEN KWANNON

In the period of Gen-roku, which lasted from 1688 to 1704, when the Shogun or military ruler Tsunayoshi's power was in full sway, he presented a solid gold figure of Kwannon, the Goddess of Mercy, to each of the three leading families of the provinces of Kii, Mito, and Owari, and they were considered as of the highest and greatest value by each of these leading Lords or Daimios, who had them kept in their inner palaces, so that they were almost impossible to get at, and were considered at least absolutely safe from robbers ; but even in spite of this the Lord of Kii took additional precautions by always having a man night and day to guard his idol.

At the same period lived a most redoubtable robber whose name was Yayegumo. He was more than an ordinary robber, and was what the people called a 'fu-in-kiri,' which means 'seal breaker' or 'seal cutter'; a first-class burglar, in fact, who never descended to robbing the poor, but only robbed the richest and most difficult palaces and castles that were to be got at, taking from them only the highest and most valuable treasures they possessed.

This bold robber broke into the Lord of Kii's Palace —no one knew how—took the idol of Kwannon, and left his name written on a piece of paper. The Lord of Kii, very angry, sent for the guard, whose name was Mumashima Iganosuke, and reprimanded him severely, asking him what excuse he had to make. 'None, my lord : tiredness overcame me and I slept. There is but one way in which I can show my regret, and that I will do by destroying myself.'

The Lord of Kii, who was a man of wisdom, answered that before he did this it would be more useful if Iganosuke would follow up the robber and try to recover the idol. Iganosuke, who had always been a faithful servant, readily consented, and, having obtained indefinite leave, went away. For fully four months he was quite unsuccessful, though he had travelled half over the country. At last he heard reports of robberies in Chugoku, and then later in Shikoku Province. Hurrying down from Izumo to Okayama, he there got on board a ship bound across the Inland Sea for Takamatsu, in Shikoku. The weather was fine and the sea smooth, and Iganosuke was in high spirits, for he had heard that one or two of the robberies had undoubtedly been done by Yayegumo, and he felt that at last he must be getting nearer the man he wished to catch—perhaps, even, he was on that very boat! Who could tell? Thinking of these possibilities, Iganosuke kept very much to himself, watching the people, whose spirits all seemed to be affected by the beautiful weather, for, though mostly strangers, they were all sociable.

Among them was a good-looking young samurai who had attracted Iganosuke by his refined appearance, as also by a beautiful gold pipe which he drew out from its case and smoked while chatting to his neighbour. By and by a samurai of some sixty years of age came up to the young man, and said :

'Sir, I have lost my pipe and tobacco-pouch somewhere on this ship. I am a confirmed smoker, and almost dying for a whiff of tobacco. Might I borrow yours for a moment or two?'

The young samurai handed both his pipe and his pouch to the old man with a bow, saying that this afforded him great pleasure.

The old samurai, after his three puffs of the pipe, was about to empty out the ash and refill it. To do so, without thinking what he was about, he knocked the pipe on the outside of the ship. To his horror the gankubi (the bowl) dropped off into the sea. The old man knew that the pipe was gold and of great value, and was utterly confused. He did not know what to say. His apologies were profuse ; but they did not bring back the end of the pipe. The young samurai, of course, was much annoyed ; but it would be no use getting angry. In any case that would have been an excessively vulgar proceeding, more especially with so old a man. He said :

'Ah ! the pipe was given to me by the lord of my clan for meritorious service rendered in the big hunt last year, and truly I do not know how I shall be able to face the disgrace of incurring his anger.' He grew pale as he mused.

Theft and Recovery of a Golden Kwannon

The old samurai felt more sorry than ever when he heard this, and said :

'There is only one way I see that you can face your lord, and that is by my death. I also was a samurai of some importance when younger, and know how to conduct myself. It is right that I should disembowel myself as an apology to you for my carelessness.' And, saying this, the old samurai drew his right arm and shoulder from under his kimono.

Surprised at the old man's high sense of honour, the young samurai seized the hand in which he held his sword and prevented him, saying :

'That will really do no good. It would not make it easier for me to explain to my lord. Your death can bring no apology to him. It was I to whom he gave the pipe, and it is I who have lost it by lending it to you. It is I, therefore, who should offer the apology to my lord by doing harakiri !' Then the young samurai prepared to kill himself.

Iganosuke, who had been watching the incident, stepped forward and said :

'Gentlemen, I also am a samurai, and I have heard what you say. Let me say that, though the pipe-end has fallen into the sea, it in no way follows that it is lost beyond recovery. Both of you appear to me to be unnecessarily hasty. I am a good diver and swimmer ; our ship is becalmed ; and the water hereabouts is not very deep. I am quite ready to try and help you to recover the pipe if you will allow me.'

Of course, both the other samurai were pleased at this idea, of which, being no swimmers themselves, they had never thought. And Iganosuke lost no time in throwing off his kimono and diving into the sea, where he was thoroughly at home, having been in his younger days so expert a swimmer that he gave lessons to many of the samurai at Kii.

Down he went to the bottom, finding not much more than seven Japanese fathoms of five feet each. The bottom was composed almost entirely of stones and was very clear. Iganosuke had not moved many feet along before he saw the end of the gold pipe, and at the same time something else gleaming between the stones. Thrusting the pipe between his teeth, he seized the other object, and to his great astonishment found it to be no less a thing than the gold figure of Kwannon which had been stolen from the castle of the Lord of Kii.

Carefully returning to the surface, Iganosuke scrambled on board, and handed the pipe-end to the grateful young samurai, who, with the old one, bowed to the ground.

When Iganosuke had thrown on his clothes, he said :

' I am a retainer of the Lord of Kii, and I have come from our castle of Takegaki to hunt for the robber who stole the very figure of Kwannon which I have just by good fortune while looking for your pipe recovered. Is it not wonderful ? Truly the old saying, " Nasakewa hito no tame naradzu "[1] is quite true ! '

Then the old man, in a wild state of delight, cried : ' Even more curious is this. My name is Matsure Fujiye of Takamatsu. Only a month ago the robber whom you name Yayegumo Fuin-kiri, the seal-breaker, came into the bedroom of my lord, and was about to steal great

[1] Favour is not for other people.

Theft and Recovery of a Golden Kwannon

valuables, when I, who was on guard, tried to take him. Though an old man, I am a fencer ; but he was too clever for me and escaped. I followed him down to the beach, but was not fast enough, and he got away. Since then I have always wondered what he had in his kimono pockets, for the bright rays of some gilded thing shot out of them. The robber had not got far from the shore before a great storm arose. He was wrecked and drowned. Both his body and the boat were recovered some days later, and I identified them ; but there was nothing in his pocket. It is clear that when his boat upset the robber lost the Kwannon, which must have been what I saw shining out of his pocket.'

Truly this was a wonderful string of coincidences !

Iganosuke, who had no further cause to travel, returned to the Lord of Kii, and reported his adventures and good fortune. So much pleased was the Daimio, he gave Iganosuke a present.

The figure of the gold Kwannon was better guarded than ever before. Undoubtedly it had miraculous power, and it may still be among the treasures of Kii.

XXV

SAIGYO HOSHI'S ROCK

SOME twelve miles south of Shodo shima (Shodo island) is the largish island of Nao or Naoshima, on the western side of the enchanting Inland Sea, which it has been my good fortune to cruise over at will, helped, instead of being hindered, by the Japanese Government, in consequence of the kindness of Sir Ernest Satow. Naoshima has but few inhabitants, not, I think, more than from sixty to a hundred ; in the time of our story, about the year 1156, there were only two,—Sobei and his good wife O Yone. These lived alone at a beautiful little bay, where they had built a fishing-hut, and cultivated some three thousand tsubo of land, with the produce of which and an unlimited supply of fish they were perfectly happy, untroubled by the quarrels of the day, which were then particularly serious, it being the Hogen period, which, lasting from 1156 to 1160, took its name from what was known as the Hogen rebellion or (to put it correctly) revolution. It was during this exciting period that the ex-Emperor Shutoku (life, 1124-1141), who was suspected of leading the rebellion, was for safety banished by those in power to the island of Naoshima.

Stranded, marooned in little else than the clothes he

stood in, he was in an unenviable plight. As far as he knew, the island was desolate. After his marooners had left him he strolled on the beach, wondering what next he should do. Should he take his life, or should he struggle to retain it? While pondering these questions night overcame Shutoku before he had thought of making a shelter, and he sat, in consequence, contemplating the past and listening to the sad waves.

Next morning, as the sun rose above the horizon, the ex-Emperor began to move. He had resolved to live. He had not gone far along the beach when he found marks of feet upon the sand, and shortly afterwards, from across a little rocky promontory, he saw smoke ascending in the still air. Lightened in heart, the ex-Emperor stepped out, and after some twenty minutes of stiff climbing came down into the bay where stood the hut of Sobei and his wife. Marching boldly up, he told them who he was, and how he had been marooned and exiled, and asked them many questions.

'Sir,' said Sobei, 'my wife and I are very humble people. We live in peace, for there are none to disturb us here, and we are passing through our lives very happily. To our humble fare you are truly welcome. Our cottage is small; but you shall have its shelter while we build another and a better for you, and at all times we shall be your servants.'

The ex-Emperor was pleased to hear these words of friendship, and became one of the family. He helped to build a lodge for himself. He helped the old couple in their fishing and agriculture, and became deeply attached to them.

In the autumn he fell ill, and was nursed through a dangerous fever, his medicines being made by O Yone from leaves, seaweeds, and other natural products of the island ; and towards the spring he began to recover. In his convalescence the ex-Emperor went out one day to sit by the sea and admire the scenery, and became so absorbed in a flock of seagulls that were following a school of sardines that he failed to notice what was going on around him. When he looked up suddenly it was to find himself surrounded by no less than fourteen knights in armour.

As soon as these noticed that the ex-Emperor had seen them, one the eldest, a grey-haired and benevolent-looking old man, stepped up to him, and, bowing, said :

'Oh, my beloved Sovereign, at last I have found you ! My name is Furuzuka Iga, and regretfully I am obliged to tell you that I am sent by the Mikado to secure your head. He fears while you live, even in banishment, for the peace of the country. Please enable me to take your head as speedily and as painlessly as possible. It is my misfortune to have to do it.'

The ex-Emperor seemed in no way surprised at this speech. Without a word, he arranged himself and stretched his neck to receive the blow from Iga's sword.

Iga, touched by his manly conduct, began to weep, and exclaimed :

'Oh, what a brave sovereign ! what a samurai ! How I grieve to be his executioner !' But his duty was plain : so he nerved himself and struck off the ex-Emperor's head with a single blow.

As soon as the head fell upon the sand the other

knights came up and respectfully placed the head in a silken bag and awaited orders from their chief.

'My friends,' said Furuzuka Iga, 'go back to the boat and take the head of Shutoku to the Emperor. Tell him that his orders have been carried out, and that he need have no future fear. Go without me, for I remain here to weep over the deed which I have had to do.'

The knights were astonished; but they departed, and Iga gave way to grief.

Soon it came to pass that Sobei and his wife went to look for the ex-Emperor, for his absence had been long. They knew the spot where he loved to sit and gaze at the beautiful scenery. Thus it was that they found Iga weeping.

'What is this?' they cried. 'What means this blood upon the sand? Who, sir, may you be, and where is our guest?'

Iga explained that he was an envoy from the Mikado, and that it had been his painful duty to kill the ex-Emperor.

The fury of Sobei and his wife knew no bounds. Instinctively they decided that they must both die after avenging the ex-Emperor by killing Iga. They proceeded to attack him with their knives—Sobei in front and his wife from behind.

Iga avoided them by his proficiency in jujitsu. In two seconds he had both of them by the wrists, and then said:

'Good people,—for I know you to be such,—listen to my story. The ex-Emperor who has been in exile on this island for nearly a year, and whom you have befriended and prevented from perishing from starvation and exposure, is not the real ex-Emperor, but my own son Furuzuka Taro!'

Sobei and his wife looked at him in bewilderment, and asked for an explanation.

'Listen, and I will tell you,' said Furuzuka Iga. 'As the result of the revolution in the Imperial Household, ex-Emperor Shutoku was taken for the enemy of the reigning Emperor, and was sentenced to exile on this island, which was supposed to be uninhabited, and is so for all but yourselves. The ex-Emperor must have died had you not been here to support him, and, though I am attached to the Imperial Court, I did not like one who had been my sovereign so to perish. It was my duty to bring the ex-Emperor here and maroon him. I marooned instead my own son, who was very much like him, and was glad to take the ex-Emperor's place. Unfortunately, the Mikado's mind became uneasy during the winter, fearing that so long as the ex-Emperor remained alive there might be further trouble, and I was again sent to Naoshima Island, this time to bring back the ex-Emperor's head. You know now what I have had to do. Was ever a father called upon to carry out so terrible a commission? Pity me; be not angered. You have lost your friend, and I my son; but the ex-Emperor still lives; moreover, he knows of my loyalty to him, and will be here shortly in secret and in disguise. That is why I have remained, and that is the whole of the story I have to tell; and both of you must know how deeply grateful I feel towards you both in your great kindness to my son Taro.'

Saigyo Hoshi's Rock

The poor samurai bowed to the ground, and the old couple, too simple to know what to do, remained silent, with tears of sorrow and of sympathy streaming down their faces.

For fully half an hour nothing was said. They remained weeping on the blood-stained beach, waiting for the tide to rise and wash away the marks; and they might have been longer had it not been that suddenly they heard the sweet strains of the biwa (a musical instrument of four strings, a lute) Then Iga arose and, drying his eyes, said, 'Here, my friends, comes the real ex-Emperor, though in disguise. He never goes anywhere without his lute, and he has signs and signals with me by certain airs he plays. He is asking now if it is safe to come forward, and if I give no answer it is safe. Listen, and see him approach!'

Sobei and his wife had never listened to such soft and bewitching music before, and, hearts full of sorrow, they sat listening. Nearer and nearer the music came, until they saw coming along the beach a man in poor clothes, whom they might almost have mistaken for their dead friend, so like was he to him.

When he came nearer, Iga went up and bowed, and then led the stranger to the fisherman and his wife, whom he made known, telling the ex-Emperor what kindness they had shown his son Taro. The ex-Emperor was pleased, and said that he was deeply grateful and considered them as part of that faithful body who had worked to save his life. Just then a ship was seen to round the point of the bay. It was the ship in which Iga had arrived, the ship which had borne away his son's head. The ex-Emperor, followed by Iga, Sobei, and his

155

wife, kneeled on the sand near the bloody stain, and prayed long for the peace of the spirit of Taro.

Next day the ex-Emperor announced his intention of remaining for the rest of his life on the island of Nao-shima with Sobei and O Yone. Iga was taken to the mainland by Sobei, and found his way back to the capital.

The ex-Emperor, attended by the faithful old couple, lived for a year on the island. His time was passed in playing on the biwa and in praying for the spirit of Taro. At the end of the year he died from mournfulness. Sobei and his wife devoted all their spare time to building a small shrine to his memory. It is said to be standing to this day.

In the third year of Ninnan the famous but eccentric priest and poet, Saigyo, who was related to the Imperial family, spent seventeen days on the island, praying night and day. During this time he sat on the favourite rock of Taro and the ex-Emperor. The rock is still known as 'Saigyo iwa' (Saigyo's Rock).

XXVI

HOW MASAKUNI REGAINED HIS SIGHT

Some seventy years ago there dwelt in Kyoto a celebrated swordmaker, a native of the province of Awa, in Tokushima. Awanokami Masakuni—for such was his name—dwelt in Kyoto for the purpose of business, and because he was nearer the homes of the grandees, for whom it paid him best to make swords. With him lived his beautiful little daughter Ai, or O Ai San ('Ai' meaning 'love'). She was fourteen, and only a child; but her beauty was enough to make her an object of affection to any one who happened to see her. O Ai thought of no one but her father, and of him she was extremely fond.

As time went on Masakuni so improved in the art of making swords and forging blades that he came to be regarded with much jealousy by the other swordmakers, all of whom, including Masakuni, lived in the Karasu-Tengu district of Kyoto, where it was the fashion for swordmakers to dwell in those days. Alas, the skill of Masakuni cost him an eye! Though the samurai and wearers of swords held ethical ideas of honour and Bushi said to be far above the average, it does not appear that the swordmakers were the same. They often committed the most horrible and cowardly crimes. One of these was to put out either one or both of the eyes of their sword-making rivals while they slept. Thus it came to pass one night that little O Ai San was awakened from her sleep by the piercing cry of her father, and found him writhing on the floor in agony, with his right eye stabbed and burst.

O Ai summoned aid ; but nothing could save the eye. It was done for ; and, though the place could be healed, Masakuni must give up all idea of ever having the use of his right eye again. There was not even the satisfaction of catching his assailant, for he did not know who it was. Amid these circumstances it was evident that Masakuni could no longer remain a swordmaker : after the loss of his eye it would be impossible for him to carry out any of the fine work needed to keep up his reputation. Consequently, he returned to his native village, Ohara, in the province of Awa, with his daughter.

Poor Masakuni had not been long settled in his old home before his left eye began to feel bad, and in less than a week there appeared to be every chance of his losing its use altogether.

Ai was disconsolate. For her dear father to lose the use of both eyes was terrible. She loved him dearly, and knew that his only remaining pleasures in life were herself and beautiful scenery. What could she do, poor child ? She waited on him day and night, cooked, and was his nurse. When she had exhausted every means in her power to do good, and her father's left eye grew worse, she betook herself to praying. Daily she toiled up the wild and rocky mountain of Shiratake, near the summit of which there was a little shrine dedicated to Fudo, sometimes thought of as the God of Wisdom. There, day after day, she prayed that she might be led to the knowledge that would cure her father, and, though it was now the icy month of January, after so doing she divested herself of clothing and stood for nearly half an hour under the waterfall from which the mountain takes its name, as was the custom of all who wished to impress upon the Deity the earnestness and sincerity of their prayers.

For three months O Ai had thus gone up the mountain daily to pray and undergo the terrible cold of the waterfall ; yet her prayer seemed unanswered, for there was no improvement in her father. O Ai, however, did not lose heart. Towards the end of February she climbed again. In spite of the severe cold (ice was hanging on to many parts of the rock), O Ai, after praying to Fudo San, divested herself of clothing and stepped under the fall, there to continue her prayers as long as she could possibly stand and live. So great was the cold, in a few moments she lost consciousness, and slipped down into the basin of the fall, receiving a severe blow on the head.

Just then, by unusual good fortune, an old man, followed by his servant, came up the mountain and was looking at and admiring the waterfall. The white body of O Ai San caught his eye while it was being churned in the basin of the fall not thirty feet from where he stood. The old man and the servant hastened to pull out the body and began to rub it, and found that life was not extinct. O Ai was half-drowned and numbed, insensible from cold and the blow, and the blood was flowing freely from the wound.

They made up their minds to save this beautiful girl, and set to with vigour. A fire was lit ; her clothes were warmed and put on ; and in less than twenty minutes she had opened her eyes and was able to speak. Seeing this, the old man asked :

' Is it by accident we find you thus nearly dead, or have you tried to take your own life ? '

' No,' said the girl : ' it is not that I wish to take my own life. It is to save the eyesight of my father that I have come here to pray ; this is the hundredth day of my prayer. To-morrow and every following day I shall be here to pray again, and so continue ; for it is against the teachings of Buddha to despair.' O Ai then related the history of her father's blindness.

The old man, answering, said :

' If devotion to duty has its reward, yours, young lady, has come. Perhaps you are not aware who I am. My name is Uozumi, Dr. Uozumi. I am the chief doctor in Kyoto, and am the only one at present who has passed his full degrees in the Medical Sciences of the Dutch. I have just been to the Palace at Yedo, and am now on my return to Kyoto. I have only put in here with my ship for to-day, and have come up this mountain to admire the scenery. Now I have found you, and so grieve with you in your trouble that I will stay here a week or two and see what can be done for your father. Do not let us lose time : put on the rest of your clothes, and let us go to your house.'

O Ai San was delighted. At last, she thought, her

33. OKUREHA IS SAVED BY THE GODDESS

34. THE GODDESS OF MOUNT DAIMUGENZAN

35. THE OLD HERMIT ENTERTAINS THE CHILDREN

36. THE SPIRIT OF FUJI SHOWS YOSOJI THE HEALTH-GIVING STREAM

37. YODA EMON FINDS HIMSELF ON A WHALE'S BACK

38. HANANO SAN TAKES THE CHERRY BRANCH FROM THE YOUTH

39. THE WOODCUTTER SAVES CHOYO FROM ROBBERS

40. MAD JOAN, THOUGH MUTTERING, IS DEAD AND A SKELETON

How Masakuni regained his Sight

prayer had been answered by Fudo San. With joy in her heart, she almost ran down the mountain, forgetting all about her own narrow escape and the long gash she had received in her head. Dr. Uozumi found it hard to keep anywhere near this healthy young maid.

Arrived at the house, Uozumi made an examination of the patient and ordered remedies after the Dutch prescriptions, the medicines for which he fortunately had with him. Day after day the doctor and O Ai attended on Masakuni, and at the end of the tenth day his left eye was perfectly cured.

Masakuni was delighted at the partial recovery of his sight, and, like his daughter, attributed the good fortune of the celebrated doctor's arrival to the mercy of Fudo San. Having purified his body and soul by living on a vegetable diet and bathing in cold water for ten days, he began making two swords, which some time afterwards he finished. One he presented to the god Fudo, and the other to Doctor Uozumi. They were afterwards known as the celebrated swords made by the semi-blind Masakuni.

The doctor thought it a pity to allow such a skilled artist as Masakuni to remain in this remote village of Awa Province, and also that the beautiful O Ai should be allowed to rust there : so he persuaded them to join him in Kyoto. Subsequently he obtained a place as maid of honour in the palace of the Duke of Karasumaru for O Ai San, where she was perfectly happy.

Five years later Masakuni died, and was buried in the cemetery of Toribeyama, at the eastern end of Kyoto. So my story-teller, Fukuga, tells me.

XXVII

SAGAMI BAY

HATSUSHIMA ISLAND is probably unknown to all foreigners, and to 9999 out of every 10,000 Japanese; consequently, it is of not much importance. Nevertheless, it has produced quite a romantic little story, which was told to me by a friend who had visited there some six years before.

The island is about seven miles south-east of Atami, in Sagami Bay (Izu Province). It is so far isolated from the mainland that very little intercourse goes on with the outer world. Indeed, it is said that the inhabitants of Hatsushima Island are a queer people, and prefer keeping to themselves. Even to-day there are only some two hundred houses, and the population cannot exceed a thousand. The principal production of the island is, of course, fish; but it is celebrated also for its jonquil flowers (suisenn). Thus it will be seen that there is hardly any trade. What little the people buy from or sell to the mainland they carry in their own fishing-boats. In matrimony also they keep to themselves, and are generally conservative and all the better for it.

Sagami Bay

There is a well-known fisherman's song of Hatsushima Island. It means something like the following, and it is of the origin of that queer verse that the story is :—

> To-day is the tenth of June. May the rain fall in torrents!
> For I long to see my dearest O Cho San.
> Hi, Hi, Ya-re-ko-no-sa! Ya-re-ko-no-sa!

Many years ago there lived on the island the daughter of a fisherman whose beauty even as a child was extraordinary. As she grew, Cho—for such was her name—improved in looks, and, in spite of her lowly birth, she had the manners and refinement of a lady. At the age of eighteen there was not a young man on the island who was not in love with her. All were eager to seek her hand in marriage; but hardly any dared to ask, even through the medium of a third party, as was usual.

Amongst them was a handsome fisherman of about twenty years whose name was Shinsaku. Being less simple than the rest, and a little more bold, he one day approached Gisuke, O Cho's brother, on the subject. Gisuke could see nothing against his sister marrying Shinsaku; indeed, he rather liked Shinsaku; and their families had always been friends. So he called his sister O Cho down to the beach, where they were sitting, and told her that Shinsaku had proposed for her hand in marriage, and that he thought it an excellent match, of which her mother would have approved had she been alive. He added : 'You must marry soon, you know. You are eighteen, and we want no spinsters on Hatsushima, or girls brought here from the mainland to marry our bachelors.'

'Stay, stay, my dear brother! I do not want all this sermon on spinsterhood,' cried O Cho. 'I have no intention of remaining single, I can tell you; and as for Shinsaku I would rather marry him than any one else— so do not worry yourself further on that account. Settle the day of the happy event.'

Needless to say, young Gisuke was delighted, and so was Shinsaku; and they settled that the marriage should be three days thence.

Soon, when all the fishing-boats had returned to the village, the news spread; and it would be difficult to describe the state of the younger men's feelings. Hitherto every one had hoped to win the pretty O Cho San; all had lived in that happy hope, and rejoiced in the uncertain state of love, which causes such happiness in its early stages. Shinsaku had hitherto been a general favourite. Now the whole of their hopes were dashed to the ground. O Cho was not for any of them. As for Shinsaku, how they suddenly hated him! What was to be done? they asked one another, little thinking of the comical side, or that in any case O Cho could marry only one of them.

No attention was paid to the fish they had caught; their boats were scarcely pulled high enough on the beach for safety; their minds were wholly given to the question how each and every one of them could marry O Cho San. First of all, it was decided to tell Shinsaku that they would prevent his marriage if possible. There were several fights on the quiet beach, which had never before been disturbed by a display of ill-feeling. At last Gisuke, O Cho's brother, consulted with his sister and Shinsaku; and they decided, for the peace of the island, to break off the marriage, O Cho and her lover determining that at all events they would marry no one else.

However, even this great sacrifice had no effect. There were fully thirty men ; in fact, the whole of the bachelors wanted to marry O Cho ; they fought daily ; the whole island was thrown into a discontent. Poor O Cho San! What could she do? Had not she and Shinsaku done enough already in sacrificing happiness for the peace of the island? There was only one more thing she could do, and, being a Japanese girl, she did it. She wrote two letters, one to her brother Gisuke, another to Shinsaku, bidding 'them farewell. 'The island of Hatsushima has never had trouble until I was born,' she said. 'For three hundred years or more our people, though poor, have lived happily and in peace. Alas ! now it is no longer so, on account of me. Farewell ! I shall be dead. Tell our people that I have died to bring them back their senses, for they have been foolish about me. Farewell ! '

After leaving the two letters where Gisuke slept, O Cho slipped stealthily out of the house (it was a pouring-wet and stormy night and the 10th of June), and cast herself into the sea from some rocks near her cottage, after well loading her sleeves with stones, so that she might rise no more.

Next morning, when Gisuke found the letters, instinctively he knew what must have happened, and rushed from the house to find Shinsaku. Brother and lover read their letters together, and were stricken with grief, as, indeed, was every one else. A search was made, and soon O Cho's straw slippers were found on the point of rocks near her house. Gisuke knew she must have jumped into the sea here, and he and Shinsaku dived down and found her body lying at the bottom. They brought it to the surface, and it was buried just beyond the rocks on which she had last stood.

From that day Shinsaku was unable to sleep at night. The poor fellow was quite distracted. O Cho's letter and straw slippers he placed beside his bed and surrounded them with flowers. His days he spent decorating and weeping over her tomb.

At last one evening Shinsaku resolved to make away with his own body, hoping that his spirit might find O Cho; and he wandered towards her tomb to take a last farewell. As he did so he thought he saw O Cho, and called her aloud three or four times, and then with outstretched arms he rushed delightedly at her. The noise awoke Gisuke, whose house was close to the grave. He came out, and found Shinsaku clasping the stone pillar which was placed at its head.

Shinsaku explained that he had seen the spirit of O Cho, and that he was about to follow her by taking his life; but from this he was dissuaded.

'Do not do that; devote your life, rather, and I will help with you in building a shrine dedicated to Cho. You will join her when you die by nature; but please her spirit here by never marrying another.'

Shinsaku promised. The young men of the place now began to be deeply sorry for Shinsaku. What selfish beasts they had been! they thought. However, they would mend their ways, and spend all their spare time in building a shrine to O Cho San; and this they did. The shrine is called 'The Shrine of O Cho San of Hatsushima,'

Sagami Bay

and a ceremony is held there every 10th of June. Curious
to relate, it invariably rains on that day, and the fishermen
say that the spirit of O Cho comes in the rain. Hence
the song :—

To-day is the tenth of June. May the rain fall in torrents!
For I long to see my dearest O Cho San.
Hi, Hi, Ya-re-ko-no-sa! Ya-re-ko-no-sa!

The shrine still stands, I am told.

XXVIII

THE KING OF TORIJIMA[1]

MANY years ago there lived a Daimio called Tarao. His castle and home were at Osaki, in Osumi Province, and amongst his retinue was a faithful and favourite servant whose name was Kume Shuzen. Kume had long been land-steward to the Lord Tarao, and indeed acted for him in everything connected with business.

One day Kume had been despatched to the capital, Kyoto, to attend to business for his master, when the Daimio Toshiro of Hyuga quarrelled with the Daimio of Osumi over some boundary question, and, Kume not being there to help his master, who was a hasty person, the two clans fought at the foot of Mount Kitamata.

---

[1] It is impossible to say exactly to which of the Torijima islands this story relates. There are two—one a rock islet some sixty miles east of Okinawajima, the main island on which is the capital of all the islands, Nafa; and the other or larger Torijima, between longitude 128° and 129°, and not far south of latitudinal line 38°. My story-teller declares the tale to be about the Rocky Island South, which charts show as 60 feet above water at high tide, by reason of there being an island adjacent called Kumeshima; while I argue that it is more probably about the northern Torijima, adjacent to which is a large island named Takuneshima, which might very well have been meant for Kumeshima. With Japanese, Chinese, and English names, these islands are very puzzling. The Japanese, though excellent map-makers, are bad geographers, changing names as they think fit.

The King of Torijima

The Lord Tarao of Osumi was killed, and so were most of his men. They were most completely beaten. The survivors retired to their lord's castle at Osaki; but the enemy followed them up, and again defeated them, taking the castle.

Messengers had been despatched to bring back Kume, of course; but Kume decided that there was only one honourable thing to do, and that was to gather the few remaining samurai he could and fight again in his dead master's behalf. Unfortunately, only some fifty men came to his call. These, with Kume, hid in the mountains with the intention of waiting until they had recruited more. One of Toshiro's spies found this out, and all except Kume were taken prisoners.

Being hotly pursued, Kume hid himself in the daytime, and made for the sea by night. After three days he reached Hizaki, and there, having bought all the provision he could carry, hid himself until an opportunity should come of seizing a boat in the darkness, hoping to baffle his pursuers.

Kume was no sailor; in fact, he had hardly ever been in a boat, and never except as a passenger. There was no difficulty in finding a boat. He pushed it off and let it drift, for he could not use the oar, and understood nothing about a sail. Fortunately, Hizaki is a long cape on the S.E. coast, facing the open Pacific, and therefore there was no difficulty in getting away, the wind being favourable and the tide as well; besides, there is here a strong current always travelling south towards the Loochoos. Kume was more or less indifferent as to where he went, and even if he had cared he could not have helped himself, for, though his knowledge of direction on land was very good, as soon as he found himself out of sight of land he was lost. All he knew was that where the sun rose there was no land which he could reach, that China lay in the direction in which it set, and that to the south there were islands which were reputed to hold savages, Nambanjin (foreign southern savages). Thus Kume drifted on, he knew not whither, lying in the bottom of the boat, and in no way economising his provisions ; and it naturally came to pass that at the end of the second day he had no water left, and suffered much in consequence.

Towards morning on the fifth day Kume lay half-asleep in the bottom of the boat. Suddenly he felt it bump.

'What ho, she bumps !' said he to himself in his native tongue, and, sitting up, he found he had drifted on to a rocky island. Kume was not long in scrambling ashore and dragging his boat as high as he was able. The first thing he set about doing was to find water to quench his thirst. As he wandered along the rocky shore hunting for a stream, Kume knew that the island could not be inhabited, for there were tens of thousands of sea-fowl perched upon the rocks, feeding along the beach and floating on the water ; others were sitting on eggs. Kume could see that he was not likely to starve while the birds were breeding, and he could see, more-over, that fish were there in abundance, for birds of the gannet species were simply gorging themselves with a kind of iwashi (sardine), which made the surface of the calm sea frizzle into foam in their endeavours to escape the larger fish that were pursuing them from underneath. Shoals of flying-fish came quite close to shore, pursued by the magnificent albacore; which clearly showed that fishermen did not visit these parts. Shell-fish were in plenty in the coral pools, and among them lay, thickly strewn, the smaller of the pearl mussels with which Kume was familiar in his own country.

There was no sand on this island—that is to say, on the seashore. Everything seemed to be of coral formation, except that there was a thick reddish substance on the top of all, out of which grew low scrubby trees bearing many fruits, which Kume found quite excellent to eat. There was no trouble in finding water : there were several streams flowing down the beach and coming from the thick scrub.

Kume returned to his boat, to make sure that it was safe, and, having found a better cove for it, he moved it thither. Then, having eaten some more fruit and shell-fish and seaweed, Kume lay down to sleep, and to think of his dead master, and wonder how he could eventually avenge him on the Daimio Toshiro of Hyuga.

When morning broke Kume was not a little surprised to see some eight or nine figures of people, as he first thought, sleeping ; but when it grew lighter he found that they were turtles, and it was not long before he was on shore and had turned one ; but then, recollecting that there was plenty of food without taking the life of a beast so much venerated, he let it go. 'Perhaps,' thought he, 'like Urashima, my kindness to the turtle may save me. Indeed, these turtles may be messengers or retainers of the Sea King's Palace!'

One thing that Kume now decided was to learn to row and sail his boat. He set to that very morning, and almost mastered the art of using the immense sculling oar used by present and ancient Japanese alike. In the afternoon he visited the highest part of his island; but it was not high enough to enable him to see land, though he thought at one time that he could discern that faint line of blue on the horizon which prophesies distant land.

However, he was safe for the time; he had food in plenty, and water; true, the birds somewhat bothered him, for they did not act as might have been expected. There seemed something uncanny in the way they sat on their perches and watched him. He did not like that, and often threw a stone at them; but even that had little effect—they only seemed to look more serious.

Though Kume was no sailor, he was a good enough swimmer, as are most Japanese who live anywhere along the sea provinces, and he was quite able to dive in moderation and up to a depth of three Japanese fathoms —fifteen feet. Thus it was that Kume spent all the time he was not practising in his boat in diving for shell-fish; he soon found that there were enormous quantities of pearl oysters, which contained beautiful pearls; and, having collected some fifty or sixty, large and small, he cut one of the sleeves of his coat and made a bag which he determined to fill. One day while Kume was diving about after his pearls and shell-fish, he found that by looking in the holes of rocks beneath the low-tide level he could find pearls that had fallen from the dead and rotten shells above; in one case they were like gravel, and he took them out of a cavity by handfuls. Discoloured they certainly were ; but Kume knew them from their roundness of shape, and rubbing with sand or earth soon proved them to be pearls. Thus it was that he worked with renewed energy, hoping all the time to make sufficient money to be able eventually to avenge his dead master.

One day, some six weeks after he had landed on the island, he saw a distant sail. Through the day he watched it carefully ; but it did not seem to come or go much nearer, and Kume came to the conclusion that it must be the sail of a stationary fishing-boat, for there was breeze enough to have taken it off out of sight twice over since he had watched, if it had wanted to go.

'Surely there must be land somewhere over there beyond the boat : it would not be there for half a day if not. To-morrow, now that I can manage to sail and row my boat, I will start on an expedition and see. I do not expect to find my own countrymen there ; but I may find Chinese who may be friendly, and if I find the southern savages I shall not, with my good Japanese sword, be afraid of them !'

Next morning Kume provisioned his boat with fruit, water, shell-fish, and eggs, and, tying his bag of pearls about him, set sail in a south-westerly direction. There was little wind, and the boat went slowly ; but Kume steered steadily all night, as was natural, considering the little he knew. He dared not go to sleep and thus perhaps lose all idea of the direction whence he had come. Thus it came that when morning broke the sun rose on his port side, and he found himself not more than some four miles from an island which lay right ahead of him. Quite elated with his first success in navigation, Kume seized his oars and helped the boat along. On reaching the land his reception was anything but pleasant. At least one hundred angry savages were on the beach with spears and staves ; but what were they (as my translator asks) to a Japanese samurai ? Fifteen of them were put out of action without his getting a scratch, for Kume was well up in all the defensive arts that his military training had given him, and the tricks in jujitsu were familiar to him.

The rest of his adversaries became frightened and began to run. Kume caught one of them, and tried to ask what island this was, and what kind of people they were. By signs he explained that he was a Japanese and in no way an enemy, but on the contrary wished to be friendly, and, as they could see, he was alone. Greatly impressed with Kume's prowess, and glad that he did not wish to resume hostilities, the natives stuck their spears point-downwards in the sand, and came forward to Kume, who sheathed his sword and proceeded to examine the fifteen men he had laid low. Eleven of these had fallen by some clever jujitsu trick, and were to all intents and purposes dead ; but Kume took them in various ways and restored them to life by a well-known art called kwatsu (really artificial breathing), which has been practised in Japan for hundreds of years in connection with some secret jujitsu tricks which are said to kill you—unless some one is present who knows the art of kwatsu you must die if left for over two hours without being restored. At present it is illegal to kill temporarily even though you know the art of kwatsu. Kume restored nine of his fallen enemies, which in itself was considered to be a marvellous performance, and gained him much respect. Two others were dead. The rest had wounds from which they recovered.

Peace being established, Kume was escorted by the chief to the village and given a hut to himself, and he found the people kind and agreeable. A wife was given to him, and Kume settled down to the life of the island, and to learn the language, which in many ways resembled his own.

Sugar and yams were the principal things planted,—with, of course, rice in the hills and where there was sufficient water for terracing,—but fishing formed the principal occupation of all. Four or five times a-year the islanders were visited by a junk which bought their produce, and exchanged things they wanted for it—such as beds, iron rods, calico, and salt. After three months' residence Kume was able to talk the language a little, and had managed to narrate his adventures ; moreover, he had explained that the island from which he had sailed—he had named it Torijima,[1] on account of the birds there —was a far better island than their own for all marine produce. ' Do, my friends,' said Kume, ' accompany me over there and see. I have shown you my pearls. I am not much of a diver ; but, for those that are divers there are as many as you can wish—also sea-slugs, bêche-de-mer, and namako of the very best kinds.'

' Do you know that the island which you call " Tori " is bewitched ? ' they asked. ' It is impossible to go there, for there is a gigantic bird which comes twice a-year and

[1] Tori-bird Island.

kills all men who have ventured to land. It could not have been there when you were, or you could not have lived a day.'

'Well, my friends,' said Kume, 'I am not afraid of a bird, and, as you have been very kind to me, I should like to show you my Torijima, for, though small, it is better than your island for all the things which come from the sea, and you would say so if you came. Please say that some of you will accompany me.'

At last thirty men said they would go; that would be three boat-loads of them.

Accordingly, next evening they started, and, as the direction was well known to the Loochooans, they reached the shores of Torijima just as the sun arose.

Kume's boat arrived first. Though he had been fully warned of the great bird which must have been absent when he was in the island, Kume landed alone, and was proceeding up the shore when an immense eagle with a body larger than his own swept down on him and began to fight. Kume, being a Japanese, immediately cut the monster in half.

From that day Torijima has been settled on by fishermen, and has afforded more pearls, coral, and fish than the other, which they named Kumijima, and sometimes Shuzen shima (both being his names); moreover, Kume Shuzen was made the king of both islands. Kume never got back to Japan to avenge his master the Lord Tarao. Indeed, he was better off than he had ever been before, and lived a happy life on the two wild Loochoo islands, which had not yet come under the Chinese rule, being too small to be thought of.

The King of Torijima

After some fifteen years Kume died and was buried on Kumijima. My story-teller says that those who visit the Loochoos and pass Kumijima will notice from the sea a monument erected to Kume Shuzen.

XXIX

THE PERPETUAL LIFE-GIVING WINE

BETWEEN the north-eastern boundary of Totomi Province
and the north-western of Suruga Province stands a lofty
mountain, Daimugenzan.   It is a wild and rugged mountain, clad nearly three-quarters up with lofty pines, yenoki,
icho, camphors, etc.   There are but few paths, and hardly
any one goes up the hill.   About half-way up through
the forest is a shrine erected to Kwannon ; but it is
so small that no priest lives there, and the building is
rotting away.   No one knows why it was put up in such
an inaccessible place—except, perhaps, one solitary girl
and her parents, who used to go there for some reason
of their own.

One day, about 1107 A.D., the girl was praying for her
mother's recovery from sickness.   Okureha was her name.
She lived at Tashiro, at the foot of the mountain, and was
the beauty of the countryside,—the daughter of a much-
loved samurai of some importance.   Amid the solemn
silence Okureha clapped her hands thrice before Kwannon
as she prayed, causing mountain echoes to resound.
Having finished her prayers, Okureha began to make her

178

way downwards, when she was suddenly sprung upon by a ruffianly-looking man, who seized her by the arm.

She cried aloud for help ; but nothing came except the echoes of her voice, and she gave herself up for lost.

Suddenly a piercing cold breeze came along, carrying the autumn leaves in little columns. Okureha struggled violently with her assailant, who seemed to weaken to the cold wind as it struck his face. Okureha weakened too. In a few seconds the man fell down as in a drunken sleep, and she was on the point of falling (she knew not why) and of sleeping (scarce could she keep her eyes open). Just then the wind came hot instead of cold, and she felt herself awake again. On looking up she saw advancing towards her a beautiful girl, apparently not many years older than herself. The stranger was dressed in white, and seemed to glide. Her face was white as the snow which capped Mount Daimugenzan ; her brows were crescent-shaped, like those of Buddha ; her mouth was like flowers. In a silvery voice she called to Okureha, saying :

'Be neither surprised nor afraid, my child. I saw that you were in danger, and I came to your rescue by putting that savage creature to sleep ; I sent the warm breeze so that you might not fall. You need not fear that the man is dead. I can revive him if I choose, or keep him as he is if I wish. What is your name ? '

Okureha fell on her knees to express her thanks, and, rising, said : 'My name is Okureha. My father is the samurai who owns the greater part of the village of Tashiro, at the foot of the mountain. My mother being

ill, I have come up to this old shrine to pray Kwannon
for her recovery. Five times have I been up before, but
never met any one until to-day, when this dreadful man
attacked me. I owe my deliverance entirely to you, holy
lady, and I am humbly and deeply grateful. I do hope
I shall be able to come here and pray at this shrine again.
My father and mother prayed here before I was born both
to Kwannon and to the Tennin [1] of the mountain. They
had no child, and I was sent to them after their prayers.
Therefore it is right that I should come here to pray for
my mother ; but this horrid man has frightened me so
that I shall be afraid to come alone again.'

The Mountain Goddess (for such was Okureha's
rescuer) smiled, and said : 'You need have no fear, my
pretty child. Come here when you will, and I shall be
your protector. Children who are as devoted to their
parents as you are deserve all that is good, and are holy
in themselves. If you wish to please me, come again
to-morrow, so that we may converse ; and bring me some
flowers from the fields, for I never descend low enough
on earth to get these, though they are my favourites—
they smell so sweet. And now you had better go home.
When you have had time to reach there I will restore this
horrid man to life and let him go. He is not likely to
return to molest you.'

'I shall be here to-morrow,' said Okureha, bowing her
thanks amid her 'Sayonaras.'

Okureha San was so much impressed by the face of
the Goddess that she could not sleep, and at daybreak
next morning was out in the fields gathering flowers,

[1] Angel.

which she took up the mountain to the shrine, where she found the goddess waiting.

They talked on many subjects, and enjoyed each other's company, and arranged to meet often. Consequently, whenever Okureha had time she always went up the mountain. This continued for nearly a year, when Okureha went up with flowers for the goddess as usual; but she was looking sad, and felt sad.

'Why is this?' asked the goddess. 'Why are you so sad?'

'Ah, your Holiness is right,' said Okureha. 'I am sad, for this may be the last day I can come up here and see you. I am now seventeen years of age, and my parents think me old enough to marry. Twelve years ago my father arranged that I should marry the son of one of his friends, Tokue, of Iwasakimura, when we were old enough. Now I am said to be old enough: so I must marry. The wedding is to be in three days. After that I shall have to stay at home and work for my husband, and I fear I shall not see you any more. That is why I am sad.' As she spoke tears ran down her cheeks, and there was for a few moments no consoling her; but the goddess soothed her, saying:

'You must not be sad, dear child. On the contrary, you are about to enter the happiest state of life, by being married. If people were not married, and did not produce children to inherit new spirits and life, there could be no continuation. Go back, my child, happily; get married and produce children. You will be happy and doing your duty to the world and to the goddess. Before we say farewell, I give you this small gourd of furoshu.[1] Take care of it on your way down the mountain, and when you are married give some to your husband. You will both remain as you are in appearance, never growing a day older though you live for centuries, as you will do; and also it will bring you perfect happiness. Now, farewell!'

Again the tears came to Okureha's eyes as she bade farewell to her benefactress; but she mustered all her pluck, and, making her last bow, took her way down the mountain, weeping as she went. Three days later Okureha was married. It was a lucky day according to the calendars, and, moreover, it was the year that the Emperor Toba came to the throne, 1108 A.D.

One day, when celebrating this event at a picnic, Okureha gave her husband some of the furoshu saké, and took the rest herself, as the goddess had bidden her. They were sitting on a beautiful green grassy spot, whereon grew wild violets of delicious fragrance; at their feet gurgled a mountain stream of sparkling clearness. To their surprise, they found petals of cherry blossom suddenly falling all round them. There were no cherry trees near, and at first they were much puzzled; but they saw in the blue sky one white cloud which had just sailed over them, and seated thereon was the Goddess of Mount Daimugenzan. Okureha recognised her, and pointed her out to her husband as their benefactress. The white cloud carried her up to the top of the mountain, where it hovered until the shades of evening hid it.

Okureha and her husband never grew older. They lived for hundreds of years as Sennins in Mount Daimugenzan.

[1] Sake wine of perpetual youth.

XXX

THE HERMIT'S CAVE

MANY years ago there lived in the village of Nomugi, in Hida Province, an old farmer named Jinnai, with his wife. They had a daughter on whom they simply doted. Her name was Yuka. She was seven years of age, and an extremely beautiful child. Unfortunately, just at this age she developed something the matter with her leg, which grew worse and worse until the limb became deformed. O Yuka suffered no pain; but her parents were much troubled. Doctors, drugs, and the advice of many friends made Yuka's leg no better.

'How sad it will be for her later on!' thought her mother and father. 'Even now it is sad that she should have a deformed leg when she plays with other children.'

There being no help, Yuka and her parents had to make the best of things. In any case, Yuka was not the only deformity in the village. There were other cases. One of Yuka's boy playmates, Tarako, had been born blind; and another, Rinkichi, was so deaf that he could hold his ear to the temple bell while the other children struck it, and he never heard the sound, though he

183

felt a vibration. Well, these two were perhaps no better off than Yuka, and at last her parents began to console themselves. The child played about and seemed perfectly happy.

Nomugi village is at the foot of the great mountain Norikuradake, which rises 10,500 feet, and is a wild place of volcanic origin.

Many of the children of Nomugi used to go daily and play on the grassy slope of an old dam at the end of the village. They would throw stones into the water, fish, sail boats, and pick flowers. The dam was a kind of club for the children. From morning to evening they were there, having with them their rice to eat.

One day, while thus playing, they were surprised by an old man with a long white beard approaching them. He came from the direction of the mountain. All stopped their games to watch him. He came on into their midst, and, patting them on the head, seemed to make friends naturally. Taking notice of Yuka's bad leg, the old man said : ' Come ! how is this ? Have not your parents tried to cure it ? ' Little Yuka answered that they had, but that they could not do any good. The old man made her lie down on the grass, and began to manipulate the leg, pulling it this way and that way, and rubbed in some red medicine which he took from a case. The old man then operated on Tarako the blind boy, and on Rinkichi the deaf one.

' Now, my children,' said he, ' you all love your fathers and mothers, and it will be a great pleasure to them to find you cured of your ailments. You are not well yet ; but you will be, if you do what I tell you, in less than three or four days. You are not to mention having seen me until I tell you that you may—after you are cured. To-morrow you will meet me at the flat rock under the cave on Mount Norikuradake. You know the place. Very well : until to-morrow good-bye, and if I find you do as I tell you I will make you all laugh by showing you some fancy tricks.' Then he trudged off in the direction whence he had come.

The children continued their play, thinking 'What a nice old man!' And, strange to say, O Yuka, as she walked home, felt her leg to be of greater use.

Very little attention is paid to Japanese children. They are nearly always good and well-behaved, little grown-up people in fact ; and therefore they ate their suppers and went to bed as such, giving no account of their day's amusements, or of the strange old man.

Next day they went to the flat rock. As it was wet, they had not started until late ; but they found the old man, and, though he had no time to play with them and show the tricks which he had promised, he attended to Yuka's leg, and to the dumb boy and the blind.

'Now go home,' he said, 'and come back here to-morrow. By the time you get home Yuka's leg will be well, Tarako will be able to see, and Rinkichi able to hear ; and I am sure your relations will be delighted. To-morrow, if it is fine, you must come early, and we shall have lots of fun.'

Even before they got home everything came about as the old man had said. The three children were recovered. The villagers and the parents rejoiced together ; but all were mystified as to who the magician could be.

Ancient Tales and Folklore of Japan

'If he returns to the mountain, as the children say, then he must live in the cave,' said one. 'He must be a Sennin,' said another. 'It is rumoured that the most famous priest, Kukai shonin, who founded the sacred temple on Mount Koyasan, in Kii Province, was able to make these wondrous cures in children,' added another. But, with all the gossiping and conjectures, none could explain how it was possible to bring sight to a boy who had been born blind. At last some one suggested that two or three should follow the children secretly on the following day : by hiding themselves they might be able to see what happened. This excellent plan was adopted.

In the morning about thirty children started off at daybreak, followed, unknown to themselves, by two men of the village.

When the children arrived at the flat rock—which is said to be large enough to measure one thousand Japanese mats of six feet by three feet—they found the old man seated at one end of it. The two men who had followed hid themselves in some fine azalea bushes.

First they saw the old man rise to his feet, and then go over to the children and hear from the three cured ones how they felt, and how their parents had been pleased. Tarako was the most delighted, perhaps, of the three ; for he had never seen the world before, or even his parents.

'Now, my children, you have come here to see me, and I am going to amuse you all. See here!' Saying this, the old man picked up some dead sticks, and, blowing at their ends, produced blossoming cherry branches, plum blossoms, and peach, and handed a branch of each to the girls.   Next he took a stone and threw it into the air, and behold ! it turned into a dove.   Another turned into a hawk, or, in fact, into any bird a boy chose to name.

'Now,' said the old man, 'I will show you some animals that will make you laugh.'   He recited some mystic verse, and monkeys came leaping on the flat rock and began to wrestle with one another.   The children clapped their hands in delight ; but one of the men who was hidden exclaimed in his astonishment :

'Who can this wizard be ?   No other but a wizard could do such things ! '

The venerable old man heard, and, looking cautiously round, said :

'Children, I can do no more tricks to-day.   My spell has gone.   I will go to my home, and you had better go to yours.   Farewell.'

So saying, the old man bowed to them, and turned up the mountain path, taking the direction of the cave.

The two men came out from their hiding, and they, with the children, tried to follow him.   In spite of his great age, he was much more nimble than they among the rocks ; but they got far enough to see him enter the cave. Some minutes later they came to the entrance, and bowed before it.   The entrance was surrounded by fragrant flowers ; but into its dark depths they did not venture.

Suddenly O Yuka pointed upwards, crying, 'There is the old grandfather ! '   They all looked up ; and standing on a cloud was the old man, right over the summit of the mountain.

'Ah, now it is quite clear ! ' cried one of the men.   ' It is the famous hermit of Mount Norikuradake.'   They all bowed low, and then went home to report to the villagers what they had seen.

Subscriptions were collected ; a small temple was built inside the cave, and they called it the 'Sendokutsu Temple,' which means The Sennin's Temple.

XXXI

YOSOJI'S CAMELLIA TREE

In the reign of the Emperor Sanjo began a particularly unlucky time. It was about the year 1013 A.D. when Sanjo came to the throne—the first year of Chowa. Plague broke out. Two years later the Royal Palace was burned down, and a war began with Korea, then known as 'Shiragi.'

In 1016 another fire broke out in the new Palace. A year later the Emperor gave up the throne, owing to blindness and for other causes. He handed over the reins of office to Prince Atsuhara, who was called the Emperor Go Ichijo, and came to the throne in the first year of Kwannin, about 1017 or 1018. The period during which the Emperor Go Ichijo reigned—about twenty years, up to 1036—was one of the worst in Japanese history. There were more wars, more fires, and worse plagues than ever. Things were in disorder generally, and even Kyoto was hardly safe to people of means, owing to the bands of brigands. In 1025 the most appalling outbreak of smallpox came; there was hardly a village or a town in Japan which escaped.

Ancient Tales and Folklore of Japan

It is at this period that our story begins. Our heroine (if such she may be called) is no less a deity than the goddess of the great mountain of Fuji, which nearly all the world has heard of, or seen depicted. Therefore, if the legend sounds stupid and childish, blame only my way of telling it (simply, as it was told to me), and think of the Great Mountain of Japan, as to which anything should be interesting ; moreover, challenge others for a better. I have been able to find none myself.

During the terrible scourge of smallpox there was a village in Suruga Province called Kamiide, which still exists, but is of little importance. It suffered more badly than most other villages. Scarce an inhabitant escaped. A youth of sixteen or seventeen years was much tried. His mother was taken with the disease, and, his father being dead, the responsibility of the household fell on Yosoji—for such was his name.

Yosoji procured all the help he could for his mother, sparing nothing in the way of medicines and attendance ; but his mother grew worse day by day, until at last her life was utterly despaired of. Having no other resource left to him, Yosoji resolved to consult a famous fortune-teller and magician, Kamo Yamakiko.

Kamo Yamakiko told Yosoji that there was but one chance that his mother could be cured, and that lay much with his own courage. 'If,' said the fortune-teller, 'you will go to a small brook which flows from the south-western side of Mount Fuji, and find a small shrine near its source, where Oki-naga-suku-neo[1] is worshipped, you may be able to cure your mother by bringing her water

[1] The God of Long Breath.

therefrom to drink. But I warn you that the place is full of dangers from wild beasts and other things, and that you may not return at all or even reach the place.'

Yosoji, in no way discouraged, made his mind up that he would start on the following morning, and, thanking the fortune-teller, went home to prepare for an early start.

At three o'clock next morning he was off.

It was a long and rough walk, one which he had never taken before; but he trudged gaily on, being sound of limb and bent on an errand of deepest concern.

Towards midday Yosoji arrived at a place where three rough paths met, and was sorely puzzled which to take. While he was deliberating the figure of a beautiful girl clad in white came towards him through the forest. At first Yosoji felt inclined to run; but the figure called to him in silvery notes, saying :

'Do not go. I know what you are here for. You are a brave lad and a faithful son. I will be your guide to the stream, and—take my word for it—its waters will cure your mother. Follow me if you will, and have no fear, though the road is bad and dangerous.'

The girl turned, and Yosoji followed in wonderment.

In silence the two went for fully four miles, always upwards and into deeper and more gloomy forests. At last a small shrine was reached, in front of which were two Torii's, and from a cleft of a rock gurgled a silvery stream, the clearness of which was such as Yosoji had never seen before.

'There,' said the white-robed girl, 'is the stream of which you are in search. Fill your gourd, and drink of it yourself, for the waters will prevent you catching the plague. Make haste, for it grows late, and it would not be well for you to be here at night. I shall guide you back to the place where I met you.'

Yosoji did as he was bid, drinking, and then filling the bottle to the brim.

Much faster did they return than they had come, for the way was all downhill. On reaching the meeting of the three paths Yosoji bowed low to his guide, and thanked her for her great kindness ; and the girl told him again that it was her pleasure to help so dutiful a son.

'In three days you will want more water for your mother,' said she, 'and I shall be at the same place to be your guide again.'

'May I not ask to whom I am indebted for this great kindness?' asked Yosoji.

'No : you must not ask, for I should not tell you,' answered the girl. Bowing again, Yosoji proceeded on his way as fast as he could, wondering greatly.

On reaching home he found his mother worse. He gave her a cup of the water, and told her of his adventures. During the night Yosoji awoke as usual to attend to his mother's wants, and to give her another bowl of water. Next morning he found that she was decidedly better. During the day he gave her three more doses, and on the morning of the third day he set forth to keep his appointment with the fair lady in white, whom he found seated waiting for him on a rock at the meeting of the three paths.

'Your mother is better : I can see from your happy face,' said she. 'Now follow me as before, and make

41. THE SENTRY FINDS WATANABE TATSUZO ON THE PINE BRANCH

42. O KIMI KILLS HERSELF ON THE ISLAND

43. THE GHOST OF THE 'KAKEMONO'

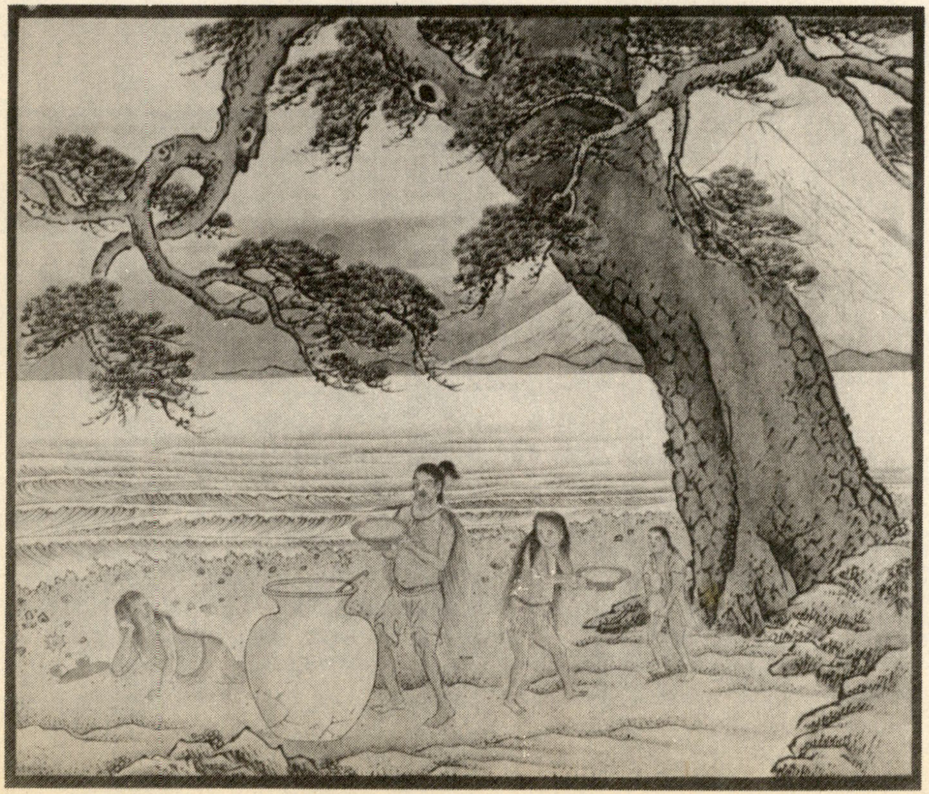

44. MAMIKIKO TASTES THE WHITE SAKE

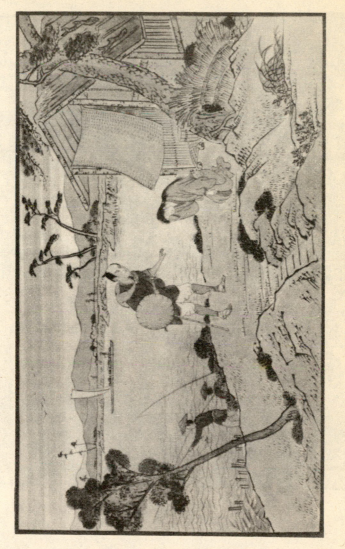

45. KICHIJIRO FINDS POOR O IMA BLIND

46. IIDAMACHI POND, HAYASHI'S HOUSE

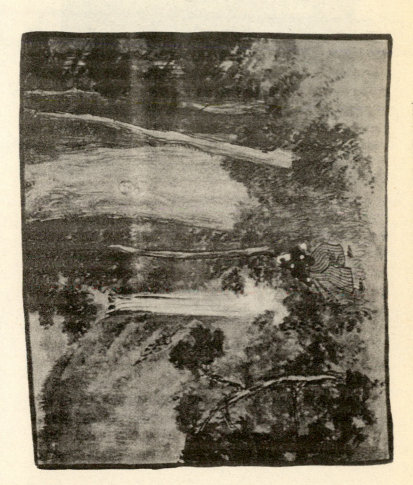

47. THE SPIRIT OF THE ONE-EYED PRIEST, YENOKI, APPEARS TO SONOBÉ

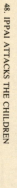

48. IPPAI ATTACKS THE CHILDREN

haste. Come again in three days, and I will meet you. It will take five trips in all, for the water must be taken fresh. You may give some to the sick villagers as well.'

Five times did Yosoji take the trip. At the end of the fifth his mother was perfectly well, and most thankful for her restoration ; besides which, most of the villagers who had not died were cured. Yosoji was the hero of the hour. Every one marvelled, and wondered who the white-robed girl was ; for, though they had heard of the shrine of Oki-naga-suku-neo, none of them knew where it was, and but few would have dared to go if they had known. Of course, all knew that Yosoji was indebted in the first place to the fortune-teller Kamo Yamakiko, to whom the whole village sent presents. Yosoji was not easy in his mind. In spite of the good he had brought about, he thought to himself that he owed the whole of his success in finding and bringing the water to the village to his fair guide, and he did not feel that he had shown sufficient gratitude. Always he had hurried home as soon as he had got the precious water, bowing his thanks. That was all, and now he felt as if more were due. Surely prayers at the shrine were due, or something ; and who was the lady in white ? He must find out. Curiosity called upon him to do so. Thus Yosoji resolved to pay one more visit to the spring, and started early in the morning.

Now familiar with the road, he did not stop at the meeting of the three paths, but pursued his way directly to the shrine. It was the first time he had travelled the road alone, and in spite of himself he felt afraid, though he could not say why. Perhaps it was the oppressive gloom of the mysterious dark forest, overshadowed by the holy mountain of Fuji, which in itself was more mysterious still, and filled one both with superstitious and religious feelings and a feeling of awe as well. No one of any imagination can approach the mountain even to-day without having one or all of these emotions.

Yosoji, however, sped on, as fast as he could go, and arrived at the shrine of Oki-naga-suku-neo. He found that the stream had dried up. There was not a drop of water left. Yosoji flung himself upon his knees before the shrine and thanked the God of Long Breath that he had been the means of curing his mother and the surviving villagers. He prayed that his guide to the spring might reveal her presence, and that he might be enabled to meet her once more to thank her for her kindness. When he arose Yosoji saw his guide standing beside him, and bowed low. She was the first to speak.

'You must not come here,' she said. 'I have told you so before. It is a place of great danger for you. Your mother and the villagers are cured. There is no reason for you to come here more.'

'I have come,' answered Yosoji, 'because I have not fully spoken my thanks, and because I wish to tell you how deeply grateful I am to you, as is my mother and as are the whole of our villagers. Moreover, they all as well as I wish to know to whom they are indebted for my guidance to the spring. Though Kamo Yamakiko told me of the spring, I should never have found it but for your kindness, which has now extended over five weeks. Surely you will let us know to whom we are so much indebted, so that we may at least erect a shrine in our temple ?'

'All that you ask is unnecessary. I am glad that you are grateful. I knew that one so truly filial as you must be so, and it is because of your filial piety and goodness that I guided you to this health-giving spring, which, as you see, is dry, having at present no further use. It is unnecessary that you should know who I am. We must now part : so farewell. End your life as you have begun it, and you shall be happy.' The beautiful maiden swung a wild camellia branch over her head as if with a beckoning motion, and a cloud came down from the top of the Mount Fuji, enveloping her at first in mist. It then arose, showing her figure to the weeping Yosoji, who now began to realise that he loved the departing figure, and that it was no less a figure than that of the great Goddess of Fujiyama. Yosoji fell on his knees and prayed to her, and the goddess, acknowledging his prayer, threw down the branch of wild camellia.

Yosoji carried it home, and planted it, caring for it with the utmost attention. The branch grew to a tree with marvellous rapidity, being over twenty feet high in two years. A shrine was built ; people came to worship the tree ; and it is said that the dewdrops from its leaves are a cure for all eye-complaints.

XXXII

WHALES

THERE are many stories and superstitions regarding whales. I take one, dating back to the period of 'Hoen' (1135), which will show the veneration and the fear in which the Japanese have always held these creatures. I will annex the translation by Mr. Ando, of our Consulate, of a newspaper paragraph of date February 12, 1907, showing that the superstitions are still current.

Some hundred and seventy-two years ago, when the 'Hoen' period began, the shrine of Atsuta at Nagoya was burned down. For some reason this calamity was said at the time to have happened because the head shrine-watcher, Yoda Emon, had startled one of the gods.[1]

Well, at any rate the holy shrine was burned down, and the caretaker was exiled to Oshima Island, in Idzu

---

[1] The gods principally worshipped at Atsuta are the Sun Goddess Amateras, her brother Susa-no-o, Prince Yamato-take, his wife Miyazu-hime, and her brother Take-ino-tane; but the object most venerated is the sword called 'Kusa-nagi no Tsurugi,' one of the three principal antique objects which form the Imperial Regalia of Japan, and of which I have previously told a story or two, notably that of 'Yamato-dake no Mikoto' (p. 56 *et seq.*).

Whales

Province, now generally known as 'Vries' Island. It is the largest and most northerly of the group of islands which run in a chain towards the south-east. The nearest to Oshima is Toshi Island, often named Rishima, of which our story is told.

Yoda Emon was a man of active mind and pursuits. Perhaps that is why he startled the god who caused the fire at Atsuta. In any case, he felt his exile greatly. He could gain no news of home or family, and he fretted and worried himself to such an extent that at last his nights became sleepless and he thought to himself that if some relief to his mind did not come soon he must either kill himself or go mad.

At last it occurred to him that possibly he might get permission to go fishing; and the permission was given him, on condition that he kept within a mile of the shore. Day after day Yoda took the boat which was lent him, and returned generally with a goodly supply of fish, singing to himself as he rowed in to and out from the shore. He soon managed to sleep soundly and regain his strength. After a month or two Yoda became quite a popular person, giving his fish away free to any who chose to take them, and he was soon allowed a wider range than the one-mile limit. He became an expert sailor, and had it not been for the loss of his family he would have been quite happy in his new home. One day, the morning being calm, Yoda ventured farther away than usual, hoping to capture some of the larger fish which were reputed to be plentiful some ten miles from Toshishima. He was lucky, and landed three magnificent fish of the mackerel family, known as 'sara' in Japan, 'seer' in India, and 'albacore' with us in England, who never see them. Unfortunately, after this the wind, instead of springing up from the south-east as usual, came out from the north-west, and, instead of being able to return to Oshima, Yoda found himself being blown farther from it. The wind came stronger and stronger, until a gale was blowing, and soon the currents caused a high and breaking sea. Darkness set in, and Yoda thought to himself that this was a visitation upon him for having caught fish. 'Oh,' cried he aloud, 'what foolish sin have I now committed? Surely my position as a banished priest should have told me that I was sinning in catching fish!' He flung himself on the bottom of the boat and prayed; but his prayers availed him nothing, for the wind increased in force, and so did the sea. Long after midnight a big wave smashed the boat to splinters. Half-stunned, half-drowned, Yoda clung to the large oar, and so remained for some three hours.

At last he felt himself being bumped against what he took to be a rock, and letting go the oar scrambled on to it more dead than alive. After many efforts, so exhausted was he and so numbed, he sat there only half-conscious in the dark.

Towards morning the turn of tide caused the sea to smooth down, and as the sun rose Yoda found to his horror that it was no rock upon which he sat, but the back of a live whale of gigantic size. Yoda knew neither what to do nor what to think; he dared not move, for fear of disturbing the whale's repose. Not even when the animal blew water and air from its spout-hole did he venture to turn his body. But silently he muttered prayers all the time. At last, when the sun was full up, the whale began to turn round, and as it did so Yoda saw a large fishing-boat not more than half a mile away. He shouted and shouted at the top of his voice, trying to attract attention ; but move he dared not, lest the whale should leave him. The wind was still high ; but the sea was smooth.

Suddenly the fishing-boat changed its course, and the whale lay still again, basking in the sunshine. The boat advanced rapidly, and when about eighty feet from the whale brought up to the wind and lay still. A life-line with a buoy attached was drifted towards the whale, and when it was near enough Yoda slid off to take it, and was hauled into the boat, thoroughly thankful for his rescue. As soon as Yoda was on board, the boat began to roll, for the whale lashed his tail and was playing about, causing quite a heavy sea ; but, to the relief of all, the creature headed south for the open Pacific.

The crew on the fishing-boat belonged to Toshi Island, and had heard of Yoda Emon, and, being good-natured fellows, felt sorry for him in his exile. After his astonishing adventure with the whale, they did not in the least mind taking him back to Oshima, which they reached about sundown.

Yoda immediately reported himself, and was congratulated on his extraordinary escape.

After this Yoda gave up fishing, and submitted without grumbling to the severe discipline of his exile. On the occasion of Prince Tanin ascending the throne, an ordinance was issued giving freedom to many prisoners and exiles. Yoda Emon was among them, and was given permission to return home; but he said he had made so many friends on the island, and his life had been saved so miraculously, that he preferred to live where he was. And he obtained official permission to do so, and to send for his family, which after building a house he did. In the first year of Koji 1142-1144, Yoda was made Mayor of Shichito—that is the seven islands lying round or south of Oshima and including itself. 'Now,' thought he, 'I shall be able to repay the kindness that the whale showed me in saving my life!' And he issued an order that no whales were to be chased or killed anywhere near the islands over which he had jurisdiction. At first there was some grumbling; but the Government sent messengers to Oshima to say that the Emperor approved Yoda Emon's order, and furthermore, that during Yoda's life no whale was to be killed anywhere in Shichito.

WHALE AND WHALER.—Some years ago there lived a wealthy fisherman called Matsushima Tomigoro at Matsushima, in Nagasaki. He made a large fortune by whale-fishing. One night he dreamed a strange dream. A whale (zato kujira), carrying a baby whale, appeared before his pillow, and requested him to let her and the baby go safely—they were going to pass a certain part of the sea at a certain time and date. Matsushima heartlessly did not accede, but took advantage of the information. He put a net in the said sea at the due time, and caught a whale and her baby. Not long after, the cruel fisherman began to reap the harvest of his

Whales

mercilessness. Misfortune after misfortune befell him, and all his wealth disappeared. 'It must be the result of his cruelty in killing the whale and its baby,' said the neighbours; and for some time they never caught whales carrying babies. (Translated by Mr. Ando.)

XXXIII

THE HOLY CHERRY TREE OF
MUSUBI-NO-KAMI TEMPLE

In the province of Mimasaka is a small town called Kagami, and in the temple grounds is a shrine which has been there for some hundreds of years, and is dedicated to Musubi-no-Kami, the God of Love. Near by once stood a magnificent old cherry tree which was given the name of Kanzakura, or Holy Cherry, and it is in honour of this tree that the shrine dedicated to the God of Love was built.

Long ago, when the village of Kagami was smaller than it is at present, it had as one of its chief residents a man called Sodayu. Sodayu was one of those men, to be found in most Japanese villages, who with but little work thrive on the work of others and grow richer than most. He bought and he sold their crops, making commission both ways, and before he was middle-aged he was a rich man.

Sodayu was a widower ; but he had a lovely daughter who was aged seventeen, and it was thought by Sodayu that the time had now arrived for him to look about for a desirable husband for Hanano. Accordingly he called her to him and said :

'The time has come, my dear child, when it is my

duty to find you a suitable husband. When I have done so you will, I trust, approve of him, for it will be your duty to marry him.'

Of course, O Hanano bowed her willingness to do just as her father decreed ; but at the same time she confided in her favourite servant Yuka that she did not care about being married to a man that she might not love.

'What can I do—what would you advise me to do—my dear O Yuka ? Do try and think how you can help me to obtain a man I can love. A handsome man he must be, and not more than twenty-two years of age.'

O Yuka answered that the advice asked for was difficult to give ; but there was one thing, she said. 'You can go to the temple and pray at the shrine of Musubi-no-Kami, the God of Love. Pray him that the husband your father finds may be handsome and after your own heart. They say that if you pray at this shrine twenty-one days in succession you will obtain the kind of lover you want.'

O Hanano was pleased with the idea, and that afternoon, accompanied by Yuka, her maid, she went to pray at the shrine of Musubi-no-Kami. Day after day they continued until the twenty-first and last day of the series had arrived. They had finished their prayers and were on their way from the temple and passing under the great cherry tree known as the 'Kanzakura' or Holy Cherry, when they saw, standing near its stem, a youth of some twenty or twenty-one years. He was handsome, with a pale face and expressive eyes. In his hand he held a branch of cherry-blossom. He smiled pleasantly at Hanano, and she at him ; then, bowing, he came forward and smilingly presented her with the blossom. Hanano blushed, and took the flowers. The youth bowed again and walked away; as did Hanano, who had a fluttering heart and felt very happy, for she thought that this youth must be the one sent by the God of Love in answer to her prayers. 'Of course it must be,' she said to O Yuka. 'This is the twenty-first, and that completes the course of prayer you spoke of. Am I not lucky? And is he not handsome? I do not think it possible that a more handsome youth was ever seen. I wish he had not gone away so soon.' This and much more did O Hanano prattle to her maid on their way home, upon reaching which the first thing she did was to put the cherry-blossom branch into a vase in her own room.

'O Yuka!' she called for the twentieth time at least. 'Now you must go and find out all you can about the young man; but say nothing to my father as yet. Possibly it is not the husband he is choosing for me; but I can love no other, at all events, and I must love him in secret if this is the case. Now go, dear Yuka. Find out all you can and you will prove yourself more faithful and dear to me than ever.' And the faithful maid went on her young mistress's errand.

Now, O Yuka found out nothing about the youth they had seen under the Holy Cherry tree; but she found out that there was another youth in the village who had fallen greatly in love with her mistress, and, as he had heard that O Hanano's father was looking out for a suitable husband, he intended to apply next day himself. His name was Tokunosuke. He was a fairly well-connected youth, and had some means; but his looks were in no way comparable with those of the youth who had handed the cherry branch to Hanano. Having discovered this much, Yuka returned to her young mistress and reported.

Next day, early in the morning, at the most formal calling hour, Tokunosuke went by appointment to see Hanano's father. Hanano was called to serve tea, and saw the young man. Tokunosuke was scrupulously formal and polite to her, and she to him ; and soon after he left Hanano was told by her father that that was the young man whom he had chosen to be her husband. 'He is desirable in every way,' he added. 'He has money. His father is my friend, and he has secretly loved you for some months. You can ask for nothing better.'

O Hanano made no answer, but burst out crying and left the room ; and Yuka was called in her stead.

'I have found a most desirable young man as husband for your mistress,' said Sodayu ; 'but instead of showing pleasure and gratitude she has flown from the room crying. Can you explain to me the reason ? You must know her secrets. Has she a lover unknown to me ?'

O Yuka was not prepared to face the anger of her mistress's father, and she thought that truth in this especial instance would further Hanano's interests best. So she told the story faithfully and boldly. Sodayu thanked her for it, and again called his daughter to him, telling her that she must either produce her lover or allow Tokunosuke to call and press his suit. Next morning Tokunosuke did call ; but Hanano told him with tears in her eyes that she could not love him, for she loved another, whose name she did not even know herself.

'This is a strange piece of news,' thought Tokunosuke to himself. 'Almost insulting to love a man whose name she does not know!' And, bowing low, he left the house, determined to find out who his nameless rival was, even if he had to disguise himself and follow Hanano to do so.

That very afternoon Hanano and Yuka went to pray as usual, and, on coming away they again found the handsome youth standing under the cherry tree, and again he advanced and smilingly handed Hanano a branch full of bloom ; but again no words came from his lips, and it was evident to Tokunosuke (who was hiding behind some stone lanterns) that they could not have known each other long.

In a few moments they bowed and separated. O Hanano and her maid walked away from the temple, while the youth under the cherry tree looked after them.

Tokunosuke was now furiously jealous. He came from his hiding-place, and accosted the youth under the cherry tree in a rude and rough tone.

'Who are you, you hateful rascal ? Give me your name and address at once ! And tell me how you dare tempt the beautiful O Hanano San to love you !' He was about to seize his enemy by the arm when the enemy jumped suddenly back a step, and before Tokunosuke had time to catch him a sudden gust of wind blew the bloom thickly off the cherry tree. So thick and quickly did the blossoms fall, they blinded Tokunosuke for some moments. When he could see again the handsome youth was gone ; but there was a strange moaning sound inside the cherry tree, while one of the temple priests came rushing at him in great anger, crying 'Ah ! you sacrilegious villain !

The Holy Cherry Tree

What do you mean by attempting violence here ? Do you not know that this cherry tree has stood here for hundreds of years? It is sacred, and contains a holy spirit, which sometimes comes forth in the form of a youth. It is he that you tried to touch with your filthy and unholy hand. Begone, I say, and never dare enter this temple again ! '

Tokunosuke did not want pressing. He took to his heels and ran, and he ran straight to the house of Sodayu, and told what he had seen, and what had befallen himself, omitting nothing, even to the names the priest had called him.

'Perhaps now your daughter may consent to marry me,' he finished by saying. 'She cannot marry a holy spirit ! '

O Hanano was called, and told the story, and was very much upset that the face to whom she had given her heart was that of a spirit. 'What sin have I committed,' she cried, 'falling in love with a god ? ' And she rushed off to implore forgiveness at the shrine. Long and earnestly she prayed that her sin might be forgiven her. She resolved to devote the rest of her life to the temple, and as she refused to marry she obtained her father's consent. Then she applied for permission to live in the temple and become one of its caretakers. She shaved her head, wore a white linen coat and the crimson pantaloons which denote that you are no longer of the world. O Hanano remained in the temple for the rest of her life, sweeping the grounds, and praying.

The temple still stands. It is highly probable that if the stump of the cherry tree remains another tree is planted beside it, as is usual.

XXXIV

A STORY OF MOUNT KANZANREI

FAR up on the north-eastern coast of Korea is a high mountain called Kanzanrei, and not far from its base, where lies the district of Kanko Fu, is a village called Teiheigun, trading in little but natural products such as mushrooms, timber, furs, fish, and a little gold.

In this village lived a pretty girl called Choyo, an orphan of some means. Her father, Choka, had been the only merchant in the district, and he had made quite a fortune for those parts, which he had left to Choyo when she was some sixteen summers old.

At the foot of the mountain of Kanzanrei lived a wood-cutter of simple and frugal habits. He dwelt alone in a broken-down hut, associated with but the few to whom he sold his wood, and was considered generally to be a morose and unsociable man. The 'Recluse' he was called, and many wondered who he was, and why he kept so much to himself, for he was not yet thirty years of age and was remarkable for his good looks and strong frame. Sawada Shigeoki was his name; but the people did not know it.

208

A Story of Mount Kanzanrei

One evening, as the Recluse was wending his way down the rough mountain path with a large load of firewood on his back, he was resting in a particularly wild and rocky pass darkened by the huge pine trees which towered on every hand, and was startled by a rustling sound close below. He looked nervously round, for the place in which he was had the reputation of being haunted by tigers, and with some truth, for several people had lately been killed by them. On this occasion, however, the sound which had startled the Recluse was caused by no tiger, but only by a pheasant which fluttered off her nest, and was imitating the sign of a wounded bird, to draw the intruder's attention away from the direction of her nest. Strange, however, was it, thought the Recluse, that the bird should have so acted, for she could neither have seen nor heard him ; and so he listened intently to find the cause. There were not many minutes to wait. Almost immediately the Recluse heard the sounds of voices and of scuffling, and, hiding himself behind the trunk of a large tree, he waited, axe in hand.

Soon he saw being carried, pushed, and dragged down the path, a girl of surpassing beauty. She was in charge of three villainous men whom the Recluse soon recognised as bandits.

As they were coming his way the Recluse retained his position, hidden behind the great pine, and grasping more firmly his axe ; and as the four approached him he sprang out and blocked their way.

'Who have you here, and what are you doing with this girl?' cried he. 'Let her go, or you will have to suffer !'

Being three to one, the robbers were in no fear, and cried back, 'Stand out of our way, you fool, and let us pass—unless you wish to lose your life.' But the woodcutter was not afraid. He raised his axe, and the robbers drew their swords. The woodcutter was too much for them. In an instant he had cut down one and pushed another over the precipice, and the third took to his heels, only too glad to get away with his life.

The Recluse then bent down to attend to the girl, who had fainted. He fetched water and bathed her face, bringing her back to her senses, and as soon as she was able to speak he asked who she was, whether she was hurt, and how she had come into the hands of such ruffians.

Amid sobs and weeping the girl answered :

'I am Choyo Choka. My home is the village of Teiheigun. This is the anniversary of my father's death, and I went to pray at his tomb at the foot of Gando Mountain. The day being fine, I decided to make a long tour and come back this way. About an hour ago I was seized by these robbers ; and the rest you know. Oh, sir, I am thankful to you for your bravery in saving me. Please tell me your name.'

The woodcutter answered :

'Ah, then, you are the famous beauty of Teiheigun village, of whom I have so often heard ! It is an honour indeed to me that I have been able to help you. As for me, I am a woodcutter. The " Recluse " they call me, and I live at the foot of this mountain. If you will come with me I will take you to my hut, where you can rest ; and then I will see you safely to your home.'

Choyo was very grateful to the woodcutter, who

shouldered his stack of wood, and, taking her by the hand, led her down the steep and dangerous path. At his hut they rested, and he made her tea; then took her to the outskirts of her village, where, bowing to her in a manner far above that of the ordinary peasant, he left her.

That night Choyo could think of nothing but the brave and handsome woodcutter who had saved her life; so much, indeed, did she think that before the morn had dawned she felt herself in love, deeply and desperately.

The day passed and night came. Choyo had told all her friends of how she had been saved and by whom. The more she talked the more she thought of the wood-cutter, until at last she made up her mind that she must go and see him, for she knew that he would not come to see her. 'I have the excuse of going to thank him,' she thought; 'and, besides, I will take him a present of some delicacies and fish.'

Accordingly, next morning she started off at daybreak, carrying her present in a basket. By good fortune she found the Recluse at home, sharpening his axes, but otherwise taking a holiday.

'I have come, sir, to thank you again for your brave rescue of myself the other day, and I have brought a small present, which, I trust, however unworthy, you will deign to accept,' said the love-sick Choyo.

'There is no reason to thank me for performing a common duty,' said the Recluse; 'but by so fair a pair of lips as yours it is pleasing to be thanked, and I feel the great honour. The gift, however, I cannot accept; for then I should be the debtor, which for a man is wrong.'

Choyo felt both flattered and rebuffed at this speech, and tried again to get the Recluse to accept her present ; but, though her attempts led to friendly conversation and to chaff, he would not do so, and Choyo left, saying :

'Well, you have beaten me to-day ; but I will return, and in time I shall beat you and make you accept a gift from me.'

'Come here when you like,' answered the Recluse. 'I shall always be glad to see you, for you are a ray of light in my miserable hut ; but never shall you place me under an obligation by making me accept a gift.'

It was a curious answer, thought Choyo as she left ; but 'Oh, how handsome he is, and how I love him ! and anyway I will visit him again, often, and see who wins in the end.'

Such was the assurance of so beautiful a girl as Choyo. She felt that she must conquer in the end.

For the next two months she visited the Recluse often, and they sat and talked. He brought her wild-flowers of great rarity and beauty from the highest mountains, and berries to eat ; but never once did he make love to her or even accept the slightest present from her hands. That did not deter Choyo from pursuing her love. She was determined to win in the end, and she even felt that in a way this strange man loved her as she loved him, but for some reason would not say so.

One day in the third month after her rescue Choyo again went to see the Recluse. He was not at home : so she sat and waited, looking round the miserable hut and thinking what a pity it was that so noble a man should live in such a state, when she, who was well off, was only too anxious to marry him ;—and of her own beauty she knew well. While she was thus musing, the woodcutter returned, not in his usual rags, but in the handsome costume of a Japanese samurai, and greatly astonished was she as she rose to greet him.

'Ah, fair Choyo, you are surprised to see me now as I am, and it is also with sorrow that I must tell you what I do, for I know well what is in both your heart and mind. To-day we must part for ever, for I am going away.'

Choyo flung herself upon the floor, weeping bitterly, and then rising, said, between her sobs : 'Oh, now, this cannot be! You must not leave me, but take me with you. Hitherto I have said nothing, because it is not for a maid to declare her love ; but I love you, and have loved you ever since the day you saved me from the robbers. Take me with you, no matter where ; even to the Cave where the Demons of Hell live will I follow you if you will but let me ! You must, for I cannot be happy without you.'

'Alas,' cried the Recluse, 'this cannot be! It is impossible ; for I am a Japanese, not a Korean. Though I love you as much as you love me, we cannot be united. My name is Sawada Shigeoki. I am a samurai from Kurume. Ten years ago I committed a political offence and had to fly from my country. I came to Korea disguised as a woodcutter, and until I met you I had not a happy day. Now our Government is changed and I am free to return home. To you I have told this story, and to you alone. Forgive my heartlessness in leaving you. I do so with tears in my eyes and sorrow in my heart. Farewell!' So saying, the 'brave samurai' (as my raconteur calls him) strode from the hut, never to see poor Choyo again.

Choyo continued to weep until darkness came on and it was too late for her to return home in safety : so she spent the night where she was, in weeping. Next morning she was found by her servants almost demented with fever. She was carried to her home, and for three months was seriously ill. On her recovery she gave most of her money to temples, and in charity ; she sold her house, keeping only enough money to buy herself rice, and spent the remainder of her days alone in the little hut at the foot of Mount Kenzanrei, where at the age of twenty-one she was found dead of a broken heart. The samurai was brave ; but was he noble in spite of his haughty national pride ? To the Japanese mind he acted as did Buddha when he renounced his worldly loves. What chance is there, if all men act thus, of a sincere friendship between Japan and Korea ?

XXXV

WHITE BONE MOUNTAIN

At the foot of Mount Shumongatake, up in the north-western province of Echigo, once stood, and probably even still stands in rotten or repaired state, a temple of some importance, inasmuch as it was the burial-ground of the feudal Lord Yamana's ancestors. The name of the temple was Fumonji, and many high and important priests kept it up generation after generation, owing to the early help received from Lord Yamana's relations. Among the priests who presided over this temple was one named Ajari Joan, who was the adopted son of the Otomo family.

Ajari was learned and virtuous, and had many followers; but one day the sight of a most attractive girl called Kiku,[1] whose age was eighteen, upset all his religious equilibrium. He fell desperately in love with her, offering to sacrifice his position and reputation if she would only listen to his prayer and marry him; but the lovely O Kiku San refused all his entreaties. A year later she was taken seriously ill with fever and died, and

[1] Chrysanthemum.

215

whispers went abroad that Ajari the priest had cursed her in his jealousy and brought about her illness and her death. The rumour was not exactly without reason, for Ajari went mad within a week of O Kiku's death. He neglected his services, and then got worse, running wildly about the temple, shrieking at night and frightening all those who came near. Finally, one night he dug up the body of O Kiku and ate part of her flesh.

People declared that he had turned into the Devil, and none dared go near the temple; even the younger priests left, until at last he was alone. So terrified were the people, none approached the temple, which soon ran to rack and ruin. Thorny bushes grew on the roof, moss on the hitherto polished and matted floors; birds built their nests inside, perched on the mortuary tablets, and made a mess of everything; the temple, which had once been a masterpiece of beauty, became a rotting ruin.

One summer evening, some six or seven months later, an old woman who owned a tea-house at the foot of Shumongatake Mountain was about to close her shutters when she was terrified at the sight of a priest with a white cap on his head approaching. 'The Devil Priest! The Devil Priest!' she cried as she slammed the last shutter in his face. 'Get away, get away! We can't have you here.'

'What do you mean by "Devil Priest"? I am a travelling or pilgrim priest, not a robber. Let me in at once, for I want both rest and refreshment,' cried the voice from outside. The old woman looked through a crack in the shutters, and saw that it was not the dreaded maniac, but a venerable pilgrim priest: so she opened the door and let him in, profuse in her apologies, and telling him how they were all frightened out of their wits by the priest of Fumonji Temple who had gone mad over a love-affair.

'Oh, sir, it is truly terrible! We hardly dare go within half a mile of the temple now, and some day the mad priest is sure to come out of it and kill some of us.'

'Do you mean to tell me that a priest has so far forgotten himself as to break through the teachings of Buddha and make himself the slave of worldly passions?' asked the traveller.

'I don't know about the worldly passions,' cried the old lady; 'but our priest has turned into a devil, as all the people hereabouts will tell you, for he has even dug up and eaten of the flesh of the poor girl whom he caused to die by his cursing!'

'There have been instances of people turning devils,' said the priest; 'but they are usually common people and not priests. A courtier of the Emperor So's turned into a serpent, the wife of Yosei into a moth, the mother of Ogan into a Yasha[1]; but I have never heard of a priest turning into a devil. Besides, Ajari Joan, your priest at Fumonji Temple, was a virtuous and clever man, I have always heard. I have come here, in fact, to do myself the honour of meeting him, and to-morrow I shall go and see him.'

The old lady served the priest with tea and begged him to think of no such thing; but he persisted, and said that on the morrow he would do as he mentioned,

---

[1] Vampire bat.

and read the mad priest a lecture ; and then he laid himself down to rest for the night.

Next afternoon the old priest, true to his word, started for the Fumonji Temple, the old lady accompanying him for the first part of the walk, to the place where the path which led to the temple turned up the mountain, and there she bade him good-bye, refusing to go another step.

The sun was beginning to set as the priest came in sight of the temple, and he saw that the place was in great disorder. The gates had tumbled off their hinges, withered leaves were thickly strewn everywhere and crumpled under his feet ; but he walked boldly on, and struck a small temple-bell with his staff. At the sound came many birds and bats from the temple, the bats flapping round his head ; but there was no other sign of life. He struck the bell again with renewed force, and it boomed and clanged in echoes. At last a thin, miserable-looking priest came out, and, looking wildly about, said :

'Who are you, and why have you come here ? The temple has long since been deserted, for some reason which I cannot understand. If you want lodging you must go to the village. There is neither food nor bedding here.'

'I am a priest from Wakasa Province. The pretty scenery and clear streams have caused me to linger long on my journey. It is too late now to go to the village, and I am too tired : so please let me remain for the night,' said the priest. The other made answer :

'I cannot order you away. This place is no longer more than a ruined shed. You can stay if you like ; but you can have neither food nor bedding.' Having said this, he sat on the corner of a rock, while the pilgrim priest sat on another, close by. Neither spoke until it was dark and the moon had risen. Then the mad priest said, 'Find what place you can inside to sleep. There are no beds; but what there is of the roof keeps the mountain dew from falling on you during the night, and it falls heavily here and wets you through.' Then he went into the temple—the pilgrim priest could not tell where, for it was dark and he could not follow, the place being littered with idols and beams and furniture which the mad priest had hacked to pieces in the early stages of his madness. The pilgrim, therefore, felt his way about until he found himself between a large fallen idol and a wall; and here he decided to spend the night, it being as safe a place in which to hide from the maniac as any he could find without knowing his way about or having a light. Fortunately for himself, he was a strong and healthy old man and was well able to do without food, and also to stand unharmed the piercing and damp cold. The pilgrim priest could hear the sound of the many streams which gurgled down the mountain-side. There was also the unpleasant sound of squeaking rats as they chased and fought, and of bats which flew in and out of the place, and of hooting owls; but beyond this nothing—nothing of the mad priest. Hour after hour passed thus until one o'clock, when suddenly, just as the pilgrim felt himself dozing off, he was aroused by a noise. The whole temple seemed as if it were being knocked down. Shutters were slammed with such violence that they fell to the floor; right and left idols and furniture were being hurled about. In and out ran the sound of the naked pattering feet of the crazed priest, who shouted :

'Oh, where is the beautiful O Kiku, my sweetly beloved Kiku ? Oh, where, oh, where is she ? The gods and the devils have combined to defraud me of her, and I care for neither and defy them all. Kiku, Kiku, come to me !'

The pilgrim, thinking his cramped position would be dangerous if the maniac came near him, availed himself of an opportunity, when the latter was in a far-off part of the temple, to get out into the grounds and hide himself again. It would be easier to see what went on, thought he, and to run if necessary.

He hid himself first in one part of the grounds and then in another. Meanwhile the mad priest paid several rushing visits to the outsides of the temple, keeping up all the time his awful cries for O Kiku. Towards morning he retired once more to the part of the temple in which he lived, and no more noise was made. Our pilgrim then went forth from his hiding, and seated himself on the rock which he had occupied the evening before, determined to see if he could not force a conversation with the demented man and read him a lesson from the sacred teachings of Buddha. He sat patiently on until the sun was high ; but all remained silent. There was no sign of the mad priest.

Towards midday the pilgrim heard sounds in the temple ; and by and by the madman came out, looking as if he had just recovered from a drunken orgy. He appeared dazed and was quiet, and started as he saw the old priest seated on the rock as he had been the night before. The old man rose, and approaching him said :

White Bone Mountain

'My friend, my name is Ungai. I am a brother priest —from the Temple of Daigoji, in Wakasa Province. I came hither to see you, hearing of your great wisdom ; but last night I heard in the village that you had broken your vows as a priest and lost your heart to a maiden, and that from love of her you have turned into a dangerous demon. I have in consequence considered it my duty to come and read you a lecture, as it is impossible to pass your conduct unnoticed. Pray listen to the lecture and tell me if I can help you.'

The mad priest answered quite meekly :

'You are indeed a Buddha. Please tell me what I can do to forget the past, and to become a holy and virtuous priest once more.'

Ungai answered :

'Come out here into the grounds and seat yourself on this rock.' Then he read a lecture out of the Buddhist Bible, and finished by saying, 'And now, if you wish to redeem your soul, you must sit on this rock until you are able to explain the following lines, which are written in this sacred book : '*The moon on the lake shines on the winds between the pine trees, and a long night grows quiet at midnight!* Having said this, Ungai bowed low and left the mad priest, Joan, seated on the rock reflecting.

For a month Ungai wandered from temple to temple, lecturing. At the end of that time he came back by way of Fumonji Temple, and thought he would go up to it and see what had happened to mad Joan. At the tea-house at which he had first put up he asked the old land-lady if she had seen or heard any more of the crazy priest.

'No,' she said : 'we have neither seen nor heard of

him. Some people say he has left; but no one knows, for none dare go up to the temple to see.'

'Well,' said Ungai, 'I will go up to-morrow morning and find out.'

Next morning Ungai went to the temple, and found Joan still seated exactly as he had left him on the rock muttering the words : '*The moon on the lake shines on the winds between the pine trees, and a long night grows quiet at midnight!*' Joan's hair and beard had become long and grey in the time, and he appeared to be miserably thin and almost transparent. Ungai was struck with pity at Joan's righteous determination and patience, and tears came to his eyes.

'Get up, get up,' said he, 'for indeed you are a holy and determined man.'

But Joan did not move. Ungai poked him with his staff, to awaken him, as he thought; but, to his horror, Joan fell to pieces, and disappeared like a flake of melting snow.

Ungai stayed in the temple for three days, praying for the soul of Joan. The villagers, hearing of this generous action, rebuilt the temple and made him their priest. Their temple had formerly belonged to the Mitsu sect; but now it was transferred to Ungai's 'Jo do' sect, and the title or name of 'Fumonji' was changed to 'Hakkotsuzan' (White Bone Mountain). The temple is said to have prospered for hundreds of years after.

XXXVI

A STORMY NIGHT'S TRAGEDY [1]

ALL who have read anything of Japanese history must have heard of Saigo Takamori, who lived between the years 1827 and 1877. He was a great Imperialist, fighting for the Emperor until 1876, when he gave over owing to his disapproval of the Europeanisation going on in the country and the abandonment of ancient national ways. As practical Commander-in-Chief of the Imperial Army, Saigo fled to Kagoshima, where he raised a body of faithful followers, which was the beginning of the Satsuma Rebellion. The Imperialists defeated them, and in September of 1877 Saigo was killed—some say in the last battle, and others that he did 'seppuku,' and that his head was cut off and secretly buried, so that it should not fall into the hands of his enemies. Saigo Takamori was highly honoured even by the Imperialists. It is hard to call him a rebel. He did not rebel against his Emperor, but only against the revolting idea of becoming Europeanised. Who can say that he was not right? He was a man of fine sentiment and great loyalty. Should all of us

---

[1] Fukuga told me this story and vouches for its accuracy.

follow meekly the Imperial order in England if we were told that we were to practise the manners and customs of South Sea Islanders? That would be hardly less revolting to us than Europeanisation was to Saigo.

In the first year of Meiji 1868 the Tokugawa army had been badly beaten by Saigo at Fushimi, and Field-Marshal Tokugawa Keiki had the greatest difficulty in getting down to the sea and escaping to Yedo. The Imperial army proceeded along the Tokaido road, determined to break up the Tokugawa force. Their advance guard had reached Hiratsuka, under Mount Fuji, on the coast.

It was a spring day, the 5th of April, and the cherry trees were in full bloom. The country folk had come in to see the victorious troops, who formed the advance guard of those who had beaten the Tokugawa. There were many beggars about, together with pedlars and sellers of sweets, roasted potatoes, and what-not. Towards evening clouds came over the skies; at five o'clock rain began; at six every one was under cover.

At the principal inn were a party of the Headquarters' Staff officers, including the gallant Saigo. They were making the best of the bad weather, and not feeling particularly lively, when they heard the soft and melodious notes of the shakuhachi at the gate.

'That is the poor blind beggar we saw playing near the temple to-day,' said one. 'Yes: so it is,' said another. 'The poor fellow must be very wet and miserable. Let us call him in.'

'A capital idea,' assented all of them, among whom was Saigo Takamori. 'We will have him in and raise a

49. THE FISHERMEN ARE ASTONISHED AT THE EXTRAORDINARY LIGHT

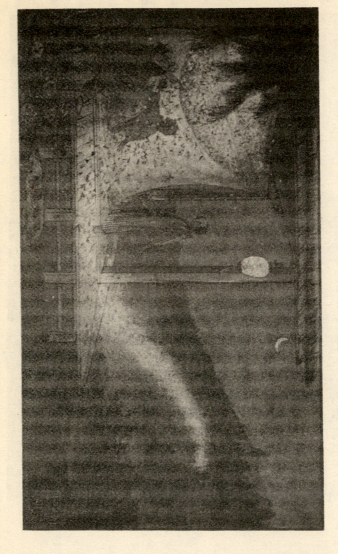

50. JIMPACHI'S MISERABLE DEATH

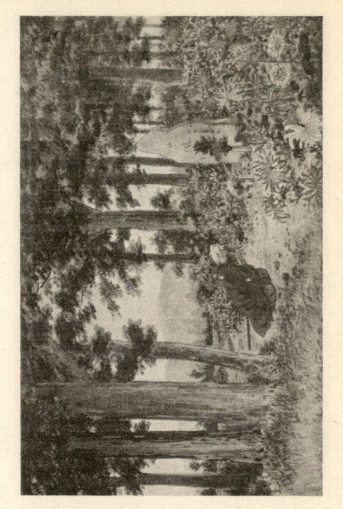

51. KIKUO PRAYS AT THE GRAVE OF HIS FEUDAL LORD

52. 'AYA HIME,' OR PRINCESS AYA, IS SAVED IN HER FALL BY THE 'BOTAN SPIRIT,' PEONY SPIRIT

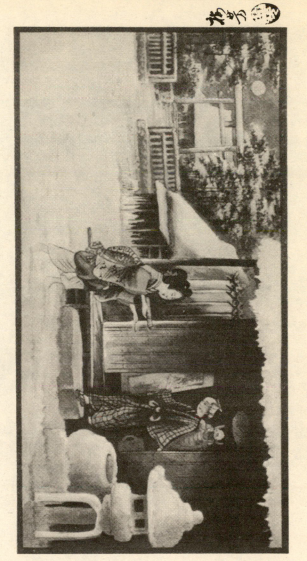

53. THE GIRL BRINGS THE KAKEMONO TO KIHACHI'S SHOP IN THE MIDDLE OF THE NIGHT

54. JIROHEI CLINGS TO THE CHERRY TREE EVEN IN DEATH

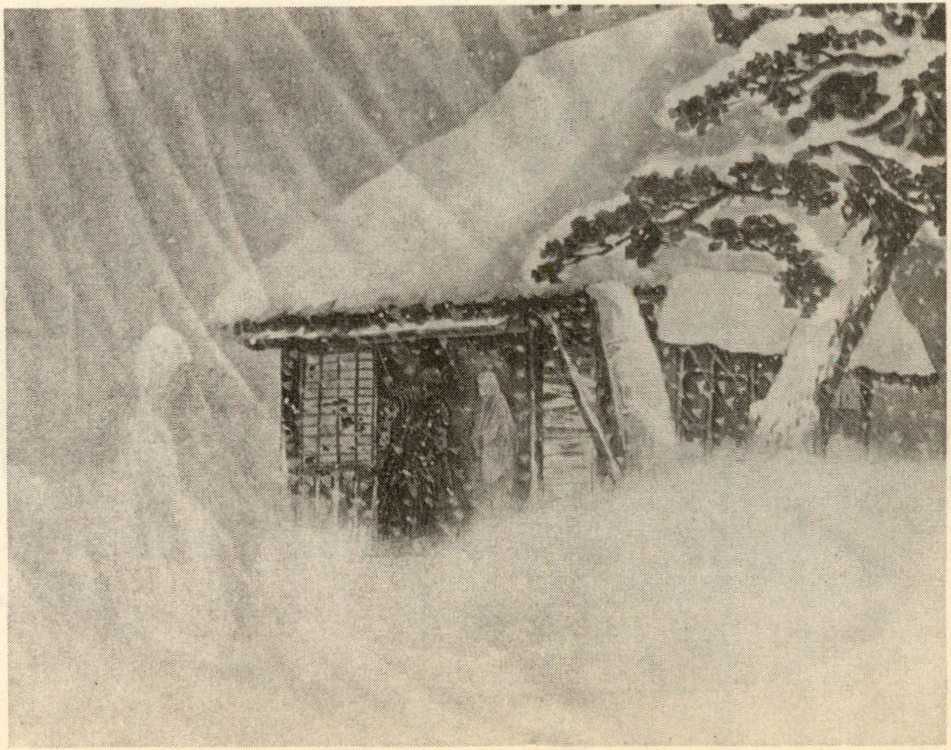

55. KYUZAEMON SEES THE 'YUKI ONNA'

56. ROKUGO SEES A GHOSTLY SPIRIT

subscription for him if he can raise our spirits in this weather.' They gave the landlord an order to admit the blind flute-player.

The poor man was led in by a side door and brought into the presence of the officers. 'Gentlemen,' said he, ' you have done me a very great honour, and a kindness, for it is not pleasant to stand outside playing in the rain with cotton clothes on. I think I can repay you, for I am said to play the shakuhachi well. Since I have been blind it has become my only pleasure, and not only that but also my only means of living. It is hard now in these unsettled days, when everything is upside-down, to earn a living. Not many travellers come to the inns while the Imperial troops occupy them. These are hard days, gentlemen.'

'They may be hard days for you, poor blind fellow ; but say nothing against the Imperial troops, for we have to be suspicious, there being spies of the Tokugawa. Three eyes, indeed, does each of us need in his head.'

'Well, well, I have no wish to say aught against the Imperial troops,' said the blind man. 'All I have to say is that it is precious hard for a blind man to earn enough rice wherewith to fill his stomach. Only once a-week on an average am I called to play to private parties or to shampoo some rheumatic person such as this wet weather produces — the blessing of the Gods be on it !'

'Well, we will see what we can do for you, poor fellow,' said Saigo. 'Go round the room, and see what you can collect, and then we will start the concert.'

Matsuichi did as he was bid, and returned to Saigo

some ten minutes later with five or six yen, to which Saigo added, saying :

'There, poor fellow : what do you think of that ? Say no more that the Imperial troops cause you to have an empty belly. Say, rather, that if you lived near them long the skin of your belly might become so overstretched as to cause you perforce to open your eyes, and then indeed you might find yourself put about for a trade. But let us hear your music. We are dull of spirit to-night, and want enlivening.'

'Oh, gentlemen, this is too much, far too much, for my poor music ! Take some of it back.'

'No, no,' they answered. 'We are troops and officers of the Imperial Army : our lives are uncertain from day to day. It is a pleasure to give, and to enjoy music when we can.'

The blind man began to play, and he played long and late. Sometimes his airs were lively, and at other times as mournful as the spring wind which blew through the cherry trees ; but his manner was enchanting, and all were grateful to him for having afforded a night's amusement. At eleven o'clock the concert finished and they went to rest ; the blind beggar left the inn ; and Kato Shichibei, the proprietor, locked it up, in spite of the sentries posted outside.

The inn was surrounded by hedges, and several clumps of bamboos stood in the corners. At the far end was an artificial mountain with a lake at its foot, and near the lake a little summer-house over which towered a huge and ancient pine tree, one of the branches of which stretched right back over the roof of the inn. At about one o'clock in the morning the form of a man might have been seen stealthily climbing this huge tree until he had reached the branch which hung over the inn. There he stretched himself flat, and began squirming along, evidently intent upon reaching the upper floor of the house. Unfortunately for himself, he cracked a small branch of dead wood, and the sound caused a sentry to look up. 'Who goes there?' cried he, bringing his musket round; but there was no answer. The sentry shouted for help, and it was not more than twenty seconds before the whole house was up and out. No escape for the man on the tree was possible. He was taken prisoner. Imagine the astonishment of all when they found that he was the blind beggar, but now not blind at all; his eyes flashed fire of indignation at his captors, for the great plan of his young life was dead.

'Who is he?' cried one and all, 'and why the trickery of being blind last evening?'

'A spy—that is what he is! A Tokugawa spy,' said one. 'Take him to Headquarters, so that the chief officers may interrogate him; and be careful to hold his hands, for he has every appearance of being a samurai and a fighter.'

And so the prisoner was led off to the Temple of Hommonji, where the Headquarters of the Staff temporarily were.

The prisoner was brought into the presence of Saigo Takamori and four other Imperial officers, one of whom was Katsura Kogoro. He was made to kneel. Then Saigo, who was the Chief, said, 'Hold your head up and give us your name.'

The prisoner answered :

' I am Watanabe Tatsuzo. I am one of those who have the honour of belonging to the bodyguard of the Tokugawa Government.'

' You are bold,' said Saigo. ' Will you have the goodness to tell us why you have been masquerading as a blind beggar, and why you were caught in an attempt to break into the inn ? '

' I found that the Imperial Ambassador was sleeping there, and our cause is not bettered by killing ordinary officers ! '

' You are a fool,' answered Saigo. ' How much better would you find yourself off if you killed Yanagiwara, Hashimoto, or Katsura ? '

' Your question is stupid,' was the unabashed answer. ' Every man of us does his little. My efforts are only a fragment ; but little by little we shall gain our ends.'

' Have you a comrade here ? ' asked Saigo.

' Oh, no,' answered the prisoner. ' We act individually as we think best for the cause. It was my intention to kill any one of importance whose death might strengthen us. I was acting entirely as I thought best.'

And Saigo said :

' Your loyalty does you credit, and I admire you for that ; but you should recognise that after the last victory of the Imperial troops at Fushimi the Tokugawa's tenure of office, extending over three hundred years, has come to an end. It is only natural that the Imperial family should return to power. Your intention is presumably to support a power that is finished. Have you never heard the proverb which says that "No single support can hold a falling tower"? Now tell me truthfully the absurd ideas which appear to exist in your mind. Do you really think that the Tokugawa have any further chance?'

'If you were any other than the heroic or admirable Saigo I should refuse to answer these questions,' said the prisoner; 'but, as you are the great Saigo Takamori and I admire your loyalty and courage, I will confess that after our defeat some two hundred of us samurai formed into a society swearing to sacrifice our lives to the cause in any way that we were able. I regret to say that nearly all ran away, and that I am (as far as I am able to judge) about the only one left. As you will execute me, there will be none.'

'Stop,' cried Saigo: 'say no more. Let me ask you: Will you not join us? Look upon the Tokugawa as dead. Too many faithful but ignorant samurai have died for them. The Imperial family must reign: nine-tenths of the country demand it. Though your guilt stands confessed, your loyalty is admirable, and we should gladly take you to our side. Think before you answer.'

No thought was necessary. Watanabe Tatsuzo answered instantly.

'No—never. Though alone, I will not be unfaithful to my cause. You had better behead me before the day dawns. I see the strength of your arguments that the Imperial family must and should reign; but that cannot alter my decision with regard to my own fate.'

Saigo stood up and said:

'Here is a man whom we must respect. There are many Tokugawa who have joined our cause through fear;

but they retain hate in their hearts. Look, all of you, at
this Watanabe, and forget him not, for he is a noble man
and true to the death.' So saying, Saigo bowed to
Watanabe, and then, turning to the guard, said :

'Take the prisoner to the Sambon matsu,[1] and behead
him as soon as the day dawns.'

Watanabe Tatsuzo was led forth and executed
accordingly.

There is a cross-road on the way leading to Mariko,
to the right of the Nitta Ferry, some five or six cho from
the hill where is the Hommonji Temple, Ikegami, in
Ebaragun, Tokio fu, where there is a little grave with a
tombstone over it and the characters :

不徹子之墓

written thereon. They mean *Tomb of Futetsu-shi*, and it
is here that Watanabe Tatsuzo is said to have been
buried.

[1] Three Pines.

XXXVII

THE KAKEMONO GHOST OF AKI PROVINCE [1]

Down the Inland Sea between Umedaichi and Kure (now a great naval port) and in the province of Aki, there is a small village called Yaiyama, in which lived a painter of some note, Abe Tenko. Abe Tenko taught more than he painted, and relied for his living mostly on the small means to which he had succeeded at his father's death and on the aspiring artists who boarded in the village for the purpose of taking daily lessons from him. The island and rock scenery in the neighbourhood afforded continual study, and Tenko was never short of pupils. Among them was one scarcely more than a boy, being only seventeen years of age. His name was Sawara Kameju, and a most promising pupil he was. He had been sent to Tenko over a year before, when scarce sixteen years of age, and, for the reason that Tenko had been a friend of his father, Sawara was taken under the roof of the artist and treated as if he had been his son.

[1] About two hundred and fifty years ago a strange legend was attached to a kakemono which was painted by an artist celebrity, Sawara Kameju by name, and, owing to the reasons given in the story, the kakemono was handed over to the safe-keeping of the head priest of the Korinji Temple.

Tenko had had a sister who went into the service of the Lord of Aki, by whom she had a daughter. Had the child been a son, it would have been adopted into the Aki family; but, being a daughter, it was, according to Japanese custom, sent back to its mother's family, with the result that Tenko took charge of the child, whose name was Kimi. The mother being dead, the child had lived with him for sixteen years. Our story opens with O Kimi grown into a pretty girl.

O Kimi was a most devoted adopted daughter to Tenko. She attended almost entirely to his household affairs, and Tenko looked upon her as if indeed she were his own daughter, instead of an illegitimate niece, trusting her in everything.

After the arrival of the young student O Kimi's heart gave her much trouble. She fell in love with him. Sawara admired O Kimi greatly; but of love he never said a word, being too much absorbed in his study. He looked upon Kimi as a sweet girl, taking his meals with her and enjoying her society. He would have fought for her, and he loved her; but he never gave himself time to think that she was not his sister, and that he might make love to her. So it came to pass at last that O Kimi one day, with the pains of love in her heart, availed herself of her guardian's absence at the temple, whither he had gone to paint something for the priests. O Kimi screwed up her courage and made love to Sawara. She told him that since he had come to the house her heart had known no peace. She loved him, and would like to marry him if he did not mind.

This simple and maidenlike request, accompanied by

The Kakemono Ghost of Aki Province

the offer of tea, was more than young Sawara was able to answer without acquiescence. After all, it did not much matter, thought he : 'Kimi is a most beautiful and charming girl, and I like her very much, and must marry some day.'

So Sawara told Kimi that he loved her and would be only too delighted to marry her when his studies were complete—say two or three years thence. Kimi was overjoyed, and on the return of the good Tenko from Korinji Temple informed her guardian of what had passed.

Sawara set to with renewed vigour, and worked diligently, improving very much in his style of painting ; and after a year Tenko thought it would do him good to finish off his studies in Kyoto under an old friend of his own, a painter named Sumiyoshi Myokei. Thus it was that in the spring of the sixth year of Kioho—that is, in 1721—Sawara bade farewell to Tenko and his pretty niece O Kimi, and started forth to the capital. It was a sad parting. Sawara had grown to love Kimi very deeply, and he vowed that as soon as his name was made he would return and marry her.

In the olden days the Japanese were even more shockingly poor correspondents than they are now, and even lovers or engaged couples did not write to each other, as several of my tales may show.

After Sawara had been away for a year, it seemed that he should write and say at all events how he was getting on ; but he did not do so. A second year passed, and still there was no news. In the meantime there had been several admirers of O Kimi's who had proposed to Tenko

233

for her hand ; but Tenko had invariably said that Kimi San was already engaged—until one day he heard from Myokei, the painter in Kyoto, who told him that Sawara was making splendid progress, and that he was most anxious that the youth should marry his daughter. He felt that he must ask his old friend Tenko first, and before speaking to Sawara.

Tenko, on the other hand, had an application from a rich merchant for O Kimi's hand. What was Tenko to do ? Sawara showed no signs of returning ; on the contrary, it seemed that Myokei was anxious to get him to marry into his family. That must be a good thing for Sawara, he thought. Myokei is a better teacher than I, and if Sawara marries his daughter he will take more interest than ever in my old pupil. Also, it is advisable that Kimi should marry that rich young merchant, if I can persuade her to do so ; but it will be difficult, for she loves Sawara still. I am afraid he has forgotten her. A little strategy I will try, and tell her that Myokei has written to tell me that Sawara is going to marry his daughter ; then, possibly, she may feel sufficiently vengeful to agree to marry the young merchant. Arguing thus to himself, he wrote to Myokei to say that he had his full consent to ask Sawara to be his son-in-law, and he wished him every success in the effort ; and in the evening he spoke to Kimi.

' Kimi,' he said, ' to-day I have had news of Sawara through my friend Myokei.'

' Oh, do tell me what ! ' cried the excited Kimi. ' Is he coming back, and has he finished his education ? How delighted I shall be to see him ! We can be married in

April, when the cherry blooms, and he can paint a picture of our first picnic.'

'I fear, Kimi, the news which I have does not talk of his coming back. On the contrary, I am asked by Myokei to allow Sawara to marry his daughter, and, as I think such a request could not have been made had Sawara been faithful to you, I have answered that I have no objection to the union. And now, as for yourself, I deeply regret to tell you this ; but as your uncle and guardian I again wish to impress upon you the advisability of marrying Yorozuya, the young merchant, who is deeply in love with you and in every way a most desirable husband ; indeed, I must insist upon it, for I think it most desirable.'

Poor O Kimi San broke into tears and deep sobs, and without answering a word went to her room, where Tenko thought it well to leave her alone for the night.

In the morning she had gone, none knew whither, there being no trace of her.

Up in Kyoto Sawara continued his studies, true and faithful to O Kimi. After receiving Tenko's letter approving of Myokei's asking Sawara to become his son-in-law, Myokei asked Sawara if he would so honour him. 'When you marry my daughter, we shall be a family of painters, and I think you will be one of the most celebrated ones that Japan ever had.'

'But, sir,' cried Sawara, 'I cannot do myself the honour of marrying your daughter, for I am already engaged—I have been for the last three years—to Kimi, Tenko's daughter. It is most strange that he should not have told you !'

Ancient Tales and Folklore of Japan

There was nothing for Myokei to say to this ; but there was much for Sawara to think about. Foolish, perhaps he then thought, were the ways of Japanese in not corresponding more freely. He wrote to Kimi twice, accordingly, but no answer came. Then Myokei fell ill of a chill and died : so Sawara returned to his village home in Aki, where he was welcomed by Tenko, who was now, without O Kimi, lonely in his old age.

When Sawara heard that Kimi had gone away leaving neither address nor letter he was very angry, for he had not been told the reason.

'An ungrateful and bad girl,' said he to Tenko, 'and I have been lucky indeed in not marrying her ! '

'Yes, yes,' said Tenko : 'you have been lucky ; but you must not be too angry. Women are queer things, and, as the saying goes, when you see water running up hill and hens laying square eggs you may expect to see a truly honest-minded woman. But come now—I want to tell you that, as I am growing old and feeble, I wish to make you the master of my house and property here. You must take my name and marry ! '

Feeling disgusted at O Kimi's conduct, Sawara readily consented. A pretty young girl, the daughter of a wealthy farmer, was found—Kiku (the Chrysanthemum) ; —and she and Sawara lived happily with old Tenko, keeping his house and minding his estate. Sawara painted in his spare time. Little by little he became quite famous. One day the Lord of Aki sent for him and said it was his wish that Sawara should paint the seven beautiful scenes of the Islands of Kabakarijima (six, probably) ; the pictures were to be mounted on gold screens.

The Kakemono Ghost of Aki Province

This was the first commission that Sawara had had from such a high official. He was very proud of it, and went off to the Upper and Lower Kabakari Islands, where he made rough sketches. He went also to the rocky islands of Shokokujima, and to the little uninhabited island of Daikokujima, where an adventure befell him.

Strolling along the shore, he met a girl, tanned by sun and wind. She wore only a red cotton cloth about her loins, and her hair fell upon her shoulders. She had been gathering shell-fish, and had a basket of them under her arm. Sawara thought it strange that he should meet a single woman in so wild a place, and more so still when she addressed him, saying, 'Surely you are Sawara Kameju—are you not?'

'Yes,' answered Sawara: 'I am; but it is very strange that you should know me. May I ask how you do so?'

'If you are Sawara, as I know you are, you should know me without asking, for I am no other than Kimi, to whom you were engaged!'

Sawara was astonished, and hardly knew what to say: so he asked her questions as to how she had come to this lonely island. O Kimi explained everything, and ended by saying, with a smile of happiness upon her face:

'And since, my dearest Sawara, I understand that what I was told is false, and that you did not marry Myokei's daughter, and that we have been faithful to each other, we can be married and happy after all. Oh, think how happy we shall be!'

'Alas, alas, my dearest Kimi, it cannot be! I was led to suppose that you had deserted our benefactor Tenko and given up all thought of me. Oh, the sadness of it

237

all, the wickedness! I have been persuaded that you were faithless, and have been made to marry another!'

O Kimi made no answer, but began to run along the shore towards a little hut, which home she had made for herself. She ran fast, and Sawara ran after her, calling, 'Kimi, Kimi, stop and speak to me'; but Kimi did not stop. She gained her hut, and, seizing a knife, plunged it into her throat, and fell back bleeding to death. Sawara, greatly grieved, burst into tears. It was horrible to see the girl who might have been his bride lying dead at his feet all covered with blood, and having suffered so horrible a death at her own hands. Greatly impressed, he drew paper from his pocket and made a sketch of the body. Then he and his boatman buried O Kimi above the tide-mark near the primitive hut. Afterwards, at home, with a mournful heart, he painted a picture of the dead girl, and hung it in his room.

On the first night that it was hung Sawara had a dreadful dream. On awakening he found the figure on the kakemono seemed to be alive: the ghost of O Kimi stepped out of it and stood near his bed. Night after night the ghost appeared, until sleep and rest for Sawara were no longer possible. There was nothing to be done, thought he, but to send his wife back to her parents, which he did; and the kakemono he presented to the Korinji Temple, where the priests kept it with great care and daily prayed for the spirit of O Kimi San. After that Sawara saw the ghost no more.

The kakemono is called the Ghost Picture of Tenko II., and is said to be still kept in the Korinji Temple, where it was placed some 230 to 240 years ago.

XXXVIII

WHITE SAKÉ

Two thousand or more years ago Lake Biwa, in Omi Province, and Mount Fuji, in Suruga Province, came into being in one night. Though my story relates this as fact, you are fully entitled to say, should you feel so inclined, 'Wonderful indeed are the ways of Nature'; but do so respectfully, if you please, and without levity, for otherwise you will grossly offend and will not understand the ethical ideas of Japanese folklore stories.

Well, at the time of this extraordinary geographical event, there lived one Yurine, a man of poor means even for those days. He loved saké wine, and scarcely ever spent a day without drinking some of it. Yurine lived near the place which is now called Sudzukawa, a little to the north of the river known as Fujikawa.

On the day which followed Fuji San's appearance Yurine became ill, and was in consequence unable to drink his cup of saké. He became worse and worse, and, at last feeling that there could be no hope for him, decided to give himself the pleasure of drinking a cup before he died. Accordingly he called to himself his only son,

239

Koyuri, a boy of fourteen years, and told him to go and fetch him a cup or two of the wine. Koyuri was sorely perplexed. He had no saké in the house, and there was not a single coin left wherewith to buy. This he did not like to tell his father, fearing that the unpleasant state of affairs might make him worse. So he took his gourd, and went wandering along the beach, wondering how he could get what his father wanted. While thus employed Koyuri heard a voice calling him by name. As he looked up towards the pines which fringed the beach, he saw a man and a woman sitting beneath an immense tree ; their hair was a scarlet red, and so were their bodies. At first Koyuri was afraid,—he had never seen their like before,— but the voice was kindly, and the man was making signs to him to approach. Koyuri did so in fear and trembling, but with that coolness which characterises the Japanese boy.

As Koyuri approached the strange people he noticed that they were drinking saké from large flat cups known as ' sakadzuki,' and that on the sand beside them was an immense jar, from which they took the liquor ; moreover, he noticed that the saké was whiter than any he had seen before.

Thinking always of his father, Koyuri unslung his gourd, reported his father's illness, and begged for saké. The red man took the gourd, and filled it. After expressing gratitude, Koyuri ran off delighted. ' Here, father, here ! ' said he as he reached his hut : ' I have got you the saké, the best I have ever seen, and I am sure it tastes as good as it looks ; try it and tell me ! '

The old man took the wine and drank greedily,

expressing great satisfaction, and said that it was indeed the best he had ever tasted. Next day he wanted more. The boy found his two red friends, and again they filled the gourd. In short, Koyuri had his gourd filled for five days in succession, and his father had regained spirits and was almost well in consequence.

Now, there lived in the next hut to Yurine an unpleasant neighbour who also was fond of saké, but too poor to procure it. His name was Mamikiko. On hearing that Yurine had been drinking saké for the last five days he became furiously jealous, and, calling Koyuri, asked where and how he had procured it. The boy explained that he had got it from the strange people with red hair who had been living near the big pine tree for some days past.

'Give me your gourd to taste,' cried Mamikiko, snatching it roughly. 'Do you think that your father is the only man who is good enough for saké?' Putting the gourd to his lips, he began to drink; but he threw it down in disgust a second later, and spat out what was in his mouth. 'What filth is this?' he cried. 'To your father you give the most excellent saké, while to me you give foul water! What is the meaning of it?' He gave Koyuri a sound beating, and then told him to lead the way to the red people on the beach, saying, 'I will beat you again if I don't get some good saké; so you had better see to it!'

Koyuri led the way, weeping the while at the loss of his saké, which Mamikiko had thrown away, and fearing the anger of his red friends. In the usual place they found the strangers, who had both been drinking and were still doing so. Mamikiko was surprised at their appearance : he had seen nothing quite like them before. Their bodies were of the pink of cherry blossom shining in the sun, while their long red hair almost frightened him ; both were naked except for a green girdle made of some curious seaweed.

'Well, boy Koyuri, what are you crying about, and why back so soon ? Has your father drunk the saké already ? If so he must be almost as fond of it as we.'

'No, no : my father has not drunk it ; but Mamikiko, here, took it from me and drank some, spitting it out and saying it was not saké ; the rest he threw away, and then made me bring him here. May I have some more for my father ? ' The red man refilled the gourd and told him not to mind, and seemed amused at Koyuri's account of Mamikiko spitting it out.

'I am as fond of saké as any one,' cried Mamikiko : 'will you give me some ? '

'Oh, yes ; help yourself,' said the red man ; 'Help yourself.' Mamikiko filled the largest of the cups, and, putting it to his nose, smelt the fragrance, which was delicious ; but as soon as he put it to his lips his face changed, and he had to spit again, for the taste was nauseating.

'What is the meaning of this ? ' he cried angrily ; and the red man answered still more angrily :

'You do not seem to be aware of who I am. Well, I will tell you that I am a shojo of high degree, and I live deep in the bottom of the ocean near the Sea Dragon's Palace. Recently we heard that a sacred mountain had arisen on the edge of the sea, and, as it is a lucky omen, and a sign that the Empire of Japan will exist in perpetuity, I have come here to see it. While enjoying the magnificent scene from Suruga coast I met this good boy Koyuri, who asked for saké for his poor sick old father, and I gave him some. Now, this saké is not ordinary saké, but sacred, and those who drink it live for ever and retain their youth ; moreover, it cures all diseases even in the aged. But you must know that any medicine is sometimes a poison, and thus it is that this sweet sacred white saké is good only in taste to the righteous, and bad-tasting and poisonous to the wicked. Thus I know that, as it tastes evil to you, you are an evil and wicked man, selfish and greedy.' And both the shojos laughed at Mamikiko, who, on hearing that the few drops which he must have swallowed would act as poison and soon kill him, began to cry with fear and to regret his conduct. He begged and implored forgiveness and that his life might be spared, and vowed that he would reform if only given a chance. The shojo, drawing some powder from a case, gave it to Mamikiko, and told him to swallow it in some saké ; ' for,' said he, ' it is better to repent and reform even in your old age than not at all.'

Mamikiko drank it down this time, finding the wine sweet and delicious ; it strengthened him and made him feel well, and he reformed and became a good man. He made friends again with Yurine and treated Koyuri well.

Some years later Mamikiko and Yurine built a hut at the southern base of Fuji San, where they brewed white saké from a recipe given them by the shojo, and they gave it to all who suffered from saké poisoning. Both Mamikiko and Yurine lived for 300 years.

In the Middle Ages a man who had heard this story

Ancient Tales and Folklore of Japan

brewed white saké at the foot of Mount Fuji; he made
it with rice yeast, and people became very fond of it.
Even to-day white saké is brewed somewhere at the foot
of the mountain, and is well known as a special liquor
belonging to Fuji. I myself drank it in 1907 without
fear of living beyond my fifty-fifth year.

XXXIX

THE BLIND BEAUTY

NEARLY three hundred years ago (or, according to my story-teller, in the second year of Kwanei, which would be 1626, the period of Kwanei having begun in 1624 and ended in 1644) there lived at Maidzuru, in the province of Tango, a youth named Kichijiro.

Kichijiro had been born at the village of Tai, where his father had been a native; but on the death of the father he had come with his elder brother, Kichisuke, to Maidzuru. The brother was his only living relation except an uncle, and had taken care of him for four years, educating him from the age of eleven until fifteen; and Kichijiro was very grateful, and determined that now he had reached the age of fifteen he must no longer be a drag on his brother, but must begin to make a way in the world for himself.

After looking about for some weeks, Kichijiro found employment with Shiwoya Hachiyemon, a merchant in Maidzuru. He worked very hard, and soon gained his master's friendship; indeed, Hachiyemon thought very highly of his apprentice; he favoured him in many ways

245

over older clerks, and finally entrusted him with the key of his safes, which contained documents and much money.

Now, Hachiyemon had a daughter of Kichijiro's age, of great beauty and promise, and she fell desperately in love with Kichijiro, who himself was at first unaware of this. The girl's name was Ima, O Ima San, and she was one of those delightful ruddy, happy-faced girls whom only Japan can produce—a mixture of yellow and red, with hair and eyebrows as black as a raven. Ima paid Kichijiro compliments now and then; but he was a boy who thought little of love. He intended to get on in the world, and marriage was a thing which had not yet entered into his mind.

After Kichijiro had been some six months in the employment of Hachiyemon he stood higher than ever in the master's estimation; but the other clerks did not like him. They were jealous. One was specially so. This was Kanshichi, who hated him not only because he was favoured by the merchant but also because he himself loved O Ima, who had given him many a rebuff when he had attempted to make love to her. So great did this secret hate become, at last Kanshichi vowed that he would be revenged upon Kichijiro, and if necessary upon his master Hachiyemon and his daughter O Ima as well; for he was a wicked and scheming man.

One day an opportunity occurred.

Kichijiro had so far secured confidence that the master had sent him off to Kasumi, in Tajima Province, there to negotiate the purchase of a junk. While he was away Kanshichi broke into the room where the safe was kept, and took therefrom two bags containing money in gold up to the value of 200 ryo. He effaced all signs of his action, and went quietly back to his work. Two or three days later Kichijiro returned, having successfully accomplished his mission, and, after reporting this to the master, set to his routine work again. On examining the safe, he found that the 200 ryo of gold were missing, and, he having reported this, the office and the household were thrown into a state of excitement.

After some hours of hunting for the money it was found in a koro (incense-burner) which belonged to Kichijiro, and no one was more surprised than he. It was Kanshichi who had found it, naturally, after having put it there himself; he did not accuse Kichijiro of having stolen the money—his plans were more deeply laid. The money having been found there, he knew that Kichijiro himself would have to say something. Of course Kichijiro said he was absolutely innocent, and that when he had left for Kasumi the money was safe—he had seen it just before leaving.

Hachiyemon was sorely distressed. He believed in the innocence of Kichijiro; but how was he to prove it? Seeing that his master did not believe Kichijiro guilty, Kanshichi decided that he must do something which would render it more or less impossible for Hachiyemon to do otherwise than to send his hated rival Kichijiro away. He went to the master and said :

'Sir, I, as your head clerk, must tell you that, though perhaps Kichijiro is innocent, things seem to prove that he is not, for how could the money have got into his koro? If he is not punished, the theft will reflect on all of us clerks, your faithful servants, and I myself should have to leave your service, for all the others would do so, and you would be unable to carry on your business. Therefore I venture to tell you, sir, that it would be advisable in your own interests to send poor Kichijiro, for whose misfortune I deeply grieve, away.'

Hachiyemon saw the force of this argument, and agreed. He sent for Kichijiro, to whom he said :

'Kichijiro, deeply as I regret it, I am obliged to send you away. I do not believe in your guilt, but I know that if I do not send you away all my clerks will leave me, and I shall be ruined. To show you that I believe in your innocence, I will tell you that my daughter Ima loves you, and that if you are willing, and after you can prove your innocence, nothing would give me greater pleasure than to have you back as my son-in-law. Go now. Try and think how you can prove your innocence. My best wishes go with you.'

Kichijiro was very sad. Now that he had to go, he found that he should more than miss the companionship of the sweet O Ima. With tears in his eyes, he vowed to the father that he would come back, prove his innocence, and marry O Ima ; and with O Ima herself he had his first love scene. They vowed that neither should rest until the scheming thief had been discovered, and they were both reunited in such a way that nothing could part them.

Kichijiro went back to his brother Kichisuke at Tai village, to consult as to what it would be best for him to do to re-establish his reputation. After a few weeks, he was employed through his brother's interest and that of his only surviving uncle in Kyoto. There he worked hard and faithfully for four long years, bringing much credit to his firm, and earning much admiration from his uncle, who made him heir to considerable landed property, and gave him a share in his own business. Kichijiro found himself at the age of twenty quite a rich man.

In the meantime calamity had come on pretty O Ima. After Kichijiro had left Maidzuru, Kanshichi began to pester her with attentions. She would have none of him ; she would not even speak to him ; and so exasperated did he become at last that he used to waylay her. On one occasion he resorted to violence and tried to carry her away by force. Of this she complained to her father, who promptly dismissed him from his service.

This made villain Kanshichi angrier than ever. As the Japanese proverb says, 'Kawaisa amatte nikusa ga hyakubai,'—which means, 'Excessive love is hatred.' So it was with Kanshichi : his love turned to hatred. He thought of how he could be avenged on Hachiyemon and O Ima. The most simple means, he thought, would be to burn down their house, the business offices, and the stores of merchandise : that must bring ruin. So one night Kanshichi set about doing these things and accomplished them most successfully—with the exception that he himself was caught in the act and sentenced to a heavy punishment. That was the only satisfaction which was got by Hachiyemon, who was all but ruined ; he sent away all his clerks and retired from business, for he was too old to begin again.

With just enough to keep life and body together, Hachiyemon and his pretty daughter lived in a little cheap cottage on the banks of the river, where it was Hachiyemon's only pleasure to fish for carp and jakko. For three years he did this, and then fell ill and died. Poor O Ima was left to herself, as lovely as ever, but mournful. The few friends she had tried to prevail on her to marry somebody—anybody, they said, sooner than live alone,—but to this advice the girl would not listen. 'It is better to live miserably alone,' she said, 'than to marry one for whom you do not care; I can love none but Kichijiro, though I shall not see him again.'

O Ima spoke the truth on that occasion, without knowing it, for, true as it is that it never rains but it pours, O Ima was to have more trouble. An eye sickness came to her, and in less than two months after her father's death the poor girl was blind, with no one to attend to her wants but an old nurse who had stuck to her through all her troubles. Ima had barely sufficient money to pay for rice.

It was just at this time that Kichijiro's success was assured : his uncle had given him a half interest in the business and made a will in which he left him his whole property. Kichijiro decided to go and report himself to his old master at Maidzuru and to claim the hand of O Ima his daughter. Having learned the sad story of downfall and ruin, and also of Ima's blindness, Kichijiro went to the girl's cottage. Poor O Ima came out and flung herself into his arms, weeping bitterly, and crying : 'Kichijiro, my beloved ! this is indeed almost the hardest blow of all. The loss of my sight was as nothing before ; but now that you have come back, I cannot see you, and how I long to do so you can but little imagine ! It is indeed the saddest blow of all. You cannot now marry me.'

Kichijiro petted her, and said, 'Dearest Ima, you must not be too hasty in your thoughts. I have never ceased thinking of you; indeed, I have grown to love you desperately. I have property now in Kyoto; but should you prefer to do so, we will live here in this cottage. I am ready to do anything you wish. It is my desire to re-establish your father's old business, for the good of your family; but first and before even this we will be married and never part again. We will do that to-morrow. Then we will go together to Kyoto and see my uncle, and ask for his advice. He is always good and kind, and you will like him—he is sure to like you.'

Next day they started on their journey to Kyoto, and Kichijiro saw his brother and his uncle, neither of whom had any objection to Kichijiro's bride on account of her blindness. Indeed, the uncle was so much pleased at his nephew's fidelity that he gave him half of his capital there and then. Kichijiro built a new house and offices in Maidzuru, just where his first master Hachiyemon's place had been. He re-established the business completely, calling his firm the Second Shiwoya Hachiyemon, as is often done in Japan (which adds much to the confusion of Europeans who study Japanese Art, for pupils often take the names of their clever masters, calling themselves the Second, or even the Third or the Fourth).

In the garden of their Maidzuru house was an artificial mountain, and on this Kichijiro had erected a tombstone or memorial dedicated to Hachiyemon, his father-in-law. At the foot of the mountain he erected a memorial to

Kanshichi. Thus he rewarded the evil wickedness of Kanshichi by kindness, but showed at the same time that evil-doers cannot expect high places. It is to be hoped that the spirits of the two dead men became reconciled.

They say in Maidzuru that the memorial tombs still stand.

XL

THE SECRET OF IIDAMACHI POND

In the first year of Bunkiu, 1861-1864, there lived a man called Yehara Keisuke in Kasumigaseki, in the district of Kojimachi. He was a hatomoto—that is, a feudatory vassal of the Shogun—and a man to whom some respect was due ; but apart from that, Yehara was much liked for his kindness of heart and general fairness in dealing with people. In Iidamachi lived another hatomoto, Hayashi Hayato. He had been married to Yehara's sister for five years. They were exceedingly happy ; their daughter, four years old now, was the delight of their hearts. Their cottage was rather dilapidated ; but it was Hayashi's own, with the pond in front of it, and two farms, the whole property comprising some two hundred acres, of which nearly half was under cultivation. Thus Hayashi was able to live without working much. In the summer he fished for carp ; in the winter he wrote much, and was considered a bit of a poet.

At the time of this story, Hayashi, having planted his rice and sweet potatoes (sato-imo), had but little to do, and

253

spent most of his time with his wife, fishing in his ponds, one of which contained large suppon (terrapin turtles) as well as koi (carp). Suddenly things went wrong.

Yehara was surprised one morning to receive a visit from his sister O Komé.

'I have come, dear brother,' she said, 'to beg you to help me to obtain a divorce or separation from my husband.'

'Divorce! Why should you want a divorce? Have you not always said you were happy with your husband, my dear friend Hayashi? For what sudden reason do you ask for a divorce? Remember you have been married for five years now, and that is sufficient to prove that your life has been happy, and that Hayashi has treated you well.'

At first O Komé would not give any reason why she wished to be separated from her husband; but at last she said:

'Brother, think not that Hayashi has been unkind. He is all that can be called kind, and we deeply love each other; but, as you know, Hayashi's family have owned the land, the farms on one of which latter we live, for some three hundred years. Nothing would induce him to change his place of abode, and I should never have wished him to do so until some twelve days ago.'

'What has happened within these twelve wonderful days?' asked Yehara.

'Dear brother, I can stand it no longer,' was his sister's answer. 'Up to twelve days ago all went well; but then a terrible thing happened. It was very dark and warm, and I was sitting outside our house looking at the clouds passing over the moon, and talking to my daughter. Suddenly there appeared, as if walking on the lilies of the pond, a white figure. Oh, so white, so wet, and so miserable to look at! It appeared to arise from the pond and float in the air, and then approached me slowly until it was within ten feet. As it came my child cried : " Why, mother, there comes O Sumi—do you know O Sumi ? " I answered her that I did not, I think ; but in truth I was so frightened I hardly know what I said. The figure was horrible to look at. It was that of a girl of eighteen or nineteen years, with hair dishevelled and hanging loose, over white and wet shoulders. " Help me ! help me ! " cried the figure, and I was so frightened that I covered my eyes and screamed for my husband, who was inside. He came out and found me in a dead faint, with my child by my side, also in a state of terror. Hayashi had seen nothing. He carried us both in, shut the doors, and told me I must have been dreaming. " Perhaps," he sarcastically added, " you saw the kappa which is said to dwell in the pond, but which none of my family have seen for over one hundred years." That is all that my husband said on the subject. Next night, however, when in bed, my child seized me suddenly, crying in terror-stricken tones, " O Sumi—here is O Sumi—how horrible she looks ! Mother, mother, do you see her ? " I did see her. She stood dripping wet within three feet of my bed, the whiteness and the wetness and the dishevelled hair being what gave her the awful look which she bore. " Help me ! Help me ! " cried the figure, and then disappeared. After that I could not sleep ; nor could I get my child to do so. On every night until now the ghost has come—O Sumi, as my child calls her. I should kill myself if I had to remain longer in that house, which has become a terror to myself and my child. My husband does not see the ghost, and only laughs at me; and that is why I see no way out of the difficulty but a separation.'

Yehara told his sister that on the following day he would call on Hayashi, and sent his sister back to her husband that night.

Next day, when Yehara called, Hayashi, after hearing what the visitor had to say, answered :

'It is very strange. I was born in this house over twenty years ago ; but I have never seen the ghost which my wife refers to, and have never heard about it. Not the slightest allusion to it was ever made by my father or mother. I will make inquiries of all my neighbours and servants, and ascertain if they ever heard of the ghost, or even of any one coming to a sudden and untimely end. There must be something : it is impossible that my little child should know the name "Sumi," she never having known any one bearing it.'

Inquiries were made ; but nothing could be learned from the servants or from the neighbours. Hayashi reasoned that, the ghost being always wet, the mystery might be solved by drying up the pond—perhaps to find the remains of some murdered person, whose bones required decent burial and prayers said over them.

The pond was old and deep, covered with water plants, and had never been emptied within his memory. It was said to contain a kappa (mythical beast, half-turtle, half-man). In any case, there were many terrapin turtle, the capture of which would well repay the cost of the empty-

57. THE SPIRIT OF THE TREE APPEARS TO KOTARO AND THE OLD MAN

58. UKON SHOWS SAYEMON THAT HE HAS ALREADY SACRIFICED HIMSELF

59. HARADA AND GUNDAYU FENCING

61. THE SPIRIT OF THE WILLOW TREE APPEARS TO GOBEI

60. WHAT SAOTOME AND TAMAJO FOUND

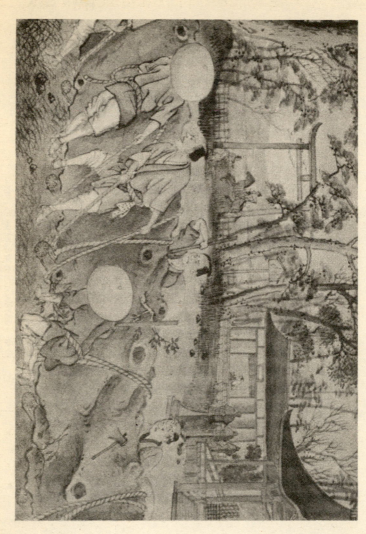

62. CHOGORO AND HIS MEN FAIL TO MOVE THE KUSUNOKI TREE

ing. The bank of the pond was cut, and next day there remained only a pool in the deepest part ; Hayashi decided to clear even this and dig into the mud below.

At this moment the grandmother of Hayashi arrived, an old woman of some eighty years, and said :

'You need go no farther. I can tell you all about the ghost. O Sumi does not rest, and it is quite true that her ghost appears. I am very sorry about it, now in my old age ; for it is my fault—the sin is mine. Listen and I will tell you all.'

Every one stood astonished at these words, feeling that some secret was about to be revealed.

The old woman continued :

'When Hayashi Hayato, your grandfather, was alive, we had a beautiful servant girl, seventeen years of age, called O Sumi. Your grandfather became enamoured of this girl, and she of him. I was about thirty at that time, and was jealous, for my better looks had passed away. One day when your grandfather was out I took Sumi to the pond and gave her a severe beating. During the struggle she fell into the water and got entangled in the weeds ; and there I left her, fully believing the water to be shallow and that she could get out. She did not succeed, and was drowned. Your grandfather found her dead on his return. In those days the police were not very particular with their inquiries. The girl was buried ; but nothing was said to me, and the matter soon blew over. Fourteen days ago was the fiftieth anniversary of this tragedy. Perhaps that is the reason of Sumi's ghost appearing ; for appear she must, or your child could not have known of her name. It must be as your child says, and that the first time she appeared Sumi communicated her name.'

The old woman was shaking with fear, and advised them all to say prayers at O Sumi's tomb. This was done, and the ghost has been seen no more. Hayashi said :

'Though I am a samurai, and have read many books, I never believed in ghosts ; but now I do.'

XLI

THE SPIRIT OF YENOKI[1]

THERE is a mountain in the province of Idsumi called Oki-yama (or Oji Yama); it is connected with the Mumaru-Yama mountains. I will not vouch that I am accurate in spelling either. Suffice it to say that the story was told to me by Fukuga Sei, and translated by Mr. Ando, the Japanese translator of our Consulate at Kobe. Both of these give the mountain's name as Oki-yama, and say that on the top of it from time immemorial there has been a shrine dedicated to Fudo-myo-o (*Achala*, in Sanskrit, which means 'immovable,' and is the god always represented as surrounded by fire and sitting uncomplainingly on as an example to others; he carries a sword in one hand, and a rope in the other, as a warning that punishment awaits those who are unable to overcome with honour the painful struggles of life).

Well, at the top of Oki-yama (high or big mountain) is this very old temple to Fudo, and many are the

---

[1] Fukuga Sei said that this was an old story told him by his nurse, who was a native of the village of Oki-yama; also, that a solid gold Buddha, eighteen inches in height, had been stolen from the temple three years ago.

pilgrimages which are made there annually. The mountain itself is covered with forest, and there are some remarkable cryptomerias, camphor and pine trees.

Many years ago, in the days of which I speak, there were only a few priests living up at this temple. Among them was a middle-aged man, half-priest, half-caretaker, called Yenoki. For twenty years had Yenoki lived at the temple; yet during that time he had never cast eyes on the figure of Fudo, over which he was partly set to guard; it was kept shut in a shrine and never seen by any one but the head priest. One day Yenoki's curiosity got the better of him. Early in the morning the door of the shrine was not quite closed. Yenoki looked in, but saw nothing. On turning to the light again, he found that he had lost the use of the eye that had looked: he was stone-blind in the right eye.

Feeling that the divine punishment served him well, and that the gods must be angry, he set about purifying himself, and fasted for one hundred days. Yenoki was mistaken in his way of devotion and repentance, and did not pacify the gods; on the contrary, they turned him into a tengu (long-nosed devil who dwells in mountains, and is the great teacher of jujitsu).

But Yenoki continued to call himself a priest—'Ichigan Hoshi,' meaning the one-eyed priest—for a year, and then died; and it is said that his spirit passed into an enormous cryptomeria tree on the east side of the mountain. After that, when sailors passed the Chinu Sea (Osaka Bay), if there was a storm they used to pray to the one-eyed priest for help, and if a light was seen on the top of Oki-yama they had a sure sign that, no matter how rough the sea, their ship would not be lost.

It may be said, in fact, that after the death of the one-eyed priest more importance was attached to his spirit and to the tree into which it had taken refuge than to the temple itself. The tree was called the Lodging of the One-eyed Priest, and no one dared approach it — not even the woodcutters who were familiar with the mountains. It was a source of awe and an object of reverence.

At the foot of Oki-yama was a lonely village, separated from others by fully two ri (five miles), and there were only one hundred and thirty houses in it.

Every year the villagers used to celebrate the 'Bon' by engaging, after it was over, in the dance called 'Bon Odori.' Like most other things in Japan, the 'Bon' and the 'Bon Odori' were in extreme contrast. The 'Bon' was a ceremony arranged for the spirits of the dead, who are supposed to return to earth for three days annually, to visit their family shrines—something like our All Saints' Day, and in any case quite a serious religious performance. The 'Bon Odori' is a dance which varies considerably in different provinces. It is confined mostly to villages—for one cannot count the pretty geisha dances in Kyoto which are practically copies of it. It is a dance of boys and girls, one may say, and continues nearly all night on the village green. For the three or four nights that it lasts, opportunities for flirtations of the most violent kind are plentiful. There are no chaperons (so to speak), and (to put it vulgarly) every one 'goes on the bust'! Hitherto - virtuous maidens spend the night out as impromptu sweethearts ; and, in the village of which this story is told, not only is it they who let themselves go, but even young brides also.

So it came to pass that the village at the foot of Oki-yama mountain—away so far from other villages—was a bad one morally. There was no restriction to what a girl might do or what she might not do during the nights of the 'Bon Odori.' Things went from bad to worse until, at the time of which I write, anarchy reigned during the festive days. At last it came to pass that after a particularly festive 'Bon,' on a beautiful moonlight night in August, the well-beloved and charming daughter of Kurahashi Yozaemon, O Kimi, aged eighteen years, who had promised her lover Kurosuke that she would meet him secretly that evening, was on her way to do so. After passing the last house in her mountain village she came to a thick copse, and standing at the edge of it was a man whom O Kimi at first took to be her lover. On approaching she found that it was not Kurosuke, but a very handsome youth of twenty-three years. He did not speak to her ; in fact, he kept a little away. If she advanced, he receded. So handsome was the youth, O Kimi felt that she loved him. 'Oh how my heart beats for him ! ' said she. 'After all, why should I not give up Kurosuke? He is not good-looking like this man, whom I love already before I have even spoken to him. I hate Kurosuke, now that I see this man.'

As she said this she saw the figure smiling and beckoning, and, being a wicked girl, loose in her morals, she followed him and was seen no more. Her family were much exercised in their minds. A week passed, and O Kimi San did not return.

A few days later Tamae, the sixteen-year-old daughter of Kinsaku, who was secretly in love with the son of the village Headman, was awaiting him in the temple grounds, standing the while by the stone figure of Jizodo (Sanskrit, *Kshitigarbha*, Patron of Women and Children). Suddenly there stood near Tamae a handsome youth of twenty-three years, as in the case of O Kimi ; she was greatly struck by the youth's beauty, so much so that when he took her by the hand and led her off she made no effort to resist, and she also disappeared.

And thus it was that nine girls of amorous nature disappeared from this small village. Everywhere for thirty miles round people talked and wondered, and said unkind things.

In Oki-yama village itself the elder people said :

' Yes : it must be that our children's immodesty since the ' Bon Odori ' has angered Yenoki San : perhaps it is he himself who appears in the form of this handsome youth and carries off our daughters.'

Nearly all agreed in a few days that they owed their losses to the Spirit of the Yenoki Tree ; and as soon as this notion had taken root the whole of the villagers locked and barred themselves in their houses both day and night. Their farms became neglected ; wood was not being cut on the mountain ; business was at a standstill. The rumour of this state of affairs spread, and the Lord of Kishiwada, becoming uneasy, summoned Sonobé Hayama, the most celebrated swordsman in that part of Japan.

'Sonobé, you are the bravest man I know of, and the best fighter. It is for you to go and inspect the tree where lodges the spirit of Yenoki. You must use your own discretion. I cannot advise as to what it is best that you should do. I leave it to you to dispose of the mystery of the disappearances of the nine girls.'

'My lord,' said Sonobé, 'my life is at your lordship's call. I shall either clear the mystery or die.'

After this interview with his master Sonobé went home. He put himself through a course of cleansing. He fasted and bathed for a week, and then repaired to Oki-yama.

This was in the month of October, when to me things always look their best. Sonobé ascended the mountain, and went first to the temple, which he reached at three o'clock in the afternoon, after a hard climb. Here he said prayers before the god Fudo for fully half an hour. Then he set out to cross the short valley which led up to the Oki-yama mountain, and to the tree which held the spirit of the one-eyed priest, Yenoki.

It was a long and steep climb, with no paths, for the mountain was avoided as much as possible by even the most adventurous of woodcutters, none of whom ever dreamed of going up as far as the Yenoki tree. Sonobé was in good training and a bold warrior. The woods were dense ; there was a chilling damp, which came from the spray of a high waterfall. The solitude was intense, and once or twice Sonobé put his hand on the hilt of his sword, thinking that he heard some one following in the gloom ; but there was no one, and by five o'clock Sonobé had reached the tree and addressed it thus :

'Oh, honourable and aged tree, that has braved

centuries of storm, thou hast become the home of Yenoki's spirit. In truth there is much honour in having so stately a lodging, and therefore he cannot have been so bad a man. I have come from the Lord of Kishiwada to upbraid him, however, and to ask what means it that Yenoki's spirit should appear as a handsome youth for the purpose of robbing poor people of their daughters. This must not continue ; else you, as the lodging of Yenoki's spirit, will be cut down, so that it may escape to another part of the country.'

At that moment a warm wind blew on the face of Sonobé, and dark clouds appeared overhead, rendering the forest dark ; rain began to fall, and the rumblings of earthquake were heard.

Suddenly the figure of an old priest appeared in ghostly form, wrinkled and thin, transparent and clammy, nerve-shattering ; but Sonobé had no fear.

'You have been sent by the Lord of Kishiwada,' said the ghost. 'I admire your courage for coming. So cowardly and sinful are most men, they fear to come near where my spirit has taken refuge. I can assure you that I do no evil to the good. So bad had morals become in the village, it was time to give a lesson. The villagers' customs defied the gods. It is true that I, hoping to improve these people and make them godly, assumed the form of a youth, and carried away nine of the worst of them. They are quite well. They deeply regret their sins, and will reform their village. Every day I have given them lectures. You will find them on the " Mino toge," or second summit of this mountain, tied to trees. Go there and release them, and afterwards tell the Lord of

Kishiwada what the spirit of Yenoki, the one-eyed priest, has done, and that it is always ready to help him to improve his people. Farewell!'

No sooner had the last word been spoken than the spirit vanished. Sonobé, who felt somewhat dazed by what the spirit had said, started off nevertheless to the 'Mino toge'; and there, sure enough, were the nine girls, tied each to a tree, as the spirit had said. He cut their bonds, gave them a lecture, took them back to the village, and reported to the Lord of Kishiwada.

Since then the people have feared more than ever the spirit of the one-eyed priest. They have become completely reformed, an example to the surrounding villages. The nine houses or families whose daughters behaved so badly contribute annually the rice eaten by the priests of Fudo-myo-o Temple. It is spoken of as 'the nine-families rice of Oki.'

XLII

THE SPIRIT OF THE LOTUS LILY

FOR some time I have been hunting for a tale about the lotus lily. My friend Fukuga has at last found one which is said to date back some two hundred years. It applies to a castle that was then situated in what was known as Kinai, now incorporated into what may be known as the Kyoto district. Probably it refers to one of the castles in that neighbourhood, though I myself know of only one, which is now called Nijo Castle.

Fukuga (who does not speak English) and my interpreter made it very difficult for me to say that the story does not really belong to a castle in the province of Idzumi, for after starting it in Kyoto they suddenly brought me to Idzumi, making the hero of it the Lord of Koriyama. In any case, I was first told that disease and sickness broke out in Kinai (Kyoto). Thousands of people died of it. It spread to Idzumi, where the feudal Lord of Koriyama lived, and attacked him also. Doctors were called from all parts; but it was no use. The disease spread, and, to the dismay of all, not only the Lord of Koriyama but also his wife and child were stricken.

There was a panic terror in the country—not that the people feared for themselves, but because they were in dread that they might lose their lord and his wife and child. The Lord Koriyama was much beloved. People flocked to the castle. They camped round its high walls, and in its empty moats, which were dry, there having been no war for some time.

One day, during the illness of this great family, Tada Samon, the highest official in the castle (next to the Lord Koriyama himself), was sitting in his room, thinking what was best to be done on the various questions that were awaiting the Daimio's recovery. While he was thus engaged, a servant announced that there was a visitor at the outer gate who requested an interview, saying that he thought he could cure the three sufferers.

Tada Samon would see the caller, whom the servant shortly after fetched.

The visitor turned out to be a yamabushi (mountain recluse) in appearance, and on entering the room bowed low to Samon, saying :

'Sir, it is an evil business—this illness of our lord and master—and it has been brought about by an evil spirit, who has entered the castle because you have put up no defence against impure and evil spirits. This castle is the centre of administration for the whole of the surrounding country, and it was unwise to allow it to remain unfortified against impure and evil spirits. The saints of old[1] have always told us to plant the lotus lily, not only

[1] Rakkan.

The Spirit of the Lotus Lily

in the one inner ditch surrounding a castle, but also in both ditches or in as many as there be, and, moreover, to plant them all around the ditches. Surely, sir, you know that the lotus, being the most emblematic flower in our religion, must be the most pure and sacred; for this reason it drives away uncleanness, which cannot cross it. Be assured, sir, that if your lord had not neglected the northern ditches of his castle, but had kept them filled with water, clean, and had planted the sacred lotus, no such evil spirit would have come as the present sent by Heaven to warn him. If I am allowed to do so, I shall enter the castle to-day and pray that the evil spirit of sickness leave; and I ask that I may be allowed to plant lotuses in the northern moats. Thus only can the Lord of Koriyama and his family be saved.'

Samon nodded in answer, for he now remembered that the northern moats had neither lotus nor water, and that this was partly his fault—a matter of economy in connection with the estates. He interviewed his master, who was more sick than ever. He called all the Court officials. It was decided that the yamabushi should have his way. He was told to carry out his ideas as he thought best. There was plenty of money, and there were hundreds of hands ready to help him—anything to save the master.

The yamabushi washed his body, and prayed that the evil spirit of sickness should leave the castle. Subsequently he superintended the cleansing and repairing of the northern moats, directing the people to fill them with water and plant lotuses. Then he disappeared mysteriously —vanished almost before the men's eyes. Wonderingly, but with more energy than ever, the men worked to carry out the orders. In less than twenty-four hours the moats had been cleaned, repaired, filled, and planted.

As was to be expected, the Lord Koriyama, his wife, and son became rapidly better. In a week all were able to be up, and in a fortnight they were as well as ever they had been.

Thanksgivings were held, and there were great rejoicings all over Idzumi. Later, people flocked to see the splendidly-kept moats of lotuses, and the villagers went so far as to rename among themselves the castle, calling it the Lotus Castle.

Some years passed before anything strange happened. The Lord Koriyama had died from natural causes, and had been succeeded by his son, who had neglected the lotus roots. A young samurai was passing along one of the moats. This was at the end of August, when the flowers of the lotus are strong and high. The samurai suddenly saw two beautiful boys, about six or seven years of age, playing at the edge of the moat.

'Boys,' said he, 'it is not safe to play so near the edge of this moat. Come along with me.'

He was about to take them by the hand and lead them off to a safer place, when they sprang into the air a little way, smiling at him the while, and fell into the water, where they disappeared with a great splash that covered him with spray.

So astonished was the samurai, he hardly knew what to think, for they did not reappear. He made sure they must be two kappas (mythical animals), and with this idea in his mind he ran to the castle and gave information.

The Spirit of the Lotus Lily

The high officials held a meeting, and arranged to have the moats dragged and cleaned ; they felt that this should have been done when the young lord had succeeded his father.

The moats were dragged accordingly from end to end ; but no kappa was found. They came to the conclusion that the samurai had been indulging in fancies, and he was chaffed in consequence.

Some few weeks later another samurai, Murata Ippai, was returning in the evening from visiting his sweetheart, and his road led along the outer moat. The lotus blossoms were luxuriant ; and Ippai sauntered slowly on, admiring them and thinking of his lady-love, when suddenly he espied a dozen or more of the beautiful little boys playing near the water's edge. They had no clothing on, and were splashing one another with water.

'Ah !' reflected the samurai, 'these, surely, are the kappas, of which we were told before. Having taken the form of human beings, they think to deceive me ! A samurai is not frightened by such as they, and they will find it difficult to escape the keen edge of my sword.'

Ippai cast off his clogs, and, drawing his sword, proceeded stealthily to approach the supposed kappas. He approached until he was within some twenty yards ; then he remained hidden behind a bush, and stood for a minute to observe.

The children continued their play. They seemed to be perfectly natural children, except that they were all extremely beautiful, and from them was wafted a peculiar scent, almost powerful, but sweet, and resembling that of the lotus lily. Ippai was puzzled, and was almost inclined to sheathe his sword on seeing how innocent and unsuspecting the children looked; but he thought that he would not be acting up to the determination of a samurai if he changed his mind. Gripping his sword with renewed vigour, therefore, he dashed out from his hiding-place and slashed right and left among the supposed kappas.

Ippai was convinced that he had done much slaughter, for he had felt his sword strike over and over again, and had heard the dull thuds of things falling; but when he looked about to see what he had killed there arose a peculiar vapour of all colours which almost blinded him by its brilliance. It fell in a watery spray all round him.

Ippai determined to wait until the morning, for he could not, as a samurai, leave such an adventure unfinished; nor, indeed, would he have liked to recount it to his friends unless he had seen the thing clean through.

It was a long and dreary wait; but Ippai was equal to it and never closed his eyes during the night.

When morning dawned he found nothing but the stalks of lotus lilies sticking up out of the water in his vicinity.

'But my sword struck more than lotus stalks,' thought he. 'If I have not killed the kappas which I saw myself in human form, they must have been the spirits of the lotus. What terrible sin have I committed? It was by the spirits of the lotus that our Lord of Koriyama and his family were saved from death! Alas, what have I done—I, a samurai, whose every drop of blood belongs to his master? I have drawn my sword on my master's most

The Spirit of the Lotus Lily

faithful friends! I must appease the spirits by disembowelling myself.'

Ippai said a prayer, and then, sitting on a stone by the
side of the fallen lotus flowers, did harakiri.

The flowers continued to bloom; but after this no
more lotus spirits were seen.

XLIII

THE TEMPLE OF THE AWABI

IN Noto Province there is a small fishing-village called Nanao. It is at the extreme northern end of the mainland. There is nothing opposite until one reaches either Korea or the Siberian coast—except the small rocky islands which are everywhere in Japan, surrounding as it were by an outer fringe the land proper of Japan itself.

Nanao contains not more than five hundred souls. Many years ago the place was devastated by an earthquake and a terrific storm, which between them destroyed nearly the whole village and killed half of the people.

On the morning after this terrible visitation, it was seen that the geographical situation had changed. Opposite Nanao, some two miles from the land, had arisen a rocky island about a mile in circumference. The sea was muddy and yellow. The people surviving were so overcome and awed that none ventured into a boat for nearly a month afterwards; indeed, most of the boats had been destroyed. Being Japanese, they took things philosophically. Every one helped some other, and within a month the village looked much as it had looked before; smaller, and less

274

populated, perhaps, but managing itself unassisted by the outside world. Indeed, all the neighbouring villages had suffered much in the same way, and after the manner of ants had put things right again.

The fishermen of Nanao arranged that their first fishing expedition should be taken together, two days before the 'Bon.' They would first go and inspect the new island, and then continue out to sea for a few miles, to find if there were still as many tai fish on their favourite ground as there used to be.

It would be a day of intense interest, and the villages of some fifty miles of coast had all decided to make their ventures simultaneously, each village trying its own grounds, of course, but all starting at the same time, with a view of eventually reporting to each other the condition of things with regard to fish, for mutual assistance is a strong characteristic in the Japanese when trouble overcomes them.

At the appointed time two days before the festival the fishermen started from Nanao. There were thirteen boats. They visited first the new island, which proved to be simply a large rock. There were many rock fish, such as wrasse and sea-perch, about it; but beyond that there was nothing remarkable. It had not had time to gather many shell-fish on its surface, and there was but little edible seaweed as yet. So the thirteen boats went farther to sea, to discover what had occurred to their old and excellent tai grounds.

These were found to produce just about what they used to produce in the days before the earthquake; but the fishermen were not able to stay long enough to

275

make a thorough test. They had meant to be away all night; but at dusk the sky gave every appearance of a storm : so they pulled up their anchors and made for home.

As they came close to the new island they were surprised to see, on one side of it, the water for the space of 240 feet square lit up with a strange light. The light seemed to come from the bottom of the sea, and in spite of the darkness the water was transparent. The fishermen, very much astonished, stopped to gaze down into the blue waters. They could see fish swimming about in thousands ; but the depth was too great for them to see the bottom, and so they gave rein to all kinds of superstitious ideas as to the cause of the light, and talked from one boat to the other about it. A few minutes afterwards they had shipped their immense paddling oars and all was quiet. Then they heard rumbling noises at the bottom of the sea, and this filled them with consternation—they feared another eruption. The oars were put out again, and to say that they went fast would in no way convey an idea of the pace that the men made their boats travel over the two miles between the mainland and the island.

Their homes were reached well before the storm came on ; but the storm lasted for fully two days, and the fishermen were unable to leave the shore.

As the sea calmed down and the villagers were looking out, on the third day cause for astonishment came. Shooting out of the sea near the island rock were rays that seemed to come from a sun in the bottom of the sea. All the village congregated on the beach to see this extraordinary spectacle, which was discussed far into the night.

The Temple of the Awabi

Not even the old priest could throw any light on the subject. Consequently, the fishermen became more and more scared, and few of them were ready to venture to sea next day ; though it was the time for the magnificent sawara (king mackerel), only one boat left the shore, and that belonged to Master Kansuke, a fisherman of some fifty years of age, who, with his son Matakichi, a youth of eighteen and a most faithful son, was always to the fore when anything out of the common had to be done.

Kansuke had been the acknowledged bold fisherman of Nanao, the leader in all things since most could remember, and his faithful and devoted son had followed him from the age of twelve through many perils ; so that no one was astonished to see their boat leave alone.

They went first to the tai grounds and fished there during the night, catching some thirty odd tai between them, the average weight of which would be four pounds. Towards break of day another storm showed on the horizon. Kansuke pulled up his anchor and started for home, hoping to take in a hobo line which he had dropped overboard near the rocky island on his way out —a line holding some two hundred hooks. They had reached the island and hauled in nearly the whole line when the rising sea caused Kansuke to lose his balance and fall overboard.

Usually the old man would soon have found it an easy matter to scramble back into the boat. On this occasion, however, his head did not appear above water ; and so his son jumped in to rescue his father. He dived into water which almost dazzled him, for bright rays were

277

shooting through it. He could see nothing of his father, but felt that he could not leave him. As the mysterious rays rising from the bottom might have something to do with the accident, he made up his mind to follow them : they must, he thought, be reflections from the eye of some monster.

It was a deep dive, and for many minutes Matakichi was under water. At last he reached the bottom, and here he found an enormous colony of the awabi (ear-shells). The space covered by them was fully 200 square feet, and in the middle of all was one of gigantic size, the like of which he had never heard of. From the holes at the top through which the feelers pass shot the bright rays which illuminated the sea,—rays which are said by the Japanese divers to show the presence of a pearl. The pearl in this shell, thought Matakichi, must be one of enormous size—as large as a baby's head. From all the awabi shells on the patch he could see that lights were coming, which denoted that they contained pearls ; but wherever he looked Matakichi could see nothing of his father. He thought his father must have been drowned, and if so, that the best thing for him to do would be to regain the surface and repair to the village to report his father's death, and also his wonderful discovery, which would be of such value to the people of Nanao. Having after much difficulty reached the surface, he, to his dismay, found the boat broken by the sea, which was now high. Matakichi was lucky, however. He saw a bit of floating wreckage, which he seized ; and as sea, wind, and current helped him, strong swimmer as he was, it was not more than half an hour before he was ashore, relating to the

The Temple of the Awabi

villagers the adventures of the day, his discoveries, and the loss of his dear father.

The fishermen could hardly credit the news that what they had taken to be supernatural lights were caused by ear-shells, for the much-valued ear-shell was extremely rare about their district ; but Matakichi was a youth of such trustworthiness that even the most sceptical believed him in the end, and had it not been for the loss of Kansuke there would have been great rejoicing in the village that evening.

Having told the villagers the news, Matakichi repaired to the old priest's house at the end of the village, and told him also.

'And now that my beloved father is dead,' said he, 'I myself beg that you will make me one of your disciples, so that I may pray daily for my father's spirit.'

The old priest followed Matakichi's wish and said, 'Not only shall I be glad to have so brave and filial a youth as yourself as a disciple, but also I myself will pray with you for your father's spirit, and on the twenty-first day from his death we will take boats and pray over the spot at which he was drowned.'

Accordingly, on the morning of the twenty-first day after the drowning of poor Kansuke, his son and the priest were anchored over the place where he had been lost, and prayers for the spirit of the dead were said.

That same night the priest awoke at midnight ; he felt ill at ease, and thought much of the spiritual affairs of his flock.

Suddenly he saw an old man standing near the head of his couch, who, bowing courteously, said :

' I am the spirit of the great ear-shell lying on the bottom of the sea near Rocky Island. My age is over 1000 years. Some days ago a fisherman fell from his boat into the sea, and I killed and ate him. This morning I heard your reverence praying over the place where I lay, with the son of the man I ate. Your sacred prayers have taught me shame, and I sorrow for the thing I have done. By way of atonement I have ordered my followers to scatter themselves, while I have determined to kill myself, so that the pearls that are in my shell may be given to Matakichi, the son of the man I ate. All I ask is that you should pray for my spirit's welfare. Farewell ! '

Saying which, the ghost of the ear-shell vanished. Early next morning, when Matakichi opened his shutters to dust the front of his door, he found thereat what he took at first to be a large rock covered with seaweed, and even with pink coral. On closer examination Matakichi found it to be the immense ear-shell which he had seen at the bottom of the sea off Rocky Island. He rushed off to the temple to tell the priest, who told Matakichi of his visitation during the night.

The shell and the body contained therein were carried to the temple with every respect and much ceremony. Prayers were said over it, and, though the shell and the immense pearl were kept in the temple, the body was buried in a tomb next to Kansuke's, with a monument erected over it, and another over Kansuke's grave. Matakichi changed his name to that of Nichige, and lived happily.

There have been no ear-shells seen near Nanao since,

The Temple of the Awabi

but on the rocky island is erected a shrine to the spirit of the ear-shell.

NOTE.—A 3000-yen pearl which I know of was sold for 12 cents by a fisherman from the west. It came from a temple, belongs now to Mikomoto, and is this size.

281

XLIV

HUMAN FIREFLIES

In Funakami mura, Omi Province, lived an old farmer called Kanshiro. The like of him for honesty, charity, and piety had never been known—no, not even among the priesthood. Annually Kanshiro made pilgrimages to various parts of the country to say his prayers and do his duty towards the various deities, never thinking of his old age or of his infirmities. He was not strong, and suffered almost always from dysentery during the hot weather; consequently, he usually made his pilgrimages in cooler times.

In the eighth year of Kwansei, however, Kanshiro felt that he could not live another year, and, feeling that he should not like to miss making another pilgrimage to the great shrines at Ise, he resolved to take all risks and go in August, the hottest month.

The people in Funakami village subscribed one hundred yen for the venerable man, so that he might have the honour and credit of presenting a decent sum to the great shrines.

On a certain day, therefore, Kanshiro started alone,

with the money hung in a bag about his neck. He had walked from sunrise to sunset for two days, when on the third in great heat he arrived at the village of Myojo, feeling nearly dead with weakness, for he had another attack of his old complaint.

Kanshiro felt that he could not continue his journey while this lasted, especially as he considered himself in an unclean condition, unfit to carry the holy money which had been entrusted to him by his friends in Funakami. He went, accordingly, to the cheapest inn he could find, and confided both his story and the hundred yen to the landlord, saying :

'Sir, I am an old man, sick with dysentery. If you will take care of me for a day or two I shall be better. Keep also until I am well this sacred money, for it would not do for me to defile it by carrying it with me while I am unwell.'

Jimpachi, the innkeeper, bowed, and gave every assurance that Kanshiro's wish should be followed.

'Fear nothing,' said he : 'I will place the money in its bag in a safe place, and myself attend upon you until you are well, for such good men as you are rare.'

For five days the poor old man was very sick indeed ; but with his indomitable pluck he recovered, and on the sixth day decided to start again.

It was a fine day. Kanshiro paid his bill, thanked the landlord for his kindness, and was handed over his money-bag at the door. He did not look into the bag, because there were many coolies and pilgrims about. He did not wish these strangers to see that he carried much money. Instead of hanging it about his neck, as he had done before, he put the bag into his sack of clothing and food, and started off.

Towards midday Kanshiro stopped to rest and eat his cold rice under a pine tree. On examining his bag he found the hundred yen gone, and stones of the same weight placed in it instead. The poor man was greatly disconcerted. He did not even wait to eat his rice, but started back to the inn, which he reached at dusk. He explained as best he could the facts to Jimpachi, the innkeeper.

At first this worthy listened to the story with some sympathy; but when Kanshiro begged him to return the money he flew into a rage.

'You old rascal!' said he. 'A nice story you are telling to try and blackmail me! I'll give you a lesson that you will not forget.' And with that he struck the old man a severe blow on the chest, and then, seizing a stick, beat him unmercifully; the coolies joined in and thrashed him until he was nearly dead.

Poor old fellow! What could he do? Alone as he was, he crawled away half-dead; but he got to the sacred Ise shrines three days later, and after saying his prayers started back to Funakami. Here he arrived seriously ill. On telling his story, some believed him; but others did not. So overcome with grief was he, he sold his small property to refund the money, and with the rest he continued his pilgrimages to various temples and shrines. At last all his money was gone; but even then he continued his pilgrimages, begging food as he went.

Three years later he again visited Myojo village on his way to Ise, and here he learned that his enemy had since made a good deal of money, and now lived in quite a good house. Kanshiro went and found him, and said : ' Three years ago you stole the money entrusted to me. I sold my property to refund the people what they had given me to take to Ise. I have been a beggar and a wanderer ever since. Think not that I shall not be avenged. I shall be. You are young ; I am old. Vengeance will overtake you soon.'

Jimpachi still protested innocence and began to get angry, saying :

'You disreputable old blackguard, if you want a meal of rice say so ; but do not dare to threaten me.'

At this moment the watchman on his rounds took Kanshiro for a real beggar, and, seizing him by the arm, dragged him to the end of the village, and ordered him not to re-enter it, on pain of arrest ; and there the poor old man died of anger and weakness.

The good priest of the neighbouring temple took the body, and buried it with respect, saying prayers.

Jimpachi in the meantime, afflicted with a guilty conscience, became sick, until after a few days he was unable to leave his bed. After he had lost all power of movement a curious thing occurred. Thousands and thousands of fireflies came out of Kanshiro's tomb and flew to the bedroom of Jimpachi. They surrounded his mosquito-curtain and tried to force their way in. The top of the curtain was pressed down with them ; the air was foul with them ; the glimmer dazzled the sick man's eyes. No rest was possible.

The villagers came in to try and kill them ; but they could make no impression, for the string of flies from

Kanshiro's tomb continued as fast as others were killed. The fireflies went nowhere else than to Jimpachi's room, and there they only surrounded his bed.

One or two villagers, seeing this, said:

'It must be true that Jimpachi stole the money from the old man, and that this is his spirit's revenge.'

Then every one feared to kill the flies. Thicker and thicker they grew until they did at last make a hole in the mosquito-net, and then they settled all over Jimpachi. They got in his mouth, his nose, his ears, and his eyes. He kicked and screamed and lived thus in agony for twenty days, and after his death the flies disappeared completely.

XLV

THE CHRYSANTHEMUM HERMIT

MANY years ago there lived at the foot of the Mountains of Nambu, in Adachi gun, Saitama Prefecture, an old man named Kikuo, which means Chrysanthemum-Old-Man.

Kikuo was a faithful retainer of Tsugaru; he was then called Sawada Hayato. Kikuo was a man of great bodily strength and fine appearance, and had much to do with the efficiency of the small fighting force which protected the feudal lord, the castle, and the estates.

Nevertheless, an evil day came. The feudal lord's small force was overthrown; the estates and castle were lost. The lord and his faithful retainer, with the few survivors, escaped to the mountains, where they continued to think that a day might come when they would be able to have their revenge.

During the enforced idleness Kikuo, knowing his lord's love of flowers (especially of the chrysanthemum), made his mind up to devote all his spare time to making chrysanthemum beds. This, he thought, would lessen the pain of defeat and exile.

Ancient Tales and Folklore of Japan

The feudal lord was greatly pleased ; but his cares and anxieties were not abated. He sickened and died in great poverty, much to the sorrow of Kikuo and the rest of his followers. Kikuo wept night and day over the humble and lonely grave ; but he busied himself again to please the spirit of his lord by planting chrysanthemums round the tomb and tending them daily. By and by the border of flowers was thirty yards broad—to the wonder of all who saw. It was because of this that Hayato got the name of Chrysanthemum-Old-Man.

The chrysanthemum is in China a holy flower. Ancient history tells of a man called Hoso (great grandson of the Emperor Juikai) who lived to the age of 800 years without showing the slightest sign of decay. This was attributed to his drinking the dew of the chrysanthemum. Besides his devotion to flowers, Kikuo delighted in children ; from the village he called them to his poor hut, and as there was no schoolmaster he taught them to write, to read, and jujitsu. The children loved him, and the good villagers revered him as if he were a kind of god.

In about his eighty-second year Kikuo caught cold, and the fever which came with it gave him great pain.

During the daytime his pupils attended to his wants ; but at night the old man was alone in his cottage.

One autumn night he awoke and found standing about his veranda some beautiful children. They did not look quite like any children he knew. They were too beautiful and noble-looking to belong to the poor of the village.

' Kikuo Sama,' cried two of them, ' do not fear us,

288

The Chrysanthemum Hermit

though we are not real children. We are the spirits of the chrysanthemum which you love so much, and of which you have taken such care. We have come to tell you how sorry we are to see you so ill, although we have heard that in China there once lived a man called Hoso who lived for 800 years by drinking the dew which falls from the flowers. We have tried all we can to prolong your life; but we find that the Heavens do not allow that you should live to a much greater age than you have already reached. In thirty more days you will die. Make ready, therefore, to depart.'

Saying this, they all wept bitterly.

'Good-bye, then,' said Kikuo. 'I have no further hopes of living. Let my death be easy. In the next world I may be able to serve my old lord and master. The only thing that makes me sad to leave this world is you : I must for ever regret to leave my chrysanthemums!' Saying this, he smiled at them in affection.

'You have been very kind to us,' said the Kiku spirits, 'and we love you for it. Man rejoices at birth, and feels sad at death ; yet now you shed no tears. You say you do not mind dying except for leaving us. If you die we shall not survive, for it would be useless misery. Believe us when we say that we shall die with you.'

As the spirits of the chrysanthemums finished speaking a puff of wind came about the house, and they disappeared. As the day dawned the old man grew worse, and, strange to say, all the chrysanthemums began to fade —even those which were just beginning to bloom ;—the leaves crumpled up and dried.

As the spirits had foretold, at the end of the thirtieth

day the old man died. The Kiku flowers died then. Not one was left in the whole district. The villagers could not account for it. They buried the old man near his lord, and, thinking to honour and please him, planted, time after time, chrysanthemums near his grave ; but all faded and died as soon as they were planted.

The two little graves were at last given up, and they remain in their solitude, with wild grasses only growing about them.

XLVI

THE PRINCESS PEONY

MANY years ago at Gamogun, in the province of Omi, was a castle called Adzuchi-no-shiro. It was a magnificent old place, surrounded by walls and a moat filled with lotus lilies. The feudal lord was a very brave and wealthy man, Yuki Naizen-no-jo. His wife had been dead for some years. He had no son; but he had a beautiful daughter aged eighteen, who (for some reason which is not quite clear to me) was given the title of Princess. For a considerable period there had been peace and quiet in the land; the feudal lords were on the best of terms, and every one was happy. Amid these circumstances Lord Naizen-no-jo perceived that there was a good opportunity to find a husband for his daughter Princess Aya; and after a time the second son of the Lord of Ako, of Harima Province, was selected, to the satisfaction of both fathers, the affair having little to do with the principals. Lord Ako's second son had viewed his bride with approval, and she him. One may say that young people are bound to approve each other when

291

it is the parents' wish that they be united. Many suicides result from this.

Princess Aya made her mind up to try and love her prospective husband. She saw nothing of him; but she thought of him, and talked of him.

One evening when Princess Aya was walking in the magnificent gardens by the moonlight, accompanied by her maids-in-waiting, she wandered down through her favourite peony bed to the pond where she loved to gaze at her reflection on the nights of the full moon, to listen to frogs, and to watch the fireflies.

When nearing the pond her foot slipped, and she would have fallen into the water had it not been that a young man appeared as if by magic and caught her. He disappeared as soon as he had put her on her feet again. The maids-of-honour saw her slip; they saw a glimmer of light, and that was all; but Princess Aya had seen more. She had seen the handsomest young man she could imagine. 'Twenty-one years old,' she said to O Sadayo San, her favourite maid, 'he must have been—a samurai of the highest order. His dress was covered with my favourite peonies, and his swords were richly mounted. Oh that I could have seen him a minute longer, to thank him for saving me from the water! Who can he be? And how could he have got into our gardens, through all the guards?'

So spoke the Princess to her maids, directing them at the same time that they were to say a word to no one, for fear that her father should hear, find the young man, and behead him for trespass.

After this evening Princess Aya fell sick. She could

not eat or sleep, and turned pale. The day for her marriage with the young Lord of Ako came and went without the event; she was far too sick for that. The best of the doctors had been sent from Kyoto, which was then the capital; but none of them had been able to do anything, and the maid grew thinner and thinner. As a last resource, the Lord Naizen-no-jo, her father, sent for her most confidential maid and friend, O Sadayo, and demanded if she could give any reason for his daughter's mysterious sickness. Had she a secret lover? Had she a particular dislike for her betrothed?

'Sir,' said O Sadayo, 'I do not like to tell secrets; but here it seems my duty to your lordship's daughter as well as to your lordship. Some three weeks ago, when the moon was at its full, we were walking in the peony beds down near the pond where the Princess loves to be. She stumbled and nearly fell into the water, when a strange thing happened. In an instant a most beautiful young samurai appeared and held her up, thus preventing her from falling into the pond. We could all see the glimmer of him; but your daughter and I saw him most distinctly. Before your daughter could thank him he had disappeared. None of us could understand how it was possible for a man to get into the gardens of the Princess, for the gates of the castle are guarded on all sides, and the Princess's garden is so much better guarded than the rest that it seems truly incredible that a man could get in. We maids were asked to say nothing for fear of your lordship's anger. Since that evening it is that our beloved Princess Aya has been sick, sir. It is sickness of the heart. She is deeply in love with the young samurai she saw for so brief a space. Indeed, my lord, there never was such a handsome man in the world before, and if we cannot find him the young Princess, I fear, will die.'

'How is it possible for a man to get into the grounds?' said Lord Yuki Naizen-no-jo. 'People say foxes and badgers assume the figures of men sometimes; but even so it is impossible for such supernatural beings to enter my castle grounds, guarded as it is at every opening.'

That evening the poor Princess was more wearily unhappy than ever before. Thinking to enliven her a little, the maids sent for a celebrated player on the biwa, called Yashaskita Kengyo. The weather being hot, they were sitting on the gallery (engawa); and while the musician was playing 'Dannoura' there appeared suddenly from behind the peonies the same handsome young samurai. He was visible to all this time—even to the peonies embroidered on his dress.

'There he is! there he is!' they cried; at which he instantly disappeared again. The Princess was highly excited, and seemed more lively than she had been for days; the old Daimio grew more puzzled than ever when he heard of it.

Next night, while two of the maids were playing for their mistress—O Yae San the flute, and O Yakumo the koto—the figure of the young man appeared again. A thorough search having been made during the day in the immense peony beds with absolutely no result, not even the sign of a footmark, the thing was increasingly strange.

A consultation was held, and it was decided by the lord of the castle to invite a veteran officer of great strength and renown, Maki Hiogo, to capture the youth

The Princess Peony

should he appear that evening. Maki Hiogo readily consented, and at the appointed time, dressed in black and consequently invisible, concealed himself among the peonies.

Music seemed to have a fascination for the young samurai. It was while music was being played that he had made his appearances. Consequently, O Yae and O Yakumo resumed their concert, while all gazed eagerly towards the peony beds. As the ladies played a piece called 'Sofuren,' there, sure enough, arose the figure of a young samurai, dressed magnificently in clothes which were covered with embroidered peonies. Every one gazed at him, and wondered why Maki Hiogo did not jump up and catch him. The fact was that Maki Hiogo was so much astonished by the noble bearing of the youth that at first he did not like to touch him. Recovering himself, and thinking of his duty to his lord, he stealthily approached the young man, and, seizing him round the waist, held him tight. After a few seconds Maki Hiogo felt a kind of wet steam falling on his face; by degrees it made him faint; and he fell to the ground, still grasping the young samurai, for he had made up his mind that he would secure him.

Every one had seen the scuffle, and some of the guards came hurrying to the place. Just as they reached the spot Maki Hiogo came to his senses, and shouted: 'Come, gentlemen! I have caught him. Come and see!' But on looking at what he held in his arms he discovered it to be only a large peony!

By this time the Lord Naizen-no-jo had arrived at the spot where Maki Hiogo lay, and so had the Princess Aya and her maids. All were astounded and mystified except the Daimio himself, who said :

'Ah ! it is as I said. No fox or badger spirit could pass our guards and get into this garden. It is the spirit of the peony flower that took the form of a prince.' Turning to his daughter and her maids, he said : 'You must take this as a compliment, and pay great respect to the peony, and show the one caught by Maki Hiogo kindness as well by taking care of it.'

The Princess Aya carried the flower back to her room, where she put it in a vase of water and placed it near her pillow. She felt as if she had her sweetheart with her. Day by day she got better. She tended the peony herself, and, strange to say, the flower seemed to get stronger and stronger, instead of fading. At last the Princess recovered. She became radiantly beautiful, while the peony continued to remain in perfect bloom, showing no sign of dying.

The Princess Aya being now perfectly well, her father could no longer put off the wedding. Consequently, some days later, the Lord of Ako and his family arrived at the Castle, and his second son was married to the Princess.

As soon as the wedding was over the peony was found still in its vase—but dead and withered. The villagers always after this, instead of speaking of the Princess Aya, or Aya Hime, called her Botan Hime or Peony Princess.

XLVII

THE MEMORIAL CHERRY TREE [1]

In the compound or enclosure of the temple called
Bukoji, at Takatsuji (high cross street), formerly called
Yabugashita, which means 'under the bush,' in Kyoto, a
curio-dealer had his little shop. His name was Kihachi.

Kihachi had not much to sell ; but what little he had
was usually good. Consequently, his was a place that the
better people looked into when they came to pray—to
see, if not to buy ;—for they knew full well if there was a
good thing to be bought, Kihachi bought it. It was a
small and ancient kind of Christie's, in fact, except that
things were not sold by auction. One day, the day on
which this story starts, Kihachi was sitting in his shop
ready either to gossip or to sell, when in walked a young
knight or court noble—'Kuge,' the Japanese called him
in those days ; and very different was such an one from a
knight of a feudal lord or of a Daimio, who was usually
a blusterer. This particular knight had been to the
temple to pray.

[1] This story begins on the 17th of February in the second year of Kenkyu. As the
first year of Kenkyu was in 1190 and the last in 1199, the precise date is February 17,
1192.

'You have many pretty and interesting things here,' said he. 'May I come in and look at them until this shower of rain has passed? My name is Sakata, and I belong to the court.'

'Come in, come in,' said Kihachi, 'by all means. Some of my things are pretty, and all are undoubtedly good; but the gentry part with little at present. One wants to live two lives of a hundred years each in my trade—one hundred of distress, revolution, and trouble, wherein one may collect the things cheap; and the next hundred of peace, wherein one may sell them and enjoy the proceeds. My business is rotten and unprofitable; yet, in spite of that, I love the things I buy, and often look at them long before I put them up for sale. Where, sir, are you bound for? I see that you are going to travel—by the clothes you wear and carry.'

'That's true,' answered Sakata: 'you are very shrewd. I am going to travel as far as Toba, in Yamato, to see my dearest friend, who has been taken suddenly and mysteriously ill. It is feared he may not live until I get there!'

'At Toba!' answered the old curio-dealer. 'Pardon me if I ask the name of your friend?'

'Certainly,' said Sakata. 'My friend's name is Matsui.'

'Then,' said the curio-dealer, 'he is the gentleman who is said to have killed the ghost or spirit of the old cherry tree near Toba, growing in the grounds of the temple in which he lives at present with the priests. The people say that this cherry tree is so old that the spirit left it. It appeared in the form of a beautiful woman, and Matsui, either fearing or not liking it,

298

The Memorial Cherry Tree

killed it, with the result, they say, that from that very evening, which was about ten days ago, your friend Matsui has been sick; and I may add that when the spirit was killed the tree withered and died.'

Sakata, thanking Kihachi for this information, went on his way, and eventually found his friend Matsui being carefully nursed by the priest of the Shonen Temple, Toba, with whom he was closely connected.

Soon after the young knight had left the old curio-dealer Kihachi in his shop it began to snow, and so it continued, and appeared likely to continue for some time. Kihachi, therefore, put up his shutters and retired to bed, as is often very sensibly done in Japan; and he no doubt retired with many old wood-carvings to rub and give an ancient appearance to during the period of darkness.

Not very late in the evening there was a knock at the shutters. Kihachi, not wishing to get out of his warm bed, shouted: 'Who are you? Come back in the morning. I do not feel well enough to get up to-night.'

'But you must—you must get up! I am sent to sell you a good kakemono,'[1] called the voice of a young girl, so sweetly and entreatingly that the old curio-dealer got up, and after much fumbling with his numbed fingers opened the door.

Snow had fallen thickly; but now it was clear moonlight, and Kihachi saw standing before him a beautiful girl of fifteen, barefooted, and holding in her hands a kakemono half-unfolded.

'See,' said she, 'I have been sent to sell you this!' She was the daughter of Matsui of Toba, she said.

[1] Picture.

299

The old man called her in, and saw that the picture was that of a beautiful woman, standing up. It was well done, and the old man took a fancy to it.

'I will give you one rio for it,' said he ; and to his astonishment the young girl accepted his offer eagerly—so much so that he thought that perhaps she had stolen it. Being a curio-dealer, he said nothing on that point, but paid her the money. She ran away with haste.

'Yes : she has stolen it—stolen it, undoubtedly,' muttered the old man. 'But what am I supposed to know about that? The kakemono is worth fully 50 rio if it is worth a cent, and not often do such chances come to me.'

So delighted was Kihachi with his purchase, he lit his lamp, hung the picture in his kakemono corner, and sat watching it. It was indeed a beautiful woman well painted, and worth more even than the 50 rio he at first thought. But, by all the saints, it seems to change ! Yes : it is no longer a beautiful woman. The face has changed to that of a fearful and horrible figure. The face of the woman has become haggard. It is covered with blood. The eyes open and shut, and the mouth gasps. Kihachi feels blood dropping on his head ; it comes from a wound in the woman's shoulder. To shut out so horrid a sight, he put his head under the bed-clothes and remained thus, sleeplessly, until dawn.

When he opened his eyes, the kakemono was the same as when he had bought it : a beautiful woman. He supposed that his delight in having made a good bargain must have made him dream : so he thought nothing more about the horror.

Kihachi, however, was mistaken. The kakemono again

kept him awake all night, showing the same bloody face, and occasionally even shrieking. Kihachi got no sleep, and perceived that instead of a cheap bargain he had got a very expensive one ; for he felt that he must go to Toba and return it to Matsui, and he knew that he could claim no expenses.

After fully two days of travel, Kihachi reached the Shonen Temple, near Toba, where he asked to see Matsui. He was ushered ceremoniously into his room. The invalid was better ; but on being handed the kakemono with the figure of a lady painted on it he turned pale, tore it to fragments, and threw it into the temple fire ('irori'[1]) ; after which he jumped in with his daughter himself, and both were burned to death.

Kihachi was sick for many days after this sight. The story soon spread over the whole surrounding country.

Prince Nijo, Governor of Kyoto, had a thorough inquiry made into the circumstances of the case ; and it was found beyond doubt that the trouble to Matsui and his family came through his having killed the spirit of the old cherry tree. The spirit, to punish him and show that there was invisible life in old and dead things and often of the best, appeared to Matsui as a beautiful woman being killed ; the spirit went into his beautiful picture and haunted him.

Prince Nijo had a fine young cherry tree planted on the spot of the old to commemorate the event, and it is called the 'Memorial Cherry Tree' to this day.

---

[1] The story says 'furnace' ; but, unless cremation went on in those days, it must have been the 'irori' (open floor fire) or else (if a Shinto temple) an open-air bonfire, which is lit on certain days.

XLVIII

THE 'JIROHEI' CHERRY TREE, KYOTO

THE Japanese say that ghosts in inanimate nature generally have more liveliness than ghosts of the dead.   There
is an old proverb which says something to the effect that
'the ghosts of trees love not the willow'; by which, I
suppose, is meant that they do not assimilate.   In Japanese
pictures of ghosts there is nearly always a willow tree.
Whether Hokusai, the ancient painter, or Okyo Maruyama, a famous painter of Kyoto of more recent date, was
responsible for the pictures with ghosts and willow trees,
I do not know; but certainly Maruyama painted many
ghosts under willow trees—the first from his wife, who
lay sick.

Exactly what this has to do with the following story I
cannot see; but my story-teller began with it.

In the northern part of Kyoto is a Shinto temple called
Hirano.   It is celebrated for the fine cherry trees that
grow there.   Among them is an old dead tree which is
called 'Jirohei,' and is much cared for; but the story
attached to it is little known, and has not been told, I
believe, to a European before.

302

The 'Jirohei' Cherry Tree, Kyoto

During the cherry blossom season many people go to view the trees, especially at night.

Close to the Jirohei cherry tree, many years ago, was a large and prosperous tea-house, once owned by Jirohei, who had started in quite a small way. So rapidly did he make money, he attributed his success to the virtue of the old cherry tree, which he accordingly venerated. Jirohei paid the greatest respect to the tree, attending to its wants. He prevented boys from climbing it and breaking its branches. The tree prospered, and so did he.

One morning a samurai (of the blood-and-thunder kind) walked up to the Hirano Temple, and sat down at Jirohei's tea-house, to take a long look at the cherry blossom. He was a powerful, dark-skinned, evil-faced man about five feet eight in height.

'Are you the landlord of this tea-house?' asked he.

'Yes, sir,' Jirohei answered meekly: 'I am. What can I bring you, sir?'

'Nothing: I thank you,' said the samurai. 'What a fine tree you have here opposite your tea-house!'

'Yes, sir: it is to the fineness of the tree that I owe my prosperity. Thank you, sir, for expressing your appreciation of it.'

'I want a branch off the tree,' quoth the samurai, 'for a geisha.'

'Deeply as I regret it, I am obliged to refuse your request. I must refuse everybody. The temple priests gave orders to this effect before they let me erect this place. No matter who it may be that asks, I must refuse. Flowers may not even be picked off the tree, though they may be gathered when they fall. Please, sir, remember that there is an old proverb which tells us to cut the plum tree for our vases, but not the cherry ! '

' You seem to be an unpleasantly argumentative person for your station in life,' said the samurai. ' When I say that I want a thing I mean to have it : so you had better go and cut it.'

' However much you may be determined, I must refuse,' said Jirohei, quietly and politely.

' And, however much you may refuse, the more determined am I to have it. I as a samurai said I should have it. Do you think that you can turn me from my purpose ? If you have not the politeness to get it, I will take it by force.' Suiting his action to his words, the samurai drew a sword about three feet long, and was about to cut off the best branch of all. Jirohei clung to the sleeve of his sword arm, crying :

' I have asked you to leave the tree alone ; but you would not. Please take my life instead.'

' You are an insolent and annoying fool : I gladly follow your request '; and saying this the samurai stabbed Jirohei slightly, to make him let go the sleeve. Jirohei did let go ; but he ran to the tree, where in a further struggle over the branch, which was cut in spite of Jirohei's defence, he was stabbed again, this time fatally. The samurai, seeing that the man must die, got away as quickly as possible, leaving the cut branch in full bloom on the ground.

Hearing the noise, the servants came out of the house, followed by Jirohei's poor old wife.

It was seen that Jirohei himself was dead ; but he clung to the tree as firmly as in life, and it was fully an hour before they were able to get him away.

The 'Jirohei' Cherry Tree, Kyoto

From this time things went badly with the tea-house. Very few people came, and such as did come were poor and spent but little money. Besides, from the day of the murder of Jirohei the tree had begun to fade and die; in less than a year it was absolutely dead. The tea-house had to be closed for want of funds to keep it open. The old wife of Jirohei had hanged herself on the dead tree a few days after her husband had been killed.

People said that ghosts had been seen about the tree, and were afraid to go there at night. Even neighbouring tea-houses suffered, and so did the temple, which for a time became unpopular.

The samurai who had been the cause of all this kept his secret, telling no one but his own father what he had done; and he expressed to his father his intention of going to the temple to verify the statements about the ghosts. Thus on the third day of March in the third year of Keio (that is, forty-two years ago) he started one night alone and well armed, in spite of his father's attempts to stop him. He went straight to the old dead tree, and hid himself behind a stone lantern.

To his astonishment, at midnight the dead tree suddenly came out into full bloom, and looked just as it had been when he cut the branch and killed Jirohei.

On seeing this he fiercely attacked the tree with his keen-edged sword. He attacked it with mad fury, cutting and slashing; and he heard a fearful scream which seemed to him to come from inside the tree.

After half an hour he became exhausted, but resolved to wait until daybreak, to see what damage he had wrought. When day dawned, the samurai found his father lying on the ground, hacked to pieces, and of course dead. Doubtless the father had followed to try and see that no harm came to the son.

The samurai was stricken with grief and shame. Nothing was left but to go and pray to the gods for forgiveness, and to offer his life to them, which he did by disembowelling himself.

From that day the ghost appeared no more, and people came as before to view the cherry-bloom by night as well as by day; so they do even now. No one has ever been able to say whether the ghost which appeared was the ghost of Jirohei, or that of his wife, or that of the cherry tree which had died when its limb had been severed.

XLIX

THE SNOW GHOST

PERHAPS there are not many, even in Japan, who have heard of the 'Yuki Onna' (Snow Ghost). It is little spoken of except in the higher mountains, which are continually snowclad in the winter. Those who have read Lafcadio Hearn's books will remember a story of the Yuki Onna, made much of on account of its beautiful telling, but in reality not better than the following.

Up in the northern province of Echigo, opposite Sado Island on the Japan Sea, snow falls heavily. Sometimes there is as much as twenty feet of it on the ground, and many are the people who have been buried in the snows and never found until the spring. Not many years ago three companies of soldiers, with the exception of three or four men, were destroyed in Aowomori; and it was many weeks before they were dug out, dead of course.

Mysterious disappearances naturally give rise to fancies in a fanciful people, and from time immemorial the Snow Ghost has been one with the people of the North; while those of the South say that those of the North take so much saké that they see snow-covered trees as women.

307

Be that as it may, I must explain what a farmer called Kyuzaemon saw.

In the village of Hoi, which consisted only of eleven houses, very poor ones at that, lived Kyuzaemon. He was poor, and doubly unfortunate in having lost both his son and his wife. He led a lonely life.

In the afternoon of the 19th of January of the third year of Tem-po—that is, 1833—a tremendous snowstorm came on. Kyuzaemon closed the shutters, and made himself as comfortable as he could. Towards eleven o'clock at night he was awakened by a rapping at his door ; it was a peculiar rap, and came at regular intervals. Kyuzaemon sat up in bed, looked towards the door, and did not know what to think of this. The rapping came again, and with it the gentle voice of a girl. Thinking that it might be one of his neighbour's children wanting help, Kyuzaemon jumped out of bed ; but when he got to the door he feared to open it. Voice and rapping coming again just as he reached it, he sprang back with a cry : 'Who are you ? What do you want ?'

'Open the door ! Open the door !' came the voice from outside.

'Open the door ! Is that likely until I know who you are and what you are doing out so late and on such a night ?'

'But you must let me in. How can I proceed farther in this deep snow ? I do not ask for food, but only for shelter.'

'I am very sorry ; but I have no quilts or bedding. I can't possibly let you stay in my house.'

'I don't want quilts or bedding,—only shelter,' pleaded the voice.

The Snow Ghost

'I can't let you in, anyway,' shouted Kyuzaemon. 'It is too late and against the rules and the law.'

Saying which, Kyuzaemon rebarred his door with a strong piece of wood, never once having ventured to open a crack in the shutters to see who his visitor might be. As he turned towards his bed, with a shudder he beheld the figure of a woman standing beside it, clad in white, with her hair down her back. She had not the appearance of a ghost; her face was pretty, and she seemed to be about twenty-five years of age. Kyuzaemon, taken by surprise and very much alarmed, called out:

'Who and what are you, and how did you get in? Where did you leave your geta.'[1]

'I can come in anywhere when I choose,' said the figure, 'and I am the woman you would not let in. I require no clogs; for I whirl along over the snow, sometimes even flying through the air. I am on my way to visit the next village; but the wind is against me. That is why I wanted you to let me rest here. If you will do so I shall start as soon as the wind goes down; in any case I shall be gone by the morning.'

'I should not so much mind letting you rest if you were an ordinary woman. I should, in fact, be glad; but I fear spirits greatly, as my forefathers have done,' said Kyuzaemon.

'Be not afraid. You have a butsudan?'[2] said the figure.

'Yes: I have a butsudan,' said Kyuzaemon; 'but what can you want to do with that?'

[1] Clogs.
[2] Family altar, in which the figures of various gods are set, and also the family mortuary tablets.

'You say you are afraid of the spirits, of the effect that I may have upon you. I wish to pay my respects to your ancestors' tablets and assure their spirits that no ill shall befall you through me. Will you open and light the butsudan?'

'Yes,' said Kyuzaemon, with fear and trembling: 'I will open the butsudan, and light the lamp. Please pray for me as well, for I am an unfortunate and unlucky man; but you must tell me in return who and what spirit you are.'

'You want to know much; but I will tell you,' said the spirit. 'I believe you are a good man. My name was Oyasu. I am the daughter of Yazaemon, who lives in the next village. My father, as perhaps you may have heard, is a farmer, and he adopted into his family, and as a husband for his daughter, Isaburo. Isaburo is a good man; but on the death of his wife, last year, he forsook his father-in-law and went back to his old home. It is principally for that reason that I am about to seek and remonstrate with him now.'

'Am I to understand,' said Kyuzaemon, 'that the daughter who was married to Isaburo was the one who perished in the snow last year? If so, you must be the spirit of Oyasu or Isaburo's wife?'

'Yes: that is right,' said the spirit. 'I was Oyasu, the wife of Isaburo, who perished now a year ago in the great snowstorm, of which to-morrow will be the anniversary.'

Kyuzaemon, with trembling hands, lit the lamp in the little butsudan, mumbling 'Namu Amida Butsu; Namu Amida Butsu' with a fervour which he had never felt before. When this was done he saw the figure of the

310

The Snow Ghost

Yuki Onna (Snow Spirit) advance ; but there was no sound
of footsteps as she glided to the altar.

Kyuzaemon retired to bed, where he promptly fell
asleep ; but shortly afterwards he was disturbed by the
voice of the woman bidding him farewell. Before he had
time to sit up she disappeared, leaving no sign ; the fire
still burned in the butsudan.

Kyuzaemon got up at daybreak, and went to the next
village to see Isaburo, whom he found living with his
father-in-law, Yazaemon.

'Yes,' said Isaburo : 'it was wrong of me to leave my
late wife's father when she died, and I am not surprised
that on cold nights when it snows I have been visited
continually by my wife's spirit as a reproof. Early this
morning I saw her again, and I resolved to return. I
have only been here two hours as it is.'

On comparing notes Kyuzaemon and Isaburo found
that directly the spirit of Oyasu had left the house of
Kyuzaemon she appeared to Isaburo, at about half-an-
hour after midnight, and stayed with him until he had
promised to return to her father's house and help him to
live in his old age.

That is roughly my story of the Yuki Onna. All
those who die by the snow and cold become spirits of
snow, appearing when there is snow ; just as the spirits of
those who are drowned in the sea only appear in stormy
seas.

Even to the present day, in the north, priests say
prayers to appease the spirits of those who have died
by snow, and to prevent them from haunting people who
are connected with them.

L

THE SNOW TOMB[1]

MANY years ago there lived a young man of the samurai class who was much famed for his skill in fencing in what was called the style of Yagyu. So adept was he, he earned by teaching, under his master, no less than thirty barrels of rice and two 'rations'—which, I am told, vary from one to five sho—a month. As one sho is ·666 feet square, our young samurai, Rokugo Yakeiji, was well off.

The seat of his success was at Minami-wari-gesui, Hongo Yedo. His teacher was Sudo Jirozaemon, and the school was at Ishiwaraku.

Rokugo was in no way proud of his skill. It was the modesty of the youth, coupled with cleverness, that had prompted the teacher to make his pupil an assistant-master. The school was one of the best in Tokio, and there were over 100 pupils.

One January the pupils were assembled to celebrate the New Year, and on this the seventh day of it were

---

[1] Told to me by Fukuchi, in connection with the fire-lights in foxes. Carefully translated by Mr. Watanabe, of the Prefectural Government.

drinking nanakusa—a kind of sloppy rice in which seven grasses and green vegetables are mixed, said to keep off all diseases for the year. The pupils were engaged in ghost stories, each trying to tell a more alarming one than his neighbour, until the hair of many was practically on end, and it was late in the evening. It was the custom to keep the 7th of January in this way, and they took their turns by drawing numbers. One hundred candles were placed in a shed at the end of the garden, and each teller of a story took his turn at bringing one away, until they had all told a story; this was to upset, if possible, the bragging of the pupil who said he did not believe in ghosts and feared nothing.

At last it came to the turn of Rokugo. After fetching his candle from the end of the garden, he spoke as follows:

'My friends, listen to my story. It is not very dreadful; but it is true. Some three years ago, when I was seventeen, my father sent me to Gifu, in Mino Province. I reached on the way a place called Nakimura about ten o'clock in the evening. Outside the village, on some wild uncultivated land, I saw a curious fireball. It moved here and there without noise, came quite close to me and then went away again, moving generally as if looking for something; it went round and round over the same ground time after time. It was generally five feet off the ground; but sometimes it went lower. I will not say that I was frightened, because subsequently I went to the Miyoshiya inn, and to bed, without mentioning what I had seen to any one; but I can assure you all that I was very glad to be in the house. Next morning my curiosity got the better of me. I told the landlord what I had seen, and he recounted to me a story. He said : " About 200 years ago a great battle was fought here, and the general who was defeated was himself killed. When his body was recovered, early in the action, it was found to be headless. The soldiers thought that the head must have been stolen by the enemy. One, more anxious than the rest to find his master's head, continued to search while the action went on. While searching he himself was killed. Since that evening, 200 years ago, the fireball has been burning after ten o'clock. The people from that time till now have called it *Kubi sagashi no hi*." [1] As the master of the inn finished relating this story, my friends, I felt an unpleasant sensation in the heart. It was the first thing of a ghostly kind that I had seen.'

The pupils agreed that the story was strange. Rokugo pushed his toes into his 'geta' (clogs), and started to fetch his candle from the end of the garden. He had not proceeded far into the garden before he heard the voice of a woman. It was not very dark, as there was snow on the ground ; but Rokugo could see no woman. He had got as far as the candles when he heard the voice again, and, turning suddenly, saw a beautiful woman of some eighteen summers. Her clothes were fine. The obi (belt) was tied in the tateyanojiri (shape of the arrow standing erect, as an arrow in a quiver). The dress was all of the pine-and-bamboo pattern, and her hair was done in the shimada style. Rokugo stood looking at her with wonder and admiration. A minute's reflection

---

[1] The head-seeking fire.

showed him that it could be no girl, and that her beauty had almost made him forget that he was a samurai.

'No : it is no real woman : it is a ghost. What an opportunity for me to distinguish myself before all my friends!'

Saying which, he drew his sword, tempered by the famous Moriye Shinkai, and with one downward cut severed head, body, and all, into halves.

He ran, seized a candle, and took it back to the room where the pupils were awaiting him ; there he told the story, and begged them to come and see the ghost. All the young men looked at one another, none of them being partial to ghosts in what you may call real life. None cared to venture ; but by and by Yamamoto Jonosuke, with better courage than the rest, said, 'I will go,' and dashed off. As soon as the other pupils saw this, they also, gathering pluck, went forth into the garden.

When they came to the spot where the dead ghost was supposed to lie, they found only the remains of a snow man which they themselves had made during the day ; and this was cut in half from head to foot, just as Rokugo had described. They all laughed. Several of the young samurai were angry, for they thought that Rokugo had been making fools of them ; but when they returned to the house they soon saw that Rokugo had not been trifling. They found him sitting with an air of great haughtiness, and thinking that his pupils would now indeed see how able a swordsman he was.

However, they looked at Rokugo scornfully, and addressed him thus :

'Indeed, we have received remarkable evidence of your ability. Even the small boy who throws a stone at a dog would have had the courage to do what you did!'

Rokugo became angry, and called them insolent. He lost his temper to such an extent that for a moment his hand flew to his sword hilt, and he even threatened to kill one or two of them.

The samurai apologised for their rudeness, but added: 'Your ghost was only the snow man we made ourselves this morning. That is why we tell you that a child need not fear to attack it.'

At this information Rokugo was confounded, and he in his turn apologised for his temper; nevertheless, he said he could not understand how it was possible for him to mistake a snow man for a female ghost. Puzzled and ashamed, he begged his friends not to say any more about the matter, but keep it to themselves; thereupon he bade them farewell and left the house.

It was no longer snowing; but the snow lay thick upon the ground. Rokugo had had a good deal of saké, and his gait was not over-steady as he made his way home to Warigesui.

When he passed near the gates of the Korinji Temple he noticed a woman coming faster than he could understand through the temple grounds. He leaned against the fence to watch her. Her hair was dishevelled, and she was all out of order. Soon a man came running behind her with a butcher's knife in his hand, and shouted as he caught her:

'You wicked woman! You have been unfaithful to

your poor husband, and I will kill you for it, for I am his friend.'

Stabbing her five or six times, he did so, and then moved away. Rukugo, resuming his way homewards, thought what a good friend must be the man who had killed the unfaithful wife. A bad woman justly rewarded with death, thought he.

Rokugo had not gone very far, however, when, to his utter astonishment, he met face to face the woman whom he had just seen killed. She was looking at him with angry eyes, and she said :

'How can a brave samurai watch so cruel a murder as you have just seen, enjoying the sight ?'

Rokugo was much astonished.

'Do not talk to me as if I were your husband,' said he, 'for I am not. I was pleased to see you killed for being unfaithful. Indeed, if you are the ghost of the woman I shall kill you myself !' Before he could draw his sword the ghost had vanished.

Rokugo continued his way, and on nearing his house he met a woman, who came up to him with horrible face and clenched teeth, as if in agony.

He had had enough troubles with women that evening. They must be foxes who had assumed the forms of women, thought he, as he continued to gaze at this last one.

At that moment he recollected that he had heard of a fact about fox-women. It was that fire coming from the bodies of foxes and badgers is always so bright that even on the darkest night you can tell the colour of their hair, or even the figures woven in the stuffs they wear, when assuming the forms of men or women ; it is clearly visible at one ken (six feet). Remembering this, Rokugo approached a little closer to the woman ; and, sure enough, he could see the pattern of her dress, shown up as if fire were underneath. The hair, too, seemed to have fire under it.

Knowing now that it was a fox he had to do with, Rokugo drew his best sword, the famous one made by Moriye, and proceeded to attack carefully, for he knew he should have to hit the fox and not the spirit of the fox in the woman's form. (It is said that whenever a fox or a badger transforms itself into human shape the real presence stands beside the apparition. If the apparition appears on the left side, the presence of the animal himself is on the right.)

Rokugo made his attack accordingly, killing the fox and consequently the apparition.

He ran to his house, and called up his relations, who came flocking out with lanterns. Near a myrtle tree which was almost two hundred years old, they found the body—not of fox or badger, but—of an otter. The animal was carried home. Next day invitations were issued to all the pupils at the fencing-school to come and see it, and a great feast was given. Rokugo had wiped away a great disgrace. The pupils erected a tomb for the beast ; it is known as 'Yukidzuka' (The Snow Tomb), and is still to be seen in the Korinji Temple at Warigesui Honjo, in Tokio.

LI

THE DRAGON-SHAPED PLUM TREE

In the year 1716 of the Kyoho Era—191 years ago—there lived at Momoyama Fushimi, an old gardener, Hambei, who was loved and respected for his kindliness of nature and his great honesty. Though a poor man, Hambei had saved enough to live on ; and he had inherited a house and garden from his father. Consequently, he was happy. His favourite pastime was tending the garden and an extraordinarily fine plum tree known in Japan as of the furyo kind (which means 'lying dragon'). Such trees are of great value, and much sought after for the arrangement of gardens. Curiously enough, though one may see many beautiful ones, trees growing on mountains or on wild islands, they are very rarely touched except near the larger commercial centres. Indeed, the Japanese have almost a veneration for some of these fantastic furyo-shaped trees, and leave them alone, whether they be pines or plums.

The tree in question Hambei loved so much that no offer people could make would induce him to part with it. So notoriously beautiful were the tints and curves of this

old stunted tree, large sums had many times been offered
for it.   Hambei loved it not only for its beauty but also
because it had belonged to his father and grandfather.
Now in his old age, with his wife in her dotage and his
children gone, it was his chief companion.   In the autumn
he tended it in its untidiness of dead and dying leaves.
He felt sorry and sympathetic for it in its cold and bare
state in November and December ; but in January he was
happily employed in watching the buds which would
blossom in February.   When they did bloom it was his
custom to let the people come at certain hours daily to
see the tree and listen to stories of historical facts, and also
to stories of romance, regarding the plum tree, of which
the Japanese mind is ever full.   When this again was over
Hambei pruned and tied the tree.   In the hot season he
lingered under it smoking his pipe, and was often rewarded
for his care by two or three dozen delicious plums, which
he valued and loved as much almost as if they had been
his own offspring.

Thus, year after year, the tree had become so much
Hambei's companion that a king's ransom would not
have bought it from him.

Alas ! no man is destined to be let alone in this world.
Some one is sure, sooner or later, to covet his property.
It came to pass that a high official at the Emperor's
court heard of Hambei's furyo tree and wanted it for his
own garden.   This dainagon sent his steward, Kotaro
Naruse, to see Hambei with a view to purchase, never
for a moment doubting that the old gardener would
readily sell if the sum offered were sufficient.

Kotaro Naruse arrived at Momoyama Fushimi, and

was received with due ceremony. After drinking a cup of tea, he announced that he had been sent to inspect and make arrangements to take the furyo plum tree for the dainagon.

Hambei was perplexed. What excuse for refusal should he make to so high a personage? He made a fumbling and rather stupid remark, of which the clever steward soon took advantage.

'On no account,' said Hambei, 'can I sell the old tree. I have refused many offers for it already.'

'I never said that I was sent to buy the tree for money,' said Kotaro. 'I said that I had come to make arrangements by which the dainagon could have it conveyed carefully to his palace, where he proposes to welcome it with ceremony and treat it with the greatest kindness. It is like taking a bride to the palace for the dainagon. Oh, what an honour for the plum tree, to be united by marriage with one of such illustrious lineage! You should indeed be proud of such a union for your tree! Please be counselled by me and grant the dainagon's wish!'

What was Hambei now to say? Such a lowly-born person, asked by a gallant samurai to grant a favour to no less a person than the dainagon!

'Sir,' he answered, 'your request in behalf of the dainagon has been so courteously made that I am completely prevented from refusing. You must, however, tell the dainagon that the tree is a present, for I cannot sell it.'

Kotaro was greatly pleased with the success of his manœuvres, and, drawing from his clothes a bag, said:

'Please, as is customary on making a gift, accept this small one in return.'

To the gardener's great astonishment, the bag contained gold. He returned it to Kotaro, saying that it was impossible to accept the gift; but on again being pressed by the smooth-tongued samurai he retracted.

The moment Kotaro had left, Hambei regretted this. He felt as if he had sold his own flesh and blood—as if he had sold his daughter—to the dainagon.

That evening he could not sleep. Towards midnight his wife rushed into his room, and, pulling him by the sleeve, shouted:

'You wicked old man! You villainous old rascal! At your age too! Where did you get that girl? I have caught you! Don't tell me lies! You are going to beat me now—I see by your eyes. I am not surprised if you avenge yourself in this way—you must feel an old fool!'

Hambei thought his wife had gone off her head for good this time. He had seen no girl.

'What is the matter with you, obaa San?'[1] he asked. 'I have seen no girl, and do not know what you are talking about.'

'Don't tell me lies! I saw her! I saw her myself when I went down to get a cup of water!'

'Saw, saw—what do you mean?' said Hambei. 'I think you have gone mad, talking of seeing girls!'

'I did see her! I saw her weeping outside the door. And a beautiful girl she was, you old sinner,—only seventeen or eighteen years of age.'

---

[1] Old woman.

The Dragon-Shaped Plum Tree

Hambei got out of bed, to see for himself whether his wife had spoken the truth or had gone truly mad.

On reaching the door he heard sobbing, and, on opening, beheld a beautiful girl.

'Who are you, and why here?' asked Hambei.

'I am the Spirit of the Plum Tree, which for so many years you have tended and loved, as did your father before you. I have heard—and grieve greatly at it—that an arrangement has been made whereby I am to be removed to the dainagon's gardens. It may seem good fortune to belong to a noble family, and an honour to be taken into it. I cannot complain; yet I grieve at being moved from where I have been so long, and from you, who have so carefully tended to my wants. Can you not let me remain here a little longer—as long as I live? I pray you, do!'

'I have made a promise to send you off on Saturday to the dainagon in Kyoto; but I cannot refuse your plea, for I love to have you here. Be easy in your mind, and I will see what can be done,' said Hambei.

The spirit dried its tears, smiled at Hambei, and disappeared as it were into the stem of the tree, while Hambei's wife stood looking on in wonder, not at all reassured that there was not some trick on her husband's part.

At last the fatal Saturday on which the tree was to be removed arrived, and Kotaro came with many men and a cart. Hambei told him what had happened—of the tree's spirit and of what it had implored of him.

'Here! take the money, please,' said the old man. 'Tell the story to the dainagon as I tell it to you, and surely he will have mercy.'

Kotaro was angry, and said :

'How has this change come about? Have you been drinking too much saké, or are you trying to fool me? You must be careful, I warn you ; else you shall find yourself headless. Even supposing the spirit of the tree did appear to you in the form of a girl, did it say that it would be sorry to leave your poor garden for a place of honour in that of the dainagon? You are a fool, and an insulting fool—how dare you return the dainagon's present? How could I explain such an insult to him, and what would he think of me? As you are not keeping your word, I will take the tree by force, or kill you in place of it.'

Kotaro was greatly enraged. He kicked Hambei down the steps, and, drawing his sword, was about to cut off his head, when suddenly there was a little puff of wind scented with plum blossom, and then there stood in front of Kotaro the beautiful girl, the Spirit of the Plum Tree!

'Get out of my way, or you will get hurt,' shouted Kotaro.

'No : I will not go away. You had better kill me, the spirit that has brought such trouble, instead of killing a poor innocent old man,' said the spirit.

'I don't believe in the spirits of plum trees,' said Kotaro. 'That you are a spirit is evident ; but you are only that of an old fox. So I will comply with your request, and at all events kill you first.'

No sooner had he said this than he made a cut with his sword, and he distinctly felt that he cut through a body. The girl disappeared, and all that fell was a branch of the plum tree and most of the flowers that were blooming.

The Dragon-Shaped Plum Tree

Kotaro now realised that what the gardener had told him was true, and made apologies accordingly.

'I will carry this branch to the dainagon,' said he, 'and see if he will listen to the story.'

Thus was Hambei's life saved by the spirit of the tree.

The dainagon heard the story, and was so moved that he sent the old gardener a kind message, and told him to keep the tree and the money, as an expression of his sorrow for the trouble which he had brought about.

Alas, however, the tree withered and died soon after Kotaro's cruel blow and in spite of Hambei's care. The dead stump was venerated for many years.

LII

THE CHESSBOARD CHERRY TREE[1]

In olden times, long before the misfortunes of Europeanisation came to Japan, there lived at Kasamatsu, in Nakasatani, near Shichikwai mura Shinji gun, Hitachi Province, a hotheaded old Daimio, Oda Sayemon. His castle stood on the top of a pine-clad hill about three miles from what is now known as Kamitachi station on the Nippon Railway. Sayemon was noted for his bravery as a soldier, for his abominable play at go (or goban), and for his bad temper and violence when he lost, which was invariably.

His most intimate friends among his retainers had tried hard to reform his manners after losing at go; but it was hopeless. All those who won from him he struck in the face with a heavy iron fan, such as was carried by warriors in those days; and he would just as readily have drawn his sword and cut his best friend's head off as be interfered with on those occasions. To be invited to

[1] This story (with the exception of the ghost) I believe to be true, for the 'seppuku' of Saito Ukon is just the kind of reasoning that would have been held out in the days of the story, and is even to-day possible in many cases. See a case—quoted by Professor Chamberlain—of the servant to an Englishman at Yokohama, and note the number of cases in the recent war.

The Chessboard Cherry Tree

play go with their lord was what all his bold samurai dreaded most. At last it was agreed among them that sooner than suffer the gross indignity of being struck by him when they won they would let him win. After all, it did not much matter, there being no money on the game. Thus Sayemon's game grew worse and worse, for he never learned anything ; yet in his conceit he thought he was better than everybody.

On the 3rd of March, in honour of his little daughter O Chio, he gave a dinner-party to his retainers. The 3rd of March is the Dolls' Day (Hina-no-sekku)—the day upon which girls bring out their dolls. People go from house to house to see them, and the little owners offer you sweet white saké in a doll's cup with much ceremony. Sayemon, no doubt, chose this day of feasting as a compliment to his daughter—for he gave sweet white saké after their food, to be drunk to the health of the dolls, instead of men's saké, which the guests would have liked much better. Sayemon himself absolutely disliked sweet saké. So as soon as the feast was over he called Saito Ukon, one of his oldest and most faithful warriors, to come and play go with him, leaving the others to drink. Ukon, curiously enough, had not played with his lord before, and he was delighted that he had been chosen. He had made up his mind to die that evening after giving his master a proper lesson.

In a luxuriously decorated room there was placed a goban (chessboard) with two go-cases containing the men, which are made of white and black stones. The white stones are usually taken by the superior player and the black by the inferior. Without any apology or explanation,

Ukon took the case containing the white stones, and began to place them as if he were without question the superior player.

Sayemon's temper began to work up; but he did not show it. So many games of go had his retainers allowed him to win lately, he was fully confident that he should win again, and that Ukon would have in addition to apologise for presuming to take the white stones.

The game ended in a win for Ukon.

'I must have another game,' said Sayemon. 'I was careless in that one. I will soon show you how I can beat you when I try.'

Again Sayemon was beaten—this time not without losing his temper, for his face turned red, his eyes looked devilish, and with a bullying voice full of passion he roared for a third game.

This also Ukon won. Sayemon's wrath knew no bounds. Seizing his iron fan, he was about to smite Ukon a violent blow in the face. His opponent caught him by the wrist, and said:

'My Lord, what ideas have you about games? Your Lordship seems to think curiously about them! It is the better player who wins; while the inferior must fail. If you fail to beat me at go, it is because you are the inferior player. Is this manner of your Lordship's in taking defeat from a superior up to the form of bushido in a samurai, as we are taught it? Be counselled by me, your faithful retainer, and be not so hasty with your anger — it ill befits one in your Lordship's high position.' And, with a look full of reproof at Sayemon, Ukon bowed almost to the ground.

The Chessboard Cherry Tree

'You insolent rascal!' roared Sayemon. 'How dare you speak to me like that? Don't move! Stand as you are, with your head bowed, so that I may take it off.'

'Your sword is to kill your enemies, not your retainers and friends,' said Ukon. 'Sheathe your sword, my Lord. You need not trouble yourself to kill me, for I have already done seppuku[1] in order to offer you the advice which I have given, and to save all others. See here, my Lord!' Ukon opened his clothes and exhibited an immense cut across his stomach.

Sayemon stood for a minute taken aback, and while he thus stood Ukon spoke to him once more, telling him how he must control his temper and treat his subjects better.

On hearing this advice again Sayemon's passion returned. Seizing his sword, he rushed upon Ukon, and, crying, 'Not even by your dying spirit will I allow myself to be advised,' made a furious cut at Ukon's head. He missed, and cut the go-board in two instead. Then, seeing that Ukon was dying rapidly, Sayemon dropped beside him, crying bitterly and saying:

'Much do I regret to see you thus die, oh faithful Ukon! In losing you I lose my oldest and most faithful retainer. You have served me faithfully and fought most gallantly in all my battles. Pardon me, I beg of you! I will take your advice. It was surely a sign by the gods that they were displeased at my conduct when they made me miss your head with my sword and cut the go-board.'

Ukon was pleased to find his lord at last repentant. He said:

[1] 'Disembowelled myself.'

'I shall not even in death forget the relation between master and servant, and my spirit shall be with you and watch over your welfare as long as you live.'

Then Ukon breathed his last.

Sayemon was so much moved by the faithfulness of Ukon that he caused him to be buried in his own garden, and he buried the broken go-board with him. From that time on the Lord Sayemon's conduct was completely reformed. He was good and kind to all his subjects, and all his people were happy.

A few months after Ukon's death, a cherry tree sprang out of his grave. In three years the tree grew to be a fine one and bloomed luxuriantly.

On the 3rd of March in the third year, the anniversary of Ukon's death, Sayemon was surprised to find it suddenly in bloom. He was looking at it, and thinking of watering it himself, as usual on that day, when he suddenly saw a faint figure standing by the stem of the tree. Just as he said, 'You are, I know, the spirit of faithful Saito Ukon,' the figure disappeared. Sayemon ran to the tree, to pour water over the roots, when he noticed that the bark of some feet of the stem had all cracked up to the size and shape of the squares of a go-board! He was much impressed. For years afterwards—until, in fact, Sayemon's death—the ghost of Ukon appeared on each 3rd of March.

A fence was built round the tree, which was held sacred ; and even to the present, they say, the tree is to be seen.

LIII

THE PRECIOUS SWORD 'NATORI NO HOTO'

IDE KAMMOTSU was a vassal of the Lord of Nakura town, in Kishu. His ancestors had all been brave warriors, and he had greatly distinguished himself in a battle at Shizugatake, which took its name from a mountain in the province of Omi. The great Hideyoshi had successfully fought in the same place so far back as in the eleventh year of the Tensho Era 1573-1592—that is, 1584—with Shibata Katsuiye. Ide Kammotsu's ancestors were loyal men. One of them as a warrior had a reputation second to none. He had cut the heads off no fewer than forty-eight men with one sword. In due time this weapon came to Ide Kammotsu, and was kept by him as a most valuable family treasure. Rather early in life Kammotsu found himself a widower. His young wife left a son, called Fujiwaka. By and by Kammotsu, feeling lonely, married a lady whose name was Sadako. Sadako later bore a son, who was called Goroh. Twelve or fourteen years after that, Kammotsu himself died, leaving the two sons in charge of Sadako. Fujiwaka was at that time nineteen years of age.

Sadako became jealous of Fujiwaka, knowing him, as the elder son, to be the heir to Kammotsu's property. She tried by every means to put her own son Goroh first.

In the meantime a little romance was secretly going on between a beautiful girl called Tae, daughter of Iwasa Shiro, and young Fujiwaka. They had fallen in love with each other, were holding secret meetings to their hearts' content, and vowing promises of marriage. At last they were found out, and Sadako made their conduct a pretext for driving Fujiwaka out of the house and depriving him of all rights in the family property.

Attached to the establishment was a faithful old nurse, Matsue, who had brought up Fujiwaka from his infancy. She was grieved at the injustice which had been done ; but little did she think of the loss of money or of property in comparison with the loss of the sword, the miraculous sword, of which the outcast son was the proper owner. She thought night and day of how she might get the heirloom for young Fujiwaka.

After many days she came to the conclusion that she must steal the sword from the Ihai (shrine—or rather a wooden tablet in the interior of the shrine, bearing the posthumous name of an ancestor, which represents the spirit of that ancestor).

One day, when her mistress and the others were absent, Matsue stole the sword. No sooner had she done so than it became apparent that it would be some months perhaps before she should be able to put it into the hands of the rightful owner. For of Fujiwaka nothing had been heard since his stepmother had driven him out. Fearing that she might be accused, the faithful Matsue dug a hole in the garden near the ayumiya—a little house, such as is kept in every Japanese gentleman's garden for performing the Tea Ceremony in,—and there she put the sword, meaning to keep it hidden until such time as she should be able to present it to Fujiwaka.

Sadako, having occasion to go to the butsudan the day after, missed the sword ; and, knowing O Matsue to have been the only servant left in the house at the time, taxed her with the theft of the sword.

Matsue denied the theft, thinking that in the cause of justice it was right of her to do so ; but it was not easy to persuade Sadako, who had Matsue confined in an outhouse and gave orders that neither rice nor water was to be given her until she confessed. No one was allowed to go near Matsue except Sadako herself, who kept the key of the shed, which she visited only once every four or five days.

About the tenth day poor Matsue died from starvation. She had stuck faithfully to her resolution that she would keep the sword and deliver it some day to her young master, the lawful heir. No one knew of Matsue's death. The evening on which she had died found Sadako seated in an old shed in a remote part of the garden, and trying to cool herself, for it was very hot.

After she had sat for about half-an-hour she suddenly saw the figure of an emaciated woman with dishevelled hair. The figure appeared from behind a stone lantern, glided along towards the place where Sadako was seated, and looked full into Sadako's face.

Sadako immediately recognised Matsue, and upbraided her loudly for breaking out of her prison.

'Go back, you thieving woman!' said she. 'I have not half finished with you yet. How dare you leave the place where you were locked up and come to confront me?'

The figure gave no answer, but glided slowly along to the spot where the sword had been buried, and dug it up.

Sadako watched carefully, and, being no coward, rushed at the figure of Matsue, intending to seize the sword. Figure and sword suddenly disappeared.

Sadako then ran at top speed to the shed where Matsue had been imprisoned, and flung the door open with violence. Before her lay Matsue dead, evidently having been so for two or three days; her body was thin and emaciated.

Sadako perceived that it must have been the ghost of O Matsue that she had seen, and mumbled 'Namu Amida Butsu; Namu Amida Butsu,' the Buddhist prayer asking for protection or mercy.

After having been driven from his family home, Ide Fujiwaka had wandered to many places, begging his food. At last he got some small employment, and was able to support himself at a very cheap inn at Umamachi Asakusa Temple.

One midnight he awoke and found standing at the foot of his bed the emaciated figure of his old nurse, bearing in her hands the precious sword, the heirloom valued beyond all others. It was wrapped in scarlet and gold brocade, as it had been before, and it was laid reverentially by the figure of O Matsue at Fujiwaka's feet.

The Precious Sword 'Natori No Hoto'

'Oh, my dear nurse,' said he, 'how glad am I ——' Before he had closed his sentence the figure had disappeared.

My story-teller did not say what became of Sadako or of her son.

LIV

THE WHITE SERPENT GOD

HARADA KURANDO was one of the leading vassals of the Lord of Tsugaru. He was a remarkable swordsman, and gave lessons in fencing. Next in seniority to Harada among the vassals was one Gundayu, who also taught fencing ; but he was no match for the famous Harada, and consequently was somewhat jealous.

One day, to encourage the art of fencing amongst his vassals, the Daimio summoned all his people and ordered them to give an exhibition in his presence.

After the younger vassals had performed, the Daimio gave an order that Harada Kurando and Hira Gundayu should have a match. To the winner, he said, he would present a gold image of the Goddess of Kwannon.

Both men fenced their best. There was great excitement. Gundayu had never done so well before ; but Harada was too good. He won the match, receiving the gold image of Kwannon from the hands of the Daimio amid loud cheering.

Gundayu left the scene of the encounter, boiling over with jealousy and vowing vengeance. Four of his most faithful companions left with him, and said they would help him to waylay and assault Harada that very evening. Having arranged this cowardly plan, they proceeded to hide on the road which Harada must traverse on his return home.

For three hours they lay there with evil intentions. At last in the moonlight they saw Harada come staggering along, for, as was natural on such an occasion, he had, with friends, been indulging in saké freely.

Gundayu and his four companions sprang out at him, Gundayu shouting, 'Now you will have to fight me to the death.'

Harada tried to draw his sword, but was slow, his head whirling. Gundayu did not wait, but cut him to the ground, killing him. The five villains then hunted through his clothes, found the golden image of Kwannon, and ran off, never again to appear on the domains of the Lord of Tsugaru.

When the body of Harada was found there was great grief.

Yonosuke, Harada's son, a boy of sixteen, vowed to avenge his father's death, and obtained from the Daimio special permission to kill Gundayu as and when he chose ; the disappearance of Gundayu was sufficient evidence that he had been the murderer.

Yonosuke set out that day on his hunt for Gundayu. He wandered about the country for five long years without getting the slightest clue ; but at the end of that time, by the guidance of Buddha, he located his enemy at Gifu, where he was acting as fencing-master to the feudal lord of that place.

Yonosuke found that it would be difficult to get at Gundayu in an ordinary way, for he hardly ever left the castle. He decided, therefore, to change his name to that of Ippai, and to apply for a place in Gundayu's house as a chugen (a samurai's private attendant).

In this Ippai (as we shall now call him) was particularly lucky, for, as Gundayu was in want of such an attendant, he got the place.

On the 24th of June a great celebration was held at the house of Gundayu, it being the fifth anniversary of his service to the clan. He put his stolen golden image of Kwannon on the tokonoma (the part of a Japanese room, raised five inches above the floor, where pictures and flowers are placed), and a dinner, with saké, was set before it. A dinner was given by Gundayu to his friends, all of whom drank so deeply that they fell asleep.

Next day the image of Kwannon had disappeared. It was not to be found. A few days later Ippai became ill, and, owing to poverty, was unable to buy proper medicine ; he went from bad to worse. His fellow-servants were kind to him ; but they could do nothing that improved his condition. Ippai did not seem to care ; he lay in his bed and seemed almost pleased to be getting weaker and weaker. All he asked was that a branch of his favourite omoto (*rhodea japonica*) should be kept in a vase before his bed, so that he might see it continually ; and this simple request was naturally complied with.

In the autumn Ippai passed quietly away and was buried. After the funeral, when the servants were cleaning out the room in which he had died, it was noticed with astonishment that a small white snake was curled round the vase containing the omoto. They tried to remove it ; but it coiled itself tighter. At last they threw the vase into the pond, not caring to have such a thing about them.

To their astonishment, the water had no effect on the snake, which continued to cling to the vase. Feeling that there was something uncanny about the snake, they wanted to get it farther away. So they cast a net, brought the vase and snake to shore again, and threw them into a stream. Even that made but little difference, the snake slightly changing its position so as to keep the branch of omoto from falling out of the vase.

By this time there was consternation among the servants, and the news spread to the different houses within the castle gates. Some samurai came down to the stream to see, and found the white snake still firmly coiled about the vase and branch. One of the samurai drew his sword and made a slash at the snake, which let go and escaped ; but the vase was broken, and, to the alarm of all, the image of the Kwannon fell out into the stream, together with a stamped permit from the Feudal Lord of Tsugaru to kill a certain man, whose name was left blank.

The samurai who had broken the vase and found the lost treasure seemed particularly pleased, and hastened to tell Gundayu the good news ; but, instead of being pleased, that person showed signs of fear. He became deadly pale when he heard the story of the death of Ippai and of the extraordinary appearance of the mysterious white snake. He trembled. He realised that Ippai was no less a person than Yonosuke, son of Harada, whose appearance after the murder he had always feared.

True to the spirit of a samurai, however, Gundayu 'pulled himself together,' and professed great pleasure to the person who had brought the image of Kwannon. Moreover, to celebrate the occasion, he gave a great feast that evening. Curiously enough, the samurai who had broken the vase and recovered the image became suddenly ill, and was unable to attend.

After he had dismissed his guests, at about 10 P.M., Gundayu retired to his bed. In the middle of the night he awoke with what he took to be a terrible nightmare. There was a choking sensation at his throat; he squirmed and twisted; gurgling noises proceeded from his mouth to such an extent that he aroused his wife, who in terror struck a light. She saw a white snake coiled tightly round her husband's throat; his face was purple, and his eyeballs stood out two inches from his face.

She called for help; but it was too late. As the young samurai came rushing in, their fencing-master was black in the face and dead.

Next day there was a close investigation. Messengers were despatched to the Lord of Tsugaru to inquire as to the history of the murdered Harada Kurando, father of Yonosuke, or 'Ippai,' and as to that of Gundayu, who had been in his employ for five years. Having ascertained the truth, the Lord of Gifu, moved by the zeal of Yonosuke in discharging his filial duties, returned the golden image of Kwannon to the bereaved family of Harada; and in commemoration he worshipped the dead snake at a shrine erected at the foot of Kodayama Mountain. The spirit is still known as Hakuja no Myojin, The White Serpent God.

LV

A FESTIVAL OF THE AWABI FISH

MANAZURU-MINATO is situated on a small promontory of the same name. It faces the Sagama Bay, famed for beauty; at its back are mountains rising gradually and overtopped in the distance by the majestic Fuji; to the north on clear days the sandy shores of Kozu and Oiso, twenty-five miles off, seem to be almost within arm's reach. Some people have compared the beauties of Manazuru-zaki from cape to river with the place in China called 'Sekiheki' by the celebrated poet of that country, Sotoba, who wrote 'Sekiheki no Fu,' the Ode to Sekiheki.

Many years ago Minamoto-no-Yoritomo, after his defeat at the battle of Ishibashiyama, fled to Manazuru-minato, and stayed there for a few days while waiting for favourable weather to cross to the opposite side, the province of Awa. One can still see, I am told, the cave in which he hid, which retains its old name, 'Shitoto-iwa.' The scenery on the coast is magnificent. The rocks rise sheer out of the sea and enclose a perfect little bay on the inside of Manazuru Zaki (Cape). There the fishermen erected a quiet little shrine, 'Kibune Jinja,' where they

341

worshipped the goddess who guards the fishing of their coast. They had but little to complain of in the Bay of Manazuru. The waters were deep, and always well-stocked with fish such as tai ; in due season came the sawara (giant mackerel) and all the smaller, migratory fishes, including the sardine and the anchovy. The fishermen had naught to complain of until about forty years ago, when a strange thing happened.

On the 24th of June, a person from some inland place arrived for a few days' sea-bathing. He was no swimmer, and he was drowned the first day. His body was never recovered, though the fishermen did all they could to find it. From this event onwards for a full two years the abundance of fish in the bay grew less and less, until it became difficult to catch enough to eat. The situation was serious in the extreme.

Some of the elder fishermen attributed the change to the stranger who had been drowned.

'It is his unrecovered body,' they said, 'that has made our sacred waters change. The uncleanness has offended Gu gun O Hime, our goddess. It will never do to go on as we are. We must hold a special festival at the temple of Kibune Jinja.'

Accordingly, the head priest, Iwata, was approached. He was pleased with the idea, and a certain day was fixed upon.

On the appointed evening hundreds of fishermen gathered together with torches in one hand and Shirayu or Gohei[1] papers fastened on a bamboo in the other.

---

[1] Gohei papers are a Shinto emblem, representing gifts of cloth to the deity, usually the god Kami. Some say Gohei represent, in their curious cutting, the Kami beating dora, a gong used in worship.

A Festival of the Awabi Fish

They formed into procession and advanced towards the shrine from various directions, beating gongs. At the temple the priest read from the sacred books, and prayed to the goddess that had watched over them and their fisheries not to desert them because their waters had been polluted by a dead body. They would search for it by every means in their power and cleanse the bay.

Suddenly, while the priest was praying, a light, the brilliance of which nearly blinded the fishermen, flashed out of the water. The priest stopped for a moment; a rumbling noise was heard at the bottom of the sea; and then there arose to the surface a goddess of surpassing beauty (probably Kwannon Gioran). She looked at the ceremony which was being held on shore for a full hour, and then disappeared with another flash, leaving the sound of roaring waves.

The priest and the elder fishermen considered matters, and came to the conclusion that what they had seen was indeed their goddess, and that she had been pleased at their ceremony. Also, they thought the dead body must still be at the bottom of the bay, directly under the spot whence the flashes of light and the goddess herself had appeared. It was arranged that two young virgins who could dive should be sent down at the spot to see, and two were accordingly chosen—Saotome and Tamajo. Wrapped in white skirts, these maidens were taken in a boat to where the flashes and the goddess had appeared. The girls dived, reached the bottom, and searched for the body of the man drowned two years before. Instead of finding it, they saw only a small but dazzling light. Curiosity led them to the spot, and there they found hundreds upon hundreds of awabi (ear-shells) fastened upon a rock six feet in height and twenty-five or thirty in length. Whenever the fish moved they were obliged to raise their shells, and it was the glitter of the pearls inside that had attracted the damsels. This rock must have been the tomb of the drowned, or else the home of the goddess.

Saotome and Tamajo returned to the surface, each having taken from the rock a large shell to show the priest. As they came to the shore cheers were given in their honour, and the priest and the fishermen crowded round them.

On learning about the awabi shells, which they had never before heard of as being in the bay, they came to the conclusion that it was not uncleanness that kept the fish away. The lights thrown from the brilliant nacreous shells, and pearls inside them, must be the cause. Many times have we heard of the awabi flying. They must have flown here at some time within two years. The fishermen resolved to remove them. It was evident that the goddess had appeared in the light so as to show what it was that kept the fish away.

No time was lost. Many hundreds of men and women went down and cleared the place ; and the fish began to return to Manazuru-minato.

At the suggestion of the priest, Iwata, there is held on every 24th of June a matsuri (festival). The fishermen light torches and go to the shrine for worship all the night through. This is called the 'Awabi Festival' of Kibune.

A Festival of the Awabi Fish

NOTE.—The story was told to me by a man who knows nothing of shell-fish. He told the story as of the osari, a kind of cockle-shell dug out of the sand at low tide. It is impossible that this story could have referred to other shell-fish than haliotis (the ear-shell), or the awabi, or the regular pearl oyster.

Diving women have seen the 'flight' of haliotis and described it to me. If one feels disposed to leave a rock, they all feel the same impulse and go. Thus it is that large old haliotis sometimes appear on a rock some fifteen fathoms deep when not one was there the day before; and they go with equal quickness. For a thousand years or more the same rocks have been haunted. And divers keep their finds at the bottom of the sea a great secret—at least, so I observe at Toshi.

LVI

THE SPIRIT OF A WILLOW TREE SAVES
FAMILY HONOUR

LONG ago there lived in Yamada village, Sarashina Gun, Shinano Province, one of the richest men in the northern part of Japan. For many generations the family had been rich, and at last the fortune descended in the eighty-third generation to Gobei Yuasa. The family had no title ; but the people treated them almost with the respect due to a princely house. Even the boys in the street, who are not given to bestowing either compliments or titles of respect, bowed ceremoniously when they met Gobei Yuasa. Gobei was the soul of good-nature, sympathetic to all in trouble.

The riches which Gobei had inherited were mainly money and land, about which he worried himself very little ; it would have been difficult to find a man who knew less and cared less about his affairs than Gobei. He spent his money freely, and when he came to think of accounts his easy nature let them all slide. His great pleasures were painting kakemono pictures, talking to his friends, and eating good things. He ordered his steward

346

not to worry him with unsatisfactory accounts of crops or any other disagreeable subjects. 'The destiny of man and his fate is arranged in Heaven,' said he. Gobei was quite celebrated as a painter, and could have made a considerable amount of money by selling his kakemonos; but no—that would not be doing credit to his ancestors and his name.

One day, while things were going from bad to worse, and Gobei was seated in his room painting, a friend came to gossip. He told Gobei that the village people were beginning to talk seriously about a spirit that had been seen by no fewer than three of them. At first they had laughed at the man who saw the ghost; the second man who saw it they were inclined not to take quite seriously; but now it had been seen by one of the village elders, and so there could be no doubt about it.

'Where do they see it?' asked Gobei.

'They say that it appears under your old willow tree between eleven and twelve o'clock at night—the tree that hangs some of its boughs out of your garden into the street.'

'That is odd,' remarked Gobei. 'I can remember hearing of no murder under that tree, nor even spirit connection with any of my ancestors; but there must be something if three of our villagers have seen it. Yet, again, where there is an old willow tree some one is sure to say, sooner or later, that he has seen a ghost. If there is a spirit there, I wonder whose it is? I should like to paint the ghost if I could see it, so as to leave it to my descendants as the last ominous sign on the road which has led to the family's ruin. That I shall make an effort to do. This very evening I will sit up to watch for the thing.'

Never had Gobei been seized with such energy before. He dismissed his friend, and went to bed at four o'clock in the afternoon, so as to allow himself to be up at ten o'clock. At that hour his servant awoke him; but even then he could not be got up before eleven. By twelve o'clock, midnight, Gobei was at last out in his garden, hidden in bushes facing the willow. It was a bright night, and there was no sign of any ghost until after one o'clock, when clouds passed over the moon. Just when Gobei was thinking of going back to bed, he beheld, arising from the ground under the willow, a thin column of white smoke, which gradually assumed the form of a charming girl.

Gobei stared in astonishment and admiration. He had never thought that a ghost could be such a vision of beauty. Rather had he expected to see a white, wild-eyed, dishevelled old woman with protruding bones, the spectacle of whom would freeze his marrow and make his teeth clatter.

Gradually the beautiful figure approached Gobei, and hung its head, as if it wished to address him.

'Who and what are you?' cried Gobei. 'You seem too beautiful, to my mind, to be the spirit of one who is dead. If you are indeed spectral, do tell me, if you may, whose spirit you are and why you appear under this willow tree!'

'I am not the spirit or ghost of man, as you say,' answered the spirit, 'but the spirit of this willow tree.'

'Then why do you leave the tree now, as they tell

me you have done several times within the last ten days?'

'I am, as I say, the spirit of this willow, which was planted here in the twenty-first generation of your family. That is now about six centuries ago. I was planted to mark the place where your wise ancestor buried a treasure —twenty feet below the ground, and fifteen from my stem, facing east. There is a vast sum of gold in a strong iron chest hidden there. The money was buried to save your house when it was about to fall. Never hitherto has there been danger; but now, in your time, ruin has come, and it is for me to step forth and tell you how by the foresight of your ancestor you have been saved from disgracing the family name by bankruptcy. Pray dig the strong box up and save the name of your house. Begin as soon as you can, and be careful in future.'

Then she vanished.

Gobei returned to his house, scarcely believing it possible that such good luck had come to him as the spirit of the willow tree planted by his wise ancestor had said. He did not go to bed, however. He summoned a few of his most faithful servants, and at daybreak began digging. What excitement there was when at nineteen feet they struck the top of an iron chest! Gobei jumped with delight; and it may almost be said that his servants did the same, for to see their honoured master's name fall into the disgrace of bankruptcy would have caused many of them to disembowel themselves.

They tore and dug with all their might, until they had the huge and weighty case out of the hole. They broke off the top with pickaxes, and then Gobei saw a

Ancient Tales and Folklore of Japan

collection of old sacks. He seized one of these; but the age of it was too great. It burst, and sent rolling out over a hundred immense old-fashioned oblong gold coins of ancient times, which must have been worth £30 each. Gobei Yuasa's hand shook. He could hardly realise as true the good fortune which had come to him. Bag after bag was pulled out, each containing a small fortune, until finally the bottom of the box was reached. Here was found a letter some six hundred years of age, saying:

'He of my descendants who is obliged to make use of the treasure to save our family reputation will read aloud and make known that this treasure has been buried by me, Fuji Yuasa, in the twenty-first generation of our family, so that in time of need or danger a future generation will be able to fall back upon it and save the family name. He whose great misfortune necessitates the use of the treasure must say: "Greatly do I repent the folly that has brought the affairs of our family so low, and necessitated the assistance of an early ancestor. I can only repay such by diligent attention to my household affairs, and also show high appreciation and give kindness to the willow tree which has so long been watching and guarding my ancestor's treasure. These things I vow to do. I shall reform entirely."'

Gobei Yuasa read this out to his servants and to his friends. He became a man of energy. His lands and farms were properly taken care of, and the Yuasa family regained its influential position.

Gobei painted a kakemono of the spirit of the willow tree as he had seen her, and this he kept in his own room during the rest of his life. It is the famous painting, in

350

A Willow Tree and Family Honour

the Yuasa Gardens to-day, which is called 'The Willow Ghost,' and perhaps it is the model from which most of the willow-tree-ghost paintings have sprung.

Gobei fenced in the famous willow tree, and attended to it himself; as did those who followed him.

LVII

THE CAMPHOR TREE TOMB

FIVE ri (ten miles) from Shirakawa, in the province of Iwaki, there is a village called Yabuki-mura. Close by is a grove some 400 feet square. The trees used to include a monster camphor nearly 150 feet in height, of untold age, and venerated by villagers and strangers alike as one of the greatest trees in Japan. A shrine was erected to it in the grove, which was known as the Nekoma-myojin forest; and a faithful old man, Hamada Tsushima, lived there, caring for the tree, the shrine, and the whole grove.

One day the tree was felled; but, instead of withering or dying, it continued to grow, and it is still flourishing, though lying on the ground. Poor Hamada Tsushima disembowelled himself when the sacred tree had been cut down. Perhaps it is because his spirit entered the sacred tree that the tree will not die. Here is the story :—

On the 17th of January in the third and last year of the Meireki period—that is, 1658—a great fire broke out in the Homyo-ji Temple, in the Maruyama Hongo district of Yedo, now Tokio. The fire spread with such rapidity that not only was that particular district burned,

352

but also a full eighth of Yedo itself was destroyed. Many of the Daimios' houses and palaces were consumed. The Lord Date Tsunamune of Sendai, one of the three greatest Daimios (who were Satsuma, Kaga, Sendai), had the whole of his seven palaces and houses destroyed by the fire; the other Daimios or feudal lords lost only one or two.

Lord Date Tsunamune resolved to build the finest palace that could be designed. It was to be at Shinzenza, in Shiba. He ordered that no time should be lost, and directed one of his high officials, Harada Kai Naonori, to see to the matter.

Harada, accordingly, sent for the greatest house-building contractor of the day, one Kinokuniya Bunzaemon, and to him he said:

'You are aware that the fire has destroyed the whole of the town mansions of Lord Date Tsunamune. I am directed to see that the finest palace should be immediately built, second to none except the Shogun's. I have sent for you as the largest contractor in Yedo. What can you do? Just make some suggestions and give me your opinion.'

'Certainly, my Lord, I can make plenty of suggestions; but to build such a palace will cost an enormous amount of money, especially now after this fire, for there is a great scarcity of large timber in the land.'

'Never mind expenses,' said Harada. 'Those I shall pay as you like and when you like; I will even advance money if you want it.'

'Oh, then,' answered the delighted contractor, 'I will start immediately. What would you think of having a palace like that of Kinkakuji in Kyoto, which was built by the Shogun Ashikaga ? What I should build would be a finer mansion than that of the present Shogun—let alone those of any Daimio. The whole of the hagi[1] to be made out of the rarest woods ; the tokobashira[2] to be of the nanten, and ceilings of unjointed camphor-tree boards, should we be able to find a tree of sufficient size. I can find nearly everything, except the last, in my own stocks ; the camphor trees are difficult. There are but few ; they are mostly sacred, and dangerous to interfere with or obtain. I know of one in the forest of Neko-ma-myojin, in Iwaki Province. If I can get that tree, I should indeed be able to make an unjointed ceiling, and that would completely put other palaces and mansions in the second rank.'

' Well, well, I must leave all this to you,' said Harada. ' You know that no expense need be spared so long as you produce speedily what is required by Lord Date Tsunamune.'

The contractor bowed low, saying that he should set to and do his best ; and he left, no doubt, delighted at so open a contract, which would enable him to fill his pockets. He set about making inquiries in every direction, and became convinced that the only camphor tree that would suit his purpose was the one before referred to—owing chiefly to its great breadth. Kinokuniya knew also that the part of the district wherein lay this tree belonged to or was under the management of Fujieda Geki, now in the Honjo district of Yedo acting as a Shogun's retainer, well off (receiving 1200 koku of rice a year), but not

---

[1] Shelves. [2] Kakumono corner-post.

over scrupulous about money, of which he was always in need.

Contractor Kinokuniya soon learned all about the man, and then went to call.

'Your name is Kinokuniya Bunzaemon, I believe. What, may I ask, do you wish to see me about?' said Fujieda.

'Sir,' said the contractor, bowing low, 'it is as you say. My name is Kinokuniya Bunzaemon, and I am a wood contractor of whom perhaps your Lordship has heard, for I have built and supplied the wood for many mansions and palaces. I come here craving assistance in the way of permission to cut trees in a small forest called Nekoma-myojin, near the village called Yabuki-mura, in the Sendai district.'

The contractor did not tell Fujieda Geki, the Shogun's retainer or agent, that he was to build a mansion for the Daimio Date Tsunamune, and that the wood which he wanted to cut was within that Daimio's domains. For he knew full well that the Lord Date would never give him permission to cut a holy tree. It was an excellent idea to take the Daimio's trees by the help of the Shogun's agent, and charge for them fully afterwards. So he continued :

'I can assure you, sir, this recent fire has cleared the whole market of wood. If you will assist me to get what I want I will build you a new house for nothing, and by way of showing my appreciation I ask you to accept this small gift of yen 200, which is only a little beginning.'

'You need not trouble with these small details,' said the delighted agent, pocketing the money, 'but do as

355

you wish. I will send for the four local managers and head-men of the district wherein you wish to cut the trees, and I will let you know when they arrive in Yedo. With them you will be able to settle the matter.'

The interview was over. The contractor was on the high road, he felt, to getting the trees he required, and the money-wanting agent was equally well pleased that so slight an effort on his part should have been the means of enriching him by yen 200, with the promise of more and a new house.

About ten days later four men, the heads of villages, arrived in Yedo, and presented themselves to Fujieda, who sent for the timber contractor, telling the four, whose names were Mosuke, Magozaemon, Yohei, and Jinyemon, that he was pleased to see them and to note how loyal they had been in their attendance on the Shogun, for that he, the Shogun, had had his palace burned down in the recent fire, and desired to have one immediately built, the great and only difficulty being the timber. 'I am told by our great contractor, to whom I shall introduce you presently, that the only timber fit for rebuilding the Shogun's palace lies in your district. I myself know nothing about these details, and I shall leave you gentlemen to settle these matters with Kinokuniya, the contractor, so soon as he arrives. I have sent for him. In the meantime consider yourselves welcome, and please accept of the meal I have arranged in the next room for you. Come along and let us enjoy it.'

Fujieda led the four countrymen into the next room, and ate with them at the meal, during which time Kinokuniya the contractor arrived, and was promptly ushered into their presence. The meal was nearly at an end.

Fujieda introduced the contractor, who in his turn said :

'Gentlemen, we cannot discuss these matters here in the house of Lord Fujieda the Shogun's agent. Now that we know one another, let me invite you to supper ; at that I can explain to you exactly what I want in the way of trees out of your district. Of course, you know my family are subjects of your feudal lords, and that we are therefore all the same.'

The four countrymen were delighted at so much hospitality. Two meals in an evening was an extraordinary dissipation for them, and that in Yedo! My word, what would they not be able to tell their wives on their return to the villages?

Kinokuniya led the four countrymen off to a restaurant called Kampanaro, in Ryogoku, where he treated them with the greatest hospitality. After the meal he said :

'Gentlemen, I hope you will allow me to hew timber from the forest in your village, for it is impossible for me otherwise to attempt any further building on a large scale.'

'Very well, you may hew,' said Mosuke, who was the senior of the four. 'Since the cutting of the trees in Nekoma-myojin forest is as it were a necessity for our lord, they must be cut ; it is, in fact, I take it, an order from our lord that the trees shall be cut ; but I must remind you that there is one tree in the grove which cannot be cut amid any circumstances whatever, and that is an enormous and sacred camphor tree which is very much revered in our district, and to which a shrine is erected. That tree we cannot consent to have cut.'

'Very well,' said the contractor. 'Just write me a little permit, giving me permission to cut any trees except the big camphor, and our business will be finished.'

Kinokuniya had by this time in the evening taken his measure of the countrymen—so shrewdly as to know that they were probably unable to write.

'Certainly,' said Mosuke. 'Just you write out a little agreement, Jinyemon.'

'No: I would rather you wrote it, Mago,' said Jinyemon.

'And I should like Yohei to write it,' said Mago.

'But I can't write at all,' said Yohei, turning to Jinyemon again.

'Well, never mind, never mind,' said Kinokuniya. 'Will you gentlemen sign the document if I write it?'

Why, of course, they all assented. That was the best way of all. They would put their stamps to the document. This they did, and after a lively evening departed pleased with themselves generally.

Kinokuniya, on the other hand, went home fully contented with his evening's business. Had he not in his pocket the permit to cut the trees, and had he not written it himself, so as to suit his own purpose? He chuckled at the thought of how neatly he had managed the business.

Next morning Kinokuniya sent off his foreman, Chogoro, accompanied by ten or a dozen men. It took them three days to reach the village called Yabuki-mura, near the Nekoma-myojin grove; they arrived on the morning of the fourth day, and proceeded to erect a scaffold round the camphor tree, so that they might the better use their axes. As they began chopping off the lower branches, Hamada Tsushima, the keeper of the shrine, came running to them.

'Here, here! What are you doing? Cutting down the sacred camphor? Curse you! Stop, I tell you! Do you hear me? Stop at once!'

Chogoro answered :

'You need not stop my men in their work. They are doing what they have been ordered to do, and with a full right to do it. I am cutting down the tree at the order of my master Kinokuniya, the timber contractor, who has permission to cut the tree from the four head-men sent to Yedo from this district.'

'I know all that,' said the caretaker ; 'but your permission is to cut down any tree except the sacred camphor.'

'There you are wrong, as this letter will show you,' said Chogoro ; 'read it yourself.' And the caretaker, in great dismay, read as follows :—

To Kinokuniya Bunzaemon,
   Timber Contractor, Yedo.

In hewing trees to build a new mansion for our lord, all the camphor trees must be spared except the large one said to be sacred in the Nekoma-myojin grove. In witness whereof we set our names.

    JINYEMON ; MAGOZAEMON ; MOSUKE ; YOHEI.
    Representing the local County Officials.

The caretaker, beside himself with grief and astonishment, sent for the four men mentioned. On their arrival each declared that he had given permission to cut anything except the big camphor; but Chogoro said that he could not believe them, and in any case he would go by the written document. Then he ordered his men to continue their work on the big camphor.

Hamada Tsushima, the caretaker, did harakiri, disembowelling himself there and then; but not before telling Chogoro that his spirit would go into the camphor tree, to take care of it, and to wreak vengeance on the wicked Kinokuniya.

At last the efforts of the men brought the stately tree down with a crash; but then they found themselves unable to move it. Pull as they might, it would not budge. Each time they tried the branches seemed to become alive; faces and eyes became painful with the hits they got from them. Pluckily they continued their efforts; but it was no use. Things got worse. Several of the men were caught and nearly crushed to death between the branches; four had broken limbs from blows given in the same way. At this moment a horseman rode up and shouted:

'My name is Matsumaye Tetsunosuke. I am one of the Lord of Sendai's retainers. The board of councillors in Sendai have refused to allow this camphor tree to be touched. You have cut it, unfortunately. It must now remain where it is. Our feudal lord of Sendai, Lord Date Tsunamune, will be furious. Kinokuniya the contractor planned an evil scheme, and will be duly punished; while as for the Shogun's agent, Fujieda Geki, he also must be reported. You yourselves return to Yedo. We cannot blame you for obeying orders. But first give me that forged permit signed by the four local fools, who, it is trusted, will destroy themselves.'

The Camphor Tree Tomb

Chogoro and his men returned to Yedo. A few days later the contractor was taken ill, and a shampooer was sent to his room. A little later Kinokuniya was found dead; the shampooer had disappeared, though it was impossible for him to have got away without being seen! It is said that the spirit of Hamada Tsushima, the caretaker, had taken the form of the shampooer, in order to kill the contractor. Chogoro became so uneasy in his mind that he returned to the camphor tree, where he spent all his savings in erecting a new shrine and putting in a caretaker. This is known as the Kusunoki Dzuka (The Camphor Tree Tomb). The tree lies there, my story-teller tells me, at the present day.

THE END